MICHAEL SHAPIRO'S

INTERNET

Travel
Planner

How to plan trips and save money online

by Michael Shapir

D1122170

The
Globe
Pequot
Press

Guilford, Connecticut

For Willow

who stuck by me

through thick and thin

and for Brian and Andrea

who dove headfirst into life

Cover and text design by Casey Shain
Production by Libby Kingsbury
Expert review by Morris Dye
Screenshot credits: Netscape Communicator browser window © 1999 Netscape Communications Corporation. Used with permission. Page 1, copyright Yahoo.com. Pages 10, 89, © At Home Corporation. Page 13, HotBot® is a registered service mark of Wired Ventures, Inc., a subsidiary of Lycos, Inc. All rights reserved. Page 19, courtesy AJR NewsLink™. Page 21, Copyright 1999 The Washington Post Company. Used with permission. Page 21, SF Gate Travel page (sfgate.com/traveler/) reprinted by permission of Chronicle Publishing Company. Page 41, courtesy American Airlines. Page 43, courtesy Southwest Airlines. Pages 51, 52, courtesy Pegasus Systems, Inc. and TravelWeb.com. Page 75, Copyright © 1999 Fodor's Travel Publications. Reprinted by permission. Page 78, Copyright, 1999, Los Angeles Times. Reprinted by permission. Page 92, Provided by MapQuest.com. Page 97, Copyright 1999, Doug Kirby, Ken Smith, Mike Wilkins. Page 105, courtesy www.ricksteves.com. Rick Steves is author of *Europe Through the Back Door* and 20 other travel guidebooks, all published by John Muir Publications. Page 118, courtesy Windjammer Barefoot Cruises, Ltd., Miami Beach, FL; 800-327-2602. Page 121, courtesy LastMinuteTravel.com. Page 132, © Mountain Travel-Sobek. Page 150, courtesy Cruise Lines International Association. Page 174, Copyright 1999 Transitions Abroad Publishing, Inc. Page 179, screen capture from biztravel.com November 1, 1999, a Rosenbluth Interactive company. Page 179, screenshot courtesy of TRIP.com. Page 180, © 1999 Cable News Network, Inc. All Rights Reserved. Used by permission of CNNfn. Page 188, Copyright 1999 Northwest Airlines. All rights reserved. Pages 210, 213, courtesy of Deja.com. Page 222, courtesy Topica Inc., a free e-mail list service. Page 224, courtesy OnNow—Your guide to live online events. Pages 212, 245, courtesy America Online, Inc. Page 246, Cruise Critic is published by The Independent Traveler, Inc., a New Jersey Corporation, www.cruisecritic.com.

Library of Congress Cataloging-in-Publication Data
Shapiro, Michael, 1962–
    [Internet travel planner]
    Michael Shapiro's internet travel planner : how to plan trips and save money online /
  Michael Shapiro.—1st Globe Pequot ed.
     p. cm.
    Includes bibliographical references (p.).
    ISBN 0-7627-0579-5
    1. Tourism—Computer network resources. 2. Internet (Computer network). 3. World Wide Web. I. Title: Internet travel planner. II. Title.

G155 .A1 S46 2000
025.06'91—dc21

                                      99-053092

Manufactured in Canada
First Globe Pequot Edition/First Printing

contents

INTRODUCTION

Is the Internet really such a great tool for travelers? With all the sites out there, wouldn't it just be easier to call a travel agent? Well, first things first: The Net is a vast, untamed frontier, but this book will point you in the right direction. Beyond site listings (and I list hundreds), *Michael Shapiro's Internet Travel Planner* focuses on instruction, so you know how to take full advantage of just about any site you come across.

The point of this book is not to tell you to ditch your travel agent—in some cases agents are the best way to go. What this book does is let you know when it's best to use the Net, and when you might want to turn to an agent. More importantly, travel planning today usually isn't an either/or proposition. Even if you want to have an agent book your trip, you can use the Net to become much more informed about your options and learn about your destination once you decide where you want to go.

The Internet Revolution

The Internet has revolutionized the way people travel, from trip planning to booking tickets to how they stay in touch while on the road. Most dramatically, the Net has broken open databases that until a few years ago were available primarily to travel agents.

The Net has matured and evolved to a point that you can now use it as a personal travel planner. With just a few clicks, you can take a virtual cruise, see what a hotel's rooms look like, or send e-mail to a tour operator on the other side of the planet. Airline fares and schedules are sorted and served up in seconds, and last-minute travel bargains are e-mailed directly to you.

These last-minute deals aren't the only online bargains: Sometimes airlines and other suppliers offer incentives for booking at their Web sites, such as a few thousand bonus frequent flier miles. Even better, some airlines offer Internet-only fares at prices well below other deals for those who book directly through the airline's Web site. Why are travel suppliers so eager to get you to book online? Simple, if you book through their sites, they don't have to pay a commission to a travel agent, so they'll pass some of the savings on to you. And airlines aren't the only travel suppliers offering online specials. You can find deals on hotel rooms, cruises, vacation packages, and tours.

Yet the Internet is much more than a place to find good deals. Although it's always great to save some money, the Net's ability to make you a more informed traveler may be even more valuable. Through the Net, you can find Web sites covering the most specific destinations and activities imaginable. Want to row a dugout canoe down the Amazon? Bungee jump in Belize? Or just find a deserted beach in Bali? Whatever your interest, you can bet someone's posted a Web page that can help you learn more—and this book will show you how to find these sites.

And don't forget the Internet is an interactive medium. Through its web of wires, you can connect with others who have recently been to your destination or who live there. They can offer insights into local customs, recommend a place to stay, or suggest an affordable restaurant where the locals go. You may even strike up a friendship online, and when you get to your destination, meet your virtual amigo for real-world sightseeing.

Some Components of *Internet Travel Planner*

The goal of this book is to familiarize you with the basics, to introduce key resources, and to help you get more familiar with techniques for planning and arranging your trips online. *Michael Shapiro's Internet Travel Planner* describes many of the best sites on the Web, of course, but offers much more. You'll find lots of instruction on how to use the Net for travel planning, booking, and communication, advice that will remain valuable even if a Web site's address changes. In addition to all the instruction and site listings, the following features are included throughout the text:

- **Siteseeing:** Detailed analysis of key Web sites that show you how to get the most from these sites.

- **First Person:** Accounts in which veteran travelers describe how they use the Net.

- **For AOL Users:** Snapshots of America Online's travel resources and advice about how to take fullest advantage of these services. (You'll also find an appendix covering AOL at the back of the book.)

- **Tips:** Sage suggestions for using the Net, broken out from the main text.

- **Glossary:** If you come across unfamiliar terms (such as *URL* or *FAQ*) while reading this book, consult the glossary, which should bring you up to speed in a nanosecond.

Who Is This Book For?

When it comes to travel planning, there seem to be two types of people: those who want to have a travel professional make their arrangements, and those who want to be in the driver's seat. Before the Internet revolution, I would sometimes go to a travel agent. While the agent was tapping on the keys, I'd sit there wishing I could turn the screen around. And when I thought about that, it became clear who this book is for: *travelers who want to turn the screen around,* who want to understand how to make it work for them.

Although this book is primarily for people who like to do their own planning, it's also valuable for those who typically use a travel agent. Even if you have an agent handle your travel arrangements, you can become more informed through online resources. Use the Net to get a better sense of what's out there, at what price, and when it's available. You can log on any time of day or night, research trips, and make more informed travel decisions.

Eleven Things *Internet Travel Planner* Can Help You Do

- **Create a custom guidebook:** Use search sites to get more specific than any guidebook can about your travel interests. By using a combination of name-brand online guidebooks, hobbyist Web sites, and online discussion groups, you can answer just about every question imaginable, and then some. Print out what you need, staple it together, and you'll have your own personalized—and free—guidebook.

Find Net-only deals: Though last-minute weekend airfare deals seem to get all the attention, there are lots of other Net-only specials, from deals on cruises to Net-only airfares available weeks or months in advance. This book shows you how to find these deals and discusses when it makes sense to book online.

Stay in touch without carrying a laptop: Free e-mail services allow you to check and send e-mail any place you can find a computer connected to the Net. This book shows you how to sign up for and use these free services and how to find Internet cafes and other places around the world to get online.

See what a hotel looks like before choosing: Get extensive descriptions of hotels, B&Bs, or hostels; and, better yet, see pictures of the hotels, rooms, and facilities. Several sites offer online audio/video hotel tours.

Map your route: Not only can you plan the ultimate road trip online, you can use online mapping sites to get turn-by-turn directions for locations in the United States. Simply enter the address for your starting point and destination, and you can quickly get directions, with mini-maps showing you where you need to turn.

Get detailed cruise reviews: Thousands of travelers have taken the time to offer insightful cruise reviews to help you choose one that's right for you. There are dozens of personal reports for every major ship on the high seas, with specific critiques of everything from the midnight buffets to shore excursions.

Find Web sites for destinations and topics: *Internet Travel Planner* lists hundreds of Web sites through the text, and hundreds more in appendixes at the back of the book. You'll find one appendix for destinations (France, New York, etc.) and another for topics (adventure, budget, etc.).

Prepare for an international journey: The Net offers almost countless tools for planning trips abroad, including ATM locators, weather forecasters, currency converters, foreign language tutorials, health advisories, and many more. We'll show you where to find these services and how to make the most of them.

Connect with other travelers: The best travel advice frequently comes from fellow travelers, and the Net makes it possible to hook up with others no matter where they live. *Internet Travel Planner* shows you how to connect with people through Web-site forums, Usenet discussion groups, mailing lists, and live chat areas. You can even get feedback from travel experts, such as guidebook writers, who sometimes host live chat events or moderate Web forums.

Find what you need on AOL: Because AOL is so popular, we've included tips in each chapter that discuss how to use the mother of all online services. Appendix B describes in detail how to use dozens of AOL travel services. Even if you're not an AOL member, you can use some of these services through AOL's Web site (aol.com).

■ **Learn how to be a savvier traveler:** *Internet Travel Planner* goes beyond tips for using the Net effectively; it includes shrewd travel advice for getting the best deals, whether you book online or not. For example, chapter 2 has tips for getting low airfares, and chapter 11 has suggestions for getting the most from your frequent flier accounts. And many of the Web sites listed in the book can make you a travel expert in no time—on subjects ranging from traveling cheap as an air courier to arranging a home-exchange vacation.

Of course, these suggestions are just a brief sampling of the hundreds of ideas, tips, and tools described in the book. Each chapter has dozens of nuggets, large and small, to help you become a more informed traveler. And the more informed you become, the more likely you are to enjoy your trip.

What the Future Holds

With such a new medium, it's hard to predict the future, but a couple of trends are clear: More people will book travel online in the coming years, and more of these bookings will be made directly with suppliers, such as US Airways or Windjammer cruises. In 1997 travelers booked just under $1 billion worth of travel online, less than 1 percent of all travel bookings in that year. According to the **PhoCusWright** analysts at **www. phocuswright.com**, online travel is projected to be a $7 billion business in 1999, almost tripling to $20 billion by 2001.

Another interesting development is how many online bookings today are handled directly through suppliers' sites (for example, United Airlines's site) compared with how many are made through an online agency (such as Travelocity). In 1996 about 80 percent of online bookings were made through online agencies. By 1999 bookings were evenly divided between agencies and suppliers, and by 2003, **Jupiter Communications (jup.com)** projects that 60 percent of online bookings will be made directly through suppliers, with online agencies capturing only 40 percent. This is an ominous trend for these agencies, who receive very little in commissions from suppliers.

More interesting for consumers may be the second wave of Net travel sites, those that deliver streaming audio and video. At this time, just a few sites deliver streaming media, but each year, more people will get the bandwidth to take full advantage of these resources. These audio/visual virtual brochures offer a more complete picture of destinations, hotels, or cruise ships, and can help you get a clearer biew of tours, cruises, hotels, and destinations. Stay tuned.

You Can Talk to Me

The Internet is an interactive medium, and some of the best anecdotes and tips in this book come from wired travelers. So if you have a story to share or a question, you can send e-mail to me at my freemail address: michaelshapiro@yahoo.com. (*Note:* I have no affiliation with Yahoo but I do like the company's freemail service.) I can't quickly respond to every e-mail, but I'll try to get back to you soon. If you have a question, all I ask is that you try to find the answer in the book or online first, but if you can't, go ahead and ask me. So now let's dive in and explore the Net—and maybe our paths will cross in cyberspace.

CREATING *a* CUSTOM GUIDEBOOK

The Internet Travel Landscape

One of the first questions many travelers ask about using the Net is, "Where should I start?" Given the thousands of travel sites out there, it's a fine question. If Lao-tzu were alive today, he might say, "A journey of a thousand miles begins with one click." One way to begin is by starting with brands you know and trust. Established travel guide publishers, such as Lonely Planet, Frommer's, and Rick Steves, have put a remarkable amount of valuable information online— free to any and all comers. And though this may be hard to believe, Rough Guides, a big guidebook publisher based in London, is placing the full texts of its more than one hundred guides on the Net.

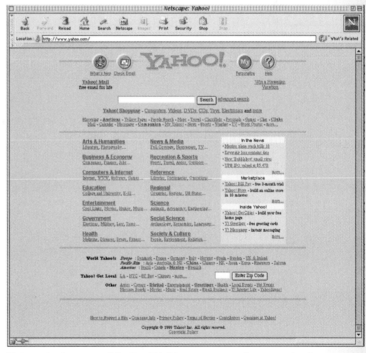

Yahoo (yahoo.com) is the Web's most popular search site.

These online guides alone could keep you busy for hours, but the Net offers much more to help you learn about destinations: magazines such as **Salon Travel (salon.com/**

travel/index.html) that take you to the ends of the Earth with just a click of your mouse, online forums that allow you to chat with others from around the world, irreverent self-published "zines" that offer insightful if sometimes quirky perspectives, and links to online versions of print newspapers, where you can take the pulse of the place you're about to visit.

If you already know what you want to do and where you want to do it, search directories such as **Yahoo (yahoo.com)** let you pinpoint information to get going. And these search sites are ideal for browsing categories that interest you; for example, skiing in the Rockies or diving in the Caribbean.

But let's be honest—the Net isn't the eighth wonder of the world. It's wild and woolly, an ungoverned and unsettled frontier, which encompasses a sometimes overwhelmingly chaotic assemblage of information. Of course, that's part of its charm—just about anyone with a Net connection can become a publisher, and those with a passion for the places they love are providing insights unavailable in mainstream guidebooks. The aim of this book is to help you make sense of this new medium and enable you to use it to enhance your travels in ways you might never have imagined possible.

Just as television isn't simply radio with pictures, the Net isn't just a convenient way to snag information that's available in other forms. The Internet is a medium unto itself with extraordinary advantages—such as Web-based freemail—that would have been hard to imagine just a few years ago. *Michael Shapiro's Internet Travel Planner* will cover many of these amazing new tools in later chapters—here we'll focus on compiling a custom guidebook, perfectly tailored to your interests and needs.

Guidebook Publishers Get Online

The popularity of print guidebooks has boomed over the past couple of decades. And for good reason: The guides provide nuts-and-bolts information that help travelers decide what to see, where to stay, and when to go. These books are indispensable, but they have some drawbacks. By the time they're printed, some of the information is inevitably out of date.

Online guides can remedy this. With timely updates, Net-based guides can be more current than their print counterparts. That doesn't mean they always are, just that the Net gives them the capability to be. Among the other advantages of online sites are the following:

■ **They're free.** This may be obvious, but for short trips it's easy to get the basics online. This could mean finding an affordable hotel in the Hamptons for a weekend getaway or getting restaurant advice for a Dallas business trip. Of course, if you're planning a three-week

tips

■ Some of the sites listed here may have changed addresses by the time you read this. For updates, see this book's companion Web site (www.internettravel planner.com).

■ When you see a rectangular box with a small arrow at the right side, this is usually a pull-down menu. Click on the arrow to see your selections. If there are more than a few, click on the scroll bar along the right side of the menu to see the rest.

trek through Nepal, it makes sense to buy a guidebook, but for a quick getaway why not save $20.

- ▨ **You can pinpoint** the information you want. If you're looking for a hotel under $100 in downtown San Francisco, or a Greek restaurant in Philly, just enter these preferences and in a few seconds, an online guidebook or dining guide can produce some recommendations tailored to your desires.
- ▨ **Discussion forums** let you post a question and get answers from fellow travelers or sometimes from a guidebook's author.
- ▨ **You can contribute** to online guidebooks. If you get to Nepal and find that a hostel recommended by **Lonely Planet (www.lonelyplanet.com)** has closed, you can drop LP a line, and they might include it in the online updates. And you may be rewarded for your help with a free guidebook or T-shirt.

Like their print counterparts, each travel Web site has its own personality and strengths. In the following section, we'll take a look at some of the best online guides and the features that make each one unique. And throughout the book—in "Siteseeing" features—we'll look at some sites in more depth.

Rough Guides Puts It All Online

Rough Guides (travel.roughguides.com) took a bold step in 1995, when the company put the full text of some of its most popular titles online. Some observers thought the company was nuts, but the strategy proved sound. From 1996 through 1998, Rough Guides' sales grew at the healthy rate of at least 20 percent a year, partially due to the company's profile on the Net.

In 1998, after piggybacking on Wired's site for three years, Rough Guides launched its own site with magazine-style features and search tools that home in on thousands of destinations. Although the magazine offers some thought-provoking features (a comparison of coffee houses in Seattle and Boston, for example), most visitors zoom in on their destinations.

Rough Guides says its site covers more than 4,000 destinations, with up-to-date information. Although it's hard to imagine RG's staff keeping current on thousands of destinations, Rough Guides offers much of the same, and in some cases updated, information that you can find in its print guides. But remember, just because a site can be updated doesn't mean it will

Rough Guides (travel.roughguides.com) has put the full text of many of their guidebooks online.

be. Some guidebook travel pages are no more current than print guides.

To get started, simply type your destination—whether it's a city, country, or state—into the search box and click on the "Search" button. Or use pull-down menus to see what cities, countries, and states Rough Guides feature. The headings typically correspond to the titles of RG's print guides: for example, "London" or "Thailand." Another section called "Rough Guide Recommends" has guides to alluring destinations, ranging from Italy's Amalfi coast to Hawaii Volcanoes National Park.

There is another search box below the pull-down menus for more advanced searches. If you were looking for a place to eat in San Francisco, you could type in "San Francisco AND dining" to take you to a list of links, including restaurants in the city, watering holes, cafes, and even quick lunch places. Click on the link of your choice to get the listings you want.

Lonely Planet's Online Upgrades

When they were in their twenties, Tony and Maureen Wheeler figured they'd travel for a year through Asia and then settle down. But after the trip, their friends kept asking for advice, so they wrote up a little guide for backpackers who wanted to follow in their footsteps. "It was totally an accident," Tony has said. "People were asking us questions, and we decided we should do something about it."

More than 400 titles later, **Lonely Planet (www. lonelyplanet.com)** covers almost every inch of the globe and is widely recognized as a source of authoritative information. The series has matured along with Tony and Maureen; although the guides are still a bible for shoestring travelers, they offer more mainstream information for those who are willing to spend a few bucks (or bhat) for a comfortable room with a private bath.

Unlike Rough Guides, Lonely Planet doesn't try to put all its content online; instead, the site provides an overview of destinations

Lonely Planet (www.lonelyplanet.com) combines timely features with some guidebook content, including online updates to its print titles.

and has well-trafficked forums where users can interact. One of the most valuable areas of this site is **Upgrades**, which are staff-written updates to dozens of its guidebooks (more on this later). Because the print guides are typically published every couple of years, the idea is to offer updates that can be printed out and carried along with the book, bringing the text up to date.

Highlighted in the Siteseeing feature on the next page are the key elements of Lonely Planet's site, with excerpts that offer a flavor of what's going on there. (*Note:* Siteseeing features appear throughout the book, taking an in-depth look at key Web sites.)

Outspoken Opinions from the Budget Travel Guru

Arthur Frommer's Budget Travel Online (www.frommers.com) is another hugely popular Web travel guide—and for good reason: It offers a wealth of ideas for budget travelers. Arthur Frommer, who still maintains a travel schedule that would wear out most people half his age, has created a site that reflects his unique blend of honesty, insight, and passion for affordable travel. Unlike some other guidebook writers, Frommer will tell you if he doesn't like a destination, hotel, or attraction. In fact he's probably the only author who ever wrote a travel guidebook telling people why they *shouldn't* visit a destination (if you're wondering, it was the country music mecca of Branson that sparked his ire).

Frommer's travel content was available only on AOL through the mid-90s, but in 1997 he opened shop on the Web, calling his guide Arthur Frommer's Outspoken Encyclopedia of Travel. Although that title suited, he changed it to match his *Budget Travel* magazine. So what does Frommer's offer its online visitors? Everything from honest cruise reviews to timely travel specials:

Arthur Frommer's Budget Travel (frommers.com) includes daily travel news and savvy strategies from the guru of affordable travel.

- **Research Destinations:** Use the pull-down menu to select a region and drill down until you find what you want. To get rates for New Orleans hotels, select "North America" and click "Go." A click on the link for New Orleans leads to a nice introduction to the city with a link to "Lodgings." This page provides an overview of lodging in New Orleans and has subcategories for budget rooms, moderately priced places, top hotels, and bed-and-breakfast inns. It sounds like a lot of clicking but, with a decent modem, it only takes a few seconds to get from page to page.

- **Daily Newsletter:** Chock full of bargains, this daily list of specials focuses mostly on package deals, such as a winter week in Paris with airfare from the East Coast for $569. Subscribe and you'll get the newsletter in your e-mail box each day. (More on e-mail newsletters in chap. 13, "Online Discussion Forums.")

- **Advance Features from *Arthur Frommer's Budget Travel* magazine:** Subjects for a recent month included "100 Money-Saving Tips That Can Change Your Travel Life," "Budget Honeymoons," and "Hosteling the California Coast."

siteseeing

Lonely Planet

■ **Destinations:** Click this link on LP's home page and you'll arrive at a page with a colorful world map. There are three ways to get where you want to go: Click on your destination on the map, choose a region and country from the pull-down menus at the top of the page and then click "Go," or type a destination into the search box near the bottom and then hit the Return or Enter key on your keyboard. Choosing the second method, I tried selecting "Americas" for region and "Guatemala" in countries. Clicking "Go" led me to LP's Guatemala page, which included information on the country's climate, geography, history, and leading attractions, as well as photos and maps. The destination pages also offer some stunning photos and insightful commentary. Here's a snippet: "The government has both touted and tortured the Maya—sticking pictures of them on its tourist brochures while sticking guns in their faces."

■ **Thorn Tree:** Those ratty bulletin boards at hostels and cafes, with their clusters of pushpins and thumb tacks, are called "thorn trees." LP has taken this idea online, with interactive forums by destination (Africa, Central Asia, etc.) and by subject (Women, Gay and Lesbian, Kids, etc.). Perhaps most interesting is the travel companions forum, which makes it easier to hook up with like-minded globe-trotters. Each post has an e-mail address (not shown here) so if you find someone you'd like to meet, you can send e-mail to that person.

Here's an excerpt:

> Cycle Ireland
> Created by: **Vanessa**
> [Timestamp: Fri 19 Feb, 0:14 Tasmanian Standard Time]
> I am keen to find someone (m or f) to join me for some or all
> of the trip as I cycle Ireland. I am planning to set off
> from Dublin on 14/15 April and heading south. I have to be
> back in Dublin 12 June. I have no set route or itinerary. I
> am a 29 yr old Australian female. If you are interested, I
> would love to hear from you.

■ **Postcards:** Veteran travelers know that fellow explorers are among the best sources of current tips and advice. In Postcards, LP offers dispatches sent by travelers from around the globe. Here's how LP describes this zone: "We get a mountain of mail from travelers on the road, covering everything from how to get a summer job in Guatemala to how to find a cold beer in Timbuktu. We want to share this stuff with other travelers ASAP, so in most cases we haven't checked the facts (letters in red have been verified, although not necessarily by Lonely Planet). The letters make great reading, but be smart and treat tips with caution until you suss things out for yourself."

■ **Upgrades:** "Borders open, hotels close, and currencies crash—the world can change a lot in one day," says the intro to Upgrades. So LP's writers and editors provide this updated information to dozens of its guides, and they verify these reports, making them more reliable than the dispatches in Postcards. The Cambodia Upgrade, penned by the author of LP's Cambodia guidebook, says, "For the traveler, Cambodia is safer now than at any time for about three decades." Although Upgrades are relatively current, LP still advises its readers to check with an embassy or consulate if there's any doubt about safety or health conditions.

LP's other sections include Scoop, with worldwide travel news; Comet, where you can sign up for a monthly e-mail dispatch of international travel news; and subWWWay, which offers links to top travel sites. It's true that all this stuff is no substitute for a handy little guidebook, but LP Online is an amazing resource in its own right.

Among other offerings are **Frommer's Tip of the Day,** reams of advice for savvy travelers, cruise reviews, discount booking, and online forums. (We'll revisit Frommer's in greater depth in chap. 7, "Budget Travel.")

Fodor's Custom Miniguides

In 1936 Eugene Fodor wrote, "The joy of travel should not be derived solely from seeing the sights, but from mingling with peoples whose customs, habits, and general outlook are different from your own." **Fodor's Travel Online (www.fodors.com)**, launched in 1996, carries that philosophy onto the Net. Fodor's site understands the medium, giving travelers the opportunity to state what they're looking for (a Santa Fe hotel for under $100) and get listings with just a couple of clicks. The following are its key features:

tips

■ **The Travel Channel (travelchannel.com),** produced in conjunction with the cable network of the same name, has destination information, travel tips, and features that complement its television programs.

■ Let's Go (www. letsgo.com), a guide-book series for young and adventurous travelers on a tight budget, offers travel advice and forums online.

- ■ **Create your own miniguides:** This is one of the coolest features on the Web. Start by choosing one of the hundred or so destinations (Santa Fe, for instance) and then click the boxes (Where to Stay, Eating Out, etc.) for the information you want. The next page lets you refine your search. For example, select centrally located hotels under $100, Italian and Mexican restaurants under $20, and tips for getting in from the airport. Click "Create My Miniguide," and you're set to jet. In seconds Fodor's produces a guide tailored to your preferences, with a concise introduction to the town and hotel listings, such as Alexander's Inn, "a 1903 two-story, Craftsman-style house in the lovely Eastside residential area, only a few blocks from the Plaza." The little red star next to the listing means the inn is recommended by Fodor's. For more information, you can call the toll-free number listed for the inn or see if Alexander's Inn has its own Web page. (We'll discuss search strategies later in this chapter.)
- ■ **Fodor's Hotel Finder:** There are two ways to search, by name or by criteria. If you're a member of a chain's award program (such as Hilton HHonors), you might try to search by name. However, if you're looking for the ideal location or best deal, try searching by criteria: price range, location, and amenities (a pool and health club sure sound nice). Fodor's also features a restaurant finder that works in a similar way.

Rick Steves' Europe Through the Back Door

In 1969, when Rick Steves was fourteen years old, he visited Europe for the first time, with his father, a piano importer. A few years later he returned, paying his way by giving piano lessons. Today, his *Europe Through the Back Door* and the many country and city guides it spawned are *the* insiders' guides to Europe, giving travelers a chance to discover intimate places that more established series sometimes overlook. **Rick Steves' Europe Through the Back Door (www.ricksteves.com)** has brought much of this advice online.

Here are the highlights:

- **Country Information:** This link leads to a page of fourteen European flags. Clicking on the Italian flag, for example, leads to dozens of headings, such as *Italian Riviera: Top Hideaways,* where you can learn about remote vacation spots, such as the Cinque Terre. Steves also recommends his favorite hotels here.
- **Back Door Travel Tips:** Steves shares much of his hard-won wisdom here, from how to avoid theft and tourist scams to strategies for coping with summer crowds: "The beaches of Greece's Peloponnesian Peninsula offer the same weather and water as the highly promoted isles of Mykonos and Ios but are out of the way, not promoted, and wonderfully deserted."

Among the other nuggets on this site are Travel News, with Steves' latest dispatches from Europe and excerpts from his most recent books; Graffiti Wall, an open forum where visitors can chat; and Railpasses Revisited, where Steves helps travelers choose the most suitable rail pass for their trips. And, of course, you can buy Steves' books through the site.

For AOL Users:

TRAVEL GUIDES

With almost 20 million subscribers, AOL has become a dominant Web presence. Throughout this book you'll find inserts discussing AOL's essential features.

Destination Guides (keyword: *destinations*): Featuring in-depth destination information from Fodor's and many other services, this is the place to start planning your trip. It also includes official tourism info from over 5,000 destinations worldwide.

Travel File (keyword: *Travel File*): Find events calendars, discounted vacation packages, tourism offices, and more. The lists of restaurants and hotels are short as only paid advertisers seem to be mentioned.

Lonely Planet Guides (keyword: *Lonely Planet*): You'll find many of the same features here that are available at LP's Web site (see earlier).

Travel News and Features (keyword: *News & Features*): Consumer and budget advice, seasonal features, and travel lit from *Salon Travel.*

Search Engines Become Portals

During the infancy of the Web, a site called Global Network Navigator (GNN) organized links by subject, reviewed leading Web sites, and recommended top picks to its readers. Though it never called itself a portal, it certainly could have. GNN was the first real window on the Web, a perfect starting point to launch a journey through cyberspace. Sadly, GNN no longer exists (it was gobbled up in 1995 by AOL), but it has been succeeded by a new generation of portals. And though you may never have heard of GNN, you're probably familiar with Yahoo, Excite, Lycos, and others.

Points of Embarkation

Today's portals are more than windows on the Web—they include such features as stock quotes, people finders, and news headlines. Among portals' most visited areas are their travel pages: These sites within sites offer destination information, ticket sales, and even flight tracking to tell you when a flight is due in. You can also get weather forecasts, maps, and trip directions, and even register for free e-mail services that will help you stay in touch, without having to carry a laptop, while you're on the road.

All the big portals started out as search engines and added commodities (weather, stock quotes, sports scores) and features (Web-based e-mail, news headlines) as they evolved. They've also dedicated pages to specific topics, such as travel, sports, and personal finance. Much of the information on a page such as Yahoo Travel comes from partners who specialize in this information: Yahoo teamed up with Travelocity for bookings, Excite chose Preview Travel, and so on.

Yahoo Travel (travel.yahoo.com)

Yahoo, Earth's biggest portal, makes it easy to find what you're looking for. You can search by destination (North America) or interest (Cruising). Most portals have partnered with top travel publishers. Yahoo has selected Lonely Planet, National Geographic Traveler, and Travelocity (for bookings), so you can count on getting useful information. Yahoo also lists Net events, such as an online discussion about planning the perfect romantic vacation. (We'll cover chats and forums in chap. 13.)

Excite Travel (www.excite.com/travel)

In the early days of the Web, a simple site called **city.net** was a great place to begin a travel search. Although city.net didn't prepare travel features, it listed excellent links for learning more about thousands of destinations. Today, city.net is part of Excite Travel and has lost much of its value: You can still go directly to city.net if you like, but that link now leads straight to Excite's travel page. On a random winter visit, features included up-to-date ski reports, frequent flyer tips, restaurant reviews, and a guide to renting cars. Of course, if you don't see what you're looking for, you can use Excite's search engine to find more.

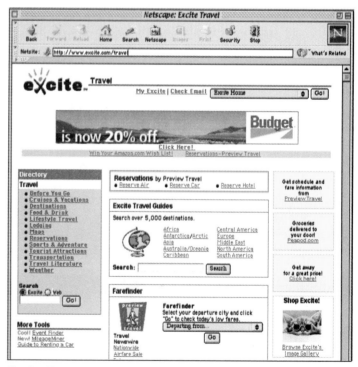

Excite Travel (www.excite.com/travel) is an example of a search site's travel page. These pages typically include online booking, destination information, and travel offers.

Go Travel (www.go.com/Center/Travel)

Until purchased by Disney, this site was known as Infoseek Travel. As part of Disney's **Go Network (go.com)**, the site now focuses on tools for travelers, such as flight booking and hotel reservations. Like many other portals, Go has teamed up with well-known partners. Its travel reservations services are handled by Microsoft's Reservation Desk, and its currency converter is provided by Xenon.

Lycos Travel Guide (www.lycos.com/travel)

If these travel guides seem to look the same, that should be no surprise, portals are famous for adopting one another's innovations. Though similar to the other big guys, Lycos Travel Guide has some nice features, such as the Lycos City Guide. Drill down from region (Europe) to country (Greece) to city (Rhodes—okay, so this is an island; it still works). This leads to a short-but-sweet introduction to the place and a selection of links, organized by headings, such as Visitor's Guide and News and Weather. Lycos Travel Guide also features trip booking, discussion forums, and a rotating list of top travel sites.

tip

■ AOL and Netscape merged shortly before press time, but each maintains its own travel pages, which are quite similar to those already listed. To see their travel sections, visit Netcenter Travel (netcenter.com/travel) or AOL Travel (www.aol.com/webcenters/travel).

Snap Travel (www.snap.com/travel)

The nice thing about the Snap Travel page is that it's more than a list of links combined with travel services. Snap's editors have focused on key travel categories, such as business travel or B&Bs, and selected top sites in each of these categories. The downside is that these listings aren't easy to find unless they're featured on the main **Travel Reservations** page. To get from Travel Reservations to the B&B page, for example, you have to plunge into Snap Categories and click the "Lodging" link. This leads to a page listing the **Bed-and-Breakfast Guide** among other categories.

About.com (www.about.com)

Though About.com (formerly known as Miningco.com) doesn't offer all the portal services of Excite or Yahoo, it can be an excellent jumping-off point for excursions through the Web. A few years ago Mining Co. recognized that some of the best pages on the Net were created by hobbyists who had tremendous interest in their topics. So they invited these people to create their own pages (called Resources) on Mining Co., for example, a guide to Las Vegas or to active travel. Each resource provides short features, extensive lists of links, forums, and the opportunity to send e-mail to the site's guide. Now that's a feature you won't often find at the biggies.

Effective *and* Efficient Searching

There are tens of thousands Web sites that can help you plan a journey—that's the good news *and* the bad news. The good part is that the information is out there; the bad news is you may have to sort through a lot of chaff to find the wheat. Sometimes, it can feel like looking for a needle in a haystack. But take heart: Once you find a couple of sites that fit the bill, these will probably lead to other useful Web pages on the same subject, and you'll be off and running.

LookSmart

A good place to start, especially if you're new to the Net, is **LookSmart (www.looksmart.com)**. This is a classic drill-down directory, meaning that you can start with broad categories and bore down until you get to a specific subcategory. To find packing tips, start by clicking on "Travel," which leads to about a dozen subcategories, including Travel Essentials. From here select Packing and Preparation and up comes a list of about fifty packing sites. And because you've been drilling through the travel category, you won't end up with, say, a link to a meat-packing facility in Iowa.

Looksmart (looksmart.com) is a classic "drill-down" directory, meaning you click on increasingly specific categories to get a manageable list of results.

Searching at Yahoo

Yahoo (yahoo.com) is really two search tools in one: first, a directory where you can drill down by subject (Travel > Budget Travel > Courier Flights), and second, a search engine, where you can input keywords and see what comes up. To drill down, visit Yahoo's home page and click "Travel" (tucked under the **Recreation & Sports** heading). This leads to dozens of subjects, from Air Travel to Virtual Field Trips. Selecting one of these topics leads you to a page with more specific subheadings and some links to Web sites.

By starting a search at Yahoo's travel page (rather than the main Yahoo page), you can limit your search to Yahoo's travel category. Just use the pull-down menu at the right of the search box and select "just this category." You can try this method in all Yahoo subcategories to refine your queries.

Searching the travel category for "amazon adventure" yields forty-four sites on this topic. You don't need to use capital letters for proper names, in fact it may limit your search if you do, so it's better to just use all lower case. Also, it's

tip

■ **If you're new to searching, take a moment to check the instructions on how to best use each search site. At Yahoo, for example, there is a "Help" icon in the upper-right-hand corner of the page. Click here to go to a tutorial about using the Web, with specific hints for searching. Many of these strategies apply to other search sites as well.**

better not to use the plural in most cases because a site listing an "Amazon adventure" might not appear if you search for "amazon adventures."

At press time, Yahoo cataloged more than 500,000 sites, organized into 25,000 categories by Yahoo editors, only a small percentage of the millions of sites on the Web. So if Yahoo doesn't have what you're looking for, you can click "Web Pages" or "Go to Web Page Matches" at the bottom of the Yahoo search results page. Doing this rolls the search over to an even larger database of sites, cataloged by automated "bots" that incessantly search for and catalog millions of sites.

tip

■ Narrow your search by limiting it to a certain category (for example, you can search just the travel section at Yahoo by using a pull-down menu).

Focusing Your Search

To refine a search, Yahoo and the other search engines employ sophisticated tools. For example, if you put a term in quotation marks ("whitewater rafting"), Yahoo will search only for Web pages that include the phrase "whitewater rafting." Without the quotations, you may get sites with just "rafting" or just "whitewater."

Using the word AND (in all capitals) will ensure that you get pages with both terms listed; for example, you could search for "vermont AND foliage" to get listings about seeing the brilliant fall colors in the Green Mountain State. You could also try searching for "vermont OR foliage," but this will produce a much longer list: sites with either the word *Vermont* or *foliage* listed. At many sites (though not at Yahoo), you can use NOT (for example "cycling NOT motorcycling").

The best way to learn how to use a search engine is by getting online and doing it. Search for topics that interest you, and when you reach a site that appears promising, have a look around. Each of the major sites has its own quirks and personality. Try a few and see which feels best for you.

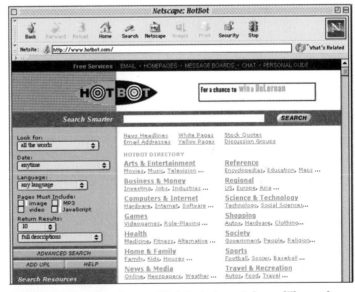

HotBot (hotbot.com), uses Web bots to catalog millions of Web sites, offering a wide range of results.

The Big Crawl

Unlike Yahoo, **AltaVista (www.altavista.com)** and **HotBot (www.hotbot.com)** don't have thousands of sites selected by editors—they have millions of Web pages cataloged by bots. They are search engines, not directories. So they'll usually offer more matches for your queries, but many of these matches may not be relevant to your search. The best advice is to try each of the major search engines and see where you feel most comfortable. Another good reason for trying more than one search engine is that each will yield different results. And because you can get thousands of matches for your query, a valuable site that's buried at one search engine may surface near the top of the list at another site.

Another option is to search most of the biggies with one click at a relatively new site called **Metacrawler (www.metacrawler.com)**. What makes Metacrawler unusual is that it searches the search engines, compiles the results, and lists them according to relevancy.

Like other search engines, Metacrawler has a travel channel, which is the best part of this site. By starting your search from the travel channel, Metacrawler combs through a small selection of excellent online travel publications (Condé Nast Traveler, Lonely Planet, Frommer's, and others) and comes up with a valuable—and rarely overwhelming—set of links. It's best to search for more general terms, such as "Maui" or "Disneyland," rather than highly specific queries, such as "Alaska summer cruises." Try your query both on Metacrawler's main page and its travel channel: You'll get different results for each search.

Though Metacrawler usually does a nice job, you'll probably want to check other search engines. Each has unique features. For example, Excite has links called "More like this," so when you find a site you like, click "More like this" and some similar sites should turn up. Like most search techniques, this one is inexact, so it pays to explore the many avenues available for finding what you want.

Book(mark) It!

Though the sheer number of Web pages out there can be daunting, you'll soon become highly adept at identifying valuable sites. When you come across one of these, use the Bookmark feature if you're using a Netscape browser, or Favorites if you roam the Web with Internet Explorer. By doing this, you'll save the Web page's address in your browser, so later you can go back to your Bookmarks (or Favorites) and go right to the page.

You can also divide your favorite Web sites into subcategories in your Bookmarks or Favorites. If you're using Netscape, go to the Bookmarks file, click on "Item," and scroll down to "Insert Folder." In Explorer, click the "Favorites" menu at the top of the page, click on "Organize Favorites," and

GoTo (www.goto.com), one of a new breed of search sites, seeks to make searching simple.

A New Wave of Search Sites

As this book went to press, several new search sites came online, each with an innovative strategy to simplify or streamline the search process. The following is a brief description of them:

■ **Google (www.google.com):** Google ranks search results according to how many sites link to it. In other words, if you search for "india travel," the site that includes the search term and has the most other sites linking to it will come up first. A button called "I'm feeling lucky" takes you directly to the top match, which works well for company names. So if you're looking for "United Airlines," Google will link you straight to United's site, rather than make you to wait for a list of search results and then click on the link to United's site. For a more detailed explanation, see **Why Use Google** (www.google.com/why_use.html).

■ **Direct Hit (www.directhit.com):** Direct Hit tracks the amount of time spent at sites that people select from the search results list. By analyzing the activity of millions of previous Internet searchers, Direct Hit attempts to determine the most popular and relevant sites for a search request. In simpler terms: Direct Hit tracks sites people select from lists of search results; the ones people visit most often are listed at the top.

tip

SMART BROWSING

■ The latest Netscape browsers include a feature called Smart Browsing, whereby instead of entering a URL, such as www.ual.com, you can enter a company's name, such as United Airlines, in the locator box, and you'll go straight to United's site. Microsoft's Internet Explorer browser has a similar feature.

■ **GoTo.com (www.goto.com):** Some sites use cagey strategies, placing their advertisers' sites on top. GoTo.com doesn't play any of these sneaky games: They blatantly sell placement to the highest bidder. So if you search for "airline tickets," the first site to come up is **Trip.com,** which at press time paid 67 cents for each person who clicks from GoTo.com over to Trip.com. Because the site lists only companies that pay for placement, results are limited, but at least they're not overwhelming.

click on the "Create New Folder" button (it looks like a folder with an asterisk popping out of it).

After surfing for a while, you'll have a nice collection of pages, and when you're ready to take off, you can print some and staple them together to compile a custom guidebook. For extended trips it may be worthwhile to invest in a three-hole punch and soft-cover binder to organize your material.

Online City Guides

Unlike the guidebook sites mentioned earlier, most online city guides don't have print counterparts. They

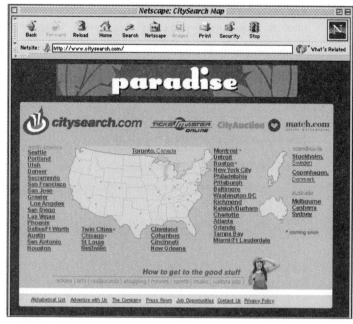

CitySearch (www.citysearch.com) is a collection of dozens of city guides that combine updated features with guidebook-style advice.

exist solely on the Net—and have rapidly developed into robust guides for the cities they cover. Though they're intended primarily for city residents, they can be superb resources for travelers, with listings for restaurants, clubs, plays, sporting events, and more.

However, they don't always deliver as much as they promise. Sometimes, they're just good for basic listings; in other cases, you can count on them to give incisive reviews about local events, restaurants, and attractions.

Despite their limitations, these city guides can be valuable sources of information. What follows are short descriptions of leading city guides with tips on how best to use them.

CitySearch (www.citysearch.com)

Produced in cooperation with local media outlets (usually newspapers and television stations), CitySearch has a section called **Visiting the City** that lists attractions and hotels. **New York CitySearch,** produced in cooperation with the *Daily News,* has some of the grit and attitude that make the city famous for welcoming travelers. CitySearch acquired Microsoft's Sidewalk city guides in 1999, and has plans to boost its coverage to 77 cities in 2000. The **Arts** guide ranges from comedy clubs to opera, with just about everything in between, while **City Scene** is a page full of features, such as a walking tour of the Lower East Side.

Digital City (www.digitalcity.com)

If you're using AOL, enter a city as your keyword, and you'll probably go straight to the Digital City site. Alternately, simply enter keyword: *digitalcity.* On the Web, visit Digital City's home page and click the city of your choice: Let's try Chicago. From there click on

destination anywhere

Entertainment and then on whatever interests you. A click on **Best Bets** led to editors' choices, including a David Mamet play and a reggae show.

Time Out (www.timeout.com)

Go to any newsstand in London and ask for a guide to the city's nightlife, and you'll get a copy of *Time Out*. On the Web, Time Out has guides for most major European cities and for several big U.S. metropolises. Because it combines an irreverent attitude with provocative features and extensive entertainment listings, Time Out is an excellent place to visit just before you take off.

CultureFinder (www.culturefinder.com)

CultureFinder lists arts events for more than 1,000 cities and makes it easy to find precisely the listings you want. Just select the dates of your visit and enter the city's name; in seconds you'll have theater, music, dance, and film listings. Inputting March 26–30 for Boston spawned 141 listings, ranging from *Ragtime* at the Colonial Theater to a Mary Cassatt retrospective at the Boston Museum of Fine Arts. If you find an event you want to attend, you can usually order tickets through the site.

FestivalFinder (www.festivalfinder.com)

OK, so this isn't a true city guide, but attending a festival is a surefire way to enliven a summer trip. Festival Finder offers two ways to search: Click on the category of your choice (folk, blues, country, reggae) or search by name, date, location, or performers. If you already have a trip planned, say to Colorado in June, enter this information and see what's going on there. My search yielded five listings, including the Telluride Bluegrass Festival and a Glen Miller festival.

Yahoo Gets Local

At the bottom of Yahoo's main page is a list of links to its regional guides, some for U.S. cities and others for countries around the world. Regional guides include event listings, lodging options, even news and sports scores for that city. A click on the metro site for Austin led to a mini-Yahoo directory for this Texas college town. Clicking on "Travel and Transportation," I found a long list of links to sites such as A Pinhole Tour of Austin, a highly personal virtual saunter past

CultureFinder (culturefinder.com) makes it easy to find arts events in more than 1,000 cities.

kitschy diners, minigolf courses, and swimming holes. Yahoo's city guides (grouped under Yahoo Gets Local) are mainly lists of links and don't have the editorial presentation you'll find on City Search or Digital City. On the other hand, I probably wouldn't have found this endearing Pinhole Tour on Sidewalk. Other portals, such as Excite, also have city guides that are based heavily on links to outside sites.

Noncorporate, Web-only Guides

Not every place you're going to visit will have a city guide devoted to it. Even if it does, it's best to balance these branded sites with information from hobbyists' sites, typically labors of love that demonstrate the authors' passions for their various destinations.

For a recent trip to the Grand Canyon, I first hit the official **U.S. National Park Service** site **(www.nps.gov)** and then searched on Yahoo for "grand canyon guide." This turned up thirty-seven site listings, including an extraordinary site called **Grand Canyon Explorer (www.kaibab.org)**.

Although the NPS site has solid official information, Grand Canyon Explorer, maintained by Canyon lover Bob Ribokas, is an online guide devoted solely to the canyon. It includes photographic tours, suggested hikes for first-timers, and advice for how much water to carry (a lot). There's a section of kids' activities, history, lodging suggestions, and canyon maps. Ribokas's adoration and respect for the canyon infuse the entire site, making it much more memorable to visit than an official government site.

The good news is that Ribokas's Grand Canyon opus is not the only one of its kind. Just about every major city or tourist attraction has at least one high-quality site—and usually several—devoted to it. Many of these are listed in the Web directories at the back of this book. It's impossible to include them all and new ones come online every month, so don't rely solely on the listings in the Web directories. Use search sites to venture into the Web's wild backcountry and see for yourself what you can track down.

If it seems too daunting to use search engines, some leading travel sites have links to their top picks by destination. **About.com (www.about.com)** has a travel area with dozens of city guides, such as **Las Vegas for Visitors**. A click on "More Links" leads to more than forty *categories* of links. Under Dining Out, I found **The Utterly Obsessive, Quite Superfluous, All-U-Can-Eat Guide to Las Vegas Buffets (www.ufomind.com/ place/us/nv/lasvegas/buffet)**. About.com has grown, and it sometimes seems almost as overwhelming as the search sites, but rest assured, its links are usually pretty well organized and hand-picked by a specialist in each subject.

Newspapers on the Net

Before the advent of the World Wide Web, savvy travelers would visit their local newsstand or library and read the newspaper for the city they were about to visit. Today, there's no need to hit the stands, just use the Net to scan the papers for your destination. Virtually every major newspaper has a free Web site, and many of these publications have special sections for entertainment listings. It's also wise to check the online newspapers' travel sections as these pages often provide information for out-of-town visitors.

So how do you find newspapers? One strategy is to go to your favorite search engine, but a better way is to use newspaper directories, which list thousands of publications from around the world. Among the best is **AJR Newslink (ajr.newslink.org/news.html)**, which categorizes U.S. papers by state and international ones by continent. You can also type your destination into the search box and see what comes up. Other top-flight newspaper directories include **Newspapers Online (www.newspapers.com)** and Editor and Publisher's **MediaInfo (www.mediainfo.com/emedia)**.

In addition to the major metro dailies, alternative newsweeklies—with their extensive arts listings—are ideal sources of information for travelers. To find altweeklies, try **NewCityNet (www.newcitynet.com)**, which lists dozens of the best from Eugene, Oregon, to Philadelphia. AJR Newslink also has a category for alternative papers, organized by state.

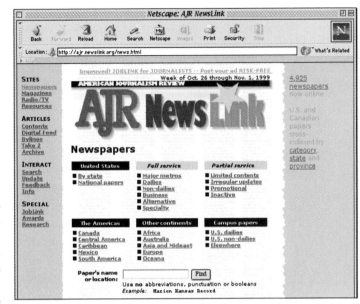

AJR Newslink (ajr.newslink.org/news.html) lets you home in on local news for your destination.

Some Superb Newspaper Travel Sections

Back in the mid-1970s, a newspaper delivery boy asked a housewife in a San Francisco suburb if she'd like to subscribe to the *Times*. Turned out she'd just moved there from New York and was thrilled to sign up for home delivery, until she realized the kid meant the *San Mateo Times*. Well, a few years later the *New York Times* launched its national edition, and she got the Old Gray Lady delivered after all. Today, just about every major newspaper in the United States and abroad offers home delivery—at no charge—through the Net. Here are a few of the best:

The New York Times (www.nytimes.com/travel)

Guidebooks are great, but more personal views are also valuable, and that's what the features at the Times offer. Much of the page is devoted to stories from the previous Sunday's travel section, but you can easily access archives through a clickable world map under **Destinations.** You'll also find archives of popular columns, such as **The Frugal Traveler.** For tech tips, click over to **Travel Log** in the CyberTimes section.

The Washington Post (www.washingtonpost.com/travel)

The *Post*'s online travel editors understand that their site isn't just for locals. They've created a **Visitors' Guide** with tours of the town, museum listings, places to stay, and much more. Click on the **"Trip Planner,"** enter the dates of your visit, and get a list of events taking place during your stay. Back at the main travel page are travel features and a nice selection of online tools, including listings for tourism offices, airport shuttles, and weather.

First Person: Larry Bleiberg

Before taking a trip, I glance at online newspapers and magazines from the area I plan to visit. In the last two years, I've been an occasional long-distance reader of the *Washington Post,* the *Vientiane* (Laos) *Times*, and the *Prince Rupert* (Canada) *Daily News,* among others.

Just by scanning the headlines, I learn about local municipal scandals and sports competitions, and, most important, I get a preview of the place I plan to visit. None of this is mandatory before a trip, but part of the joy of travel is that it provides a peek inside another way of life. Before a recent trip to the Middle East, I used online newspaper directories to link to local news outlets from Israel and Jordan. Following are a couple of items I found:

- The annual horse-endurance race across Jordan's Arabian Desert was a nail-biter. Dubai's crown prince finished the 80-mile course in 7 hours, 26 minutes. Quite a gentleman, the prince donated his prize, a Land Rover, to charity.

- In Israel, leaders marked the closure of a fifty-year-old garbage dump with a cocktail party and music provided by the Tel Aviv Fire and Rescue Service band. One of the politicians used the occasion to campaign for mayor, but another kept his speech short, declaring the site too "hot and smelly."

Reading local media outlets not only makes my stay more meaningful, but it can make it more comfortable. While it's wonderful to visit a new place and become immersed in the swirl of daily life, it also can be intimidating.

The only danger is that knowing too much about a place can remove some of its romance. For example, by reading the online version of the *Jordan Times,* I learned that the early morning music in Amman isn't the lyrical call of the ancient city. It's gas cylinder delivery trucks.

According to the newspaper, the vehicles prowl the streets honking their horns to attract customers, much like an ice-cream truck's siren song. But the early deliveries of the popular fuel source have annoyed many residents, so the city has required the trucks to play classical music instead of honking.

Not an exotic explanation, granted. But at least it was one less thing I had to wonder about when I got there.

Larry Bleiberg is assistant travel editor of the *Dallas Morning News.*
Reprinted with permission of the *Dallas Morning News.*

The Planet (www.the-planet.co.uk)

A publication of the London-based electronic Telegraph, the Planet combines recent features (riding a camel train through the Australian outback) with an extensive database of travel stories and classifieds for holiday seekers. Use pull-down menus to search by region or country and by activity. A search for "cycling" and "Europe" turned up twelve stories, including "Wheeling in a Kent Wonderland." Travel news, last-minute deals, and seasonal features, such as ski reports, round out this fine site.

SF Gate Traveler (www.sfgate.com/travel)

SF Gate, a collaboration between the *San Francisco Examiner* and *Chronicle,* produces this lively guide to the city. Recent features included SF's top one hundred restaurants and advice on where to celebrate Chinese New Year. Click on the "Visitors Guide" and find a tour for "virgins" (first-time visitors to the city) and **The Ten Best Things to Do in SF,** such as watching the surf crash at Fort Point. At the bottom of the SF Gate Traveler home page is a link to the *San Francisco Examiner* Sunday Travel section and a column called **Follow the Reader,** where you can peruse tips from travelers who discuss their favorite off-the-beaten-path secrets.

Keep in mind that travel and entertainment aren't the only sections worth checking. It's

In addition to lively travel features, the Washington Post's travel section (washingtonpost.com/travel) has a visitor's guide listing local attractions, hotels, and restaurants.

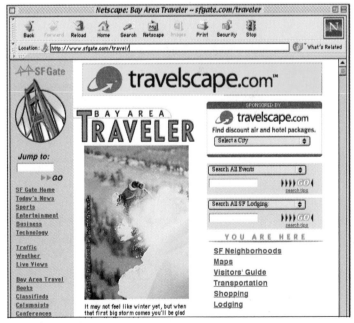

SF Gate's Bay Area Traveler (www.sfgate.com/travel) is an example of a city guide produced by local media outlets.

often best to start with the home page (formerly known as the front page) and scan the news and metro sections to get a sense of what's happening at your destination. And even if you don't speak the language of the place you're headed, you can often find superb English-language newspapers, such as the **Jerusalem Post (www.jpost.co.il)** and **Russia Today (www.russiatoday.com)**, online.

Magazines Get Online

Just as most top newspapers have taken to the Net, so have leading magazines. Yet there are many excellent publications that exist solely on the Web, from the literary **Salon Travel (salon.com/travel)** to the quirky **Split (www.splitnews.com)**. And of course, well-known names such as **CNN** and **Condé Nast Traveler** have jumped into the online publishing fray with mixed results. CNN and CNT do a fine job by adapting their content to the capabilities of the Web, while other leading brands have simply slapped stories online, with less compelling results.

For a more complete roundup of online travel publications, visit Yahoo's list of travel magazines at **dir.yahoo.com/Recreation/Travel/News_and_Media/ Magazines**. If this address is too unwieldy, simply go to **yahoo.com**, and click "Travel" then "News and Media," and finally "Magazines" and scroll down to see the list. (Or see the Web directories at the back of this book.)

> ## tip
> ■ **Some parts of a URL (Web address) are case sensitive, meaning that upper and lower cases are significant. In the Yahoo URL, everything after "yahoo.com" is case sensitive, so if you don't use capitals in the right places, it might not work.**

A selection of leading online magazines follows. Keep in mind that these publications are as varied as print publications and take wildly divergent approaches. As you might imagine, CNN is a solid general resource, while The Connected Traveler offers a more personal viewpoint.

CNN Travelguide (www.cnn.com/TRAVEL)

With breaking travel news, destination features, and tools, such as maps and trip directions, **Travelguide** aims to be an all-in-one travel site. Though no single site will satisfy all your desires, CNN does a good job with its wide range of offerings. Its destination guides are at the heart of this site, with timely reports from around the globe, as well as light-hearted features, such as a tour of Seattle's funky Fremont neighborhood. You can also search CNN to get news reports about your destination.

Concierge.com: The Travel Supersite (concierge.com)

Pulling together magazine features from *Condé Nast Traveler* with reviews from Fodor's and booking by Expedia.com, **Concierge.com** promises one-stop shopping for the upscale traveler. Those familiar with Condé Nast Traveler's print edition know the magazine loves lists, such as the Top 50 Golf Resorts. Following the link to top golf resorts lets you sort by course design, nearby accommodations and dining, or even speed of play. But this is just one of many features. The clickable world map lets you zoom in on destinations and get recommendations for lodging, dining, events, and more. The Search button is another way to quickly access destination information. Before searching, choose whether you want to find essentials, dining, lodging, or photos. Other sections linked from the home page include **Bargains, Advice, Features, Discussion,** and **CN Traveler,** which has features from the magazine.

Salon Travel (www.salon.com/travel/index.html)

Even if you're not planning a trip, *Salon* magazine's travel section, formerly known as Wanderlust, is a destination in its own right. This is perhaps the ultimate watering hole for armchair travelers, where you can read stirring dispatches from leading travel writers. They go places you might not want to, such as war-torn Kosovo, where the writer had a gun pointed to her head and realized in a heartbeat that journalists are not immune from strife.

Editor Don George, a veteran of newspaper and magazine journalism, says he loves the ability to post stories immediately. "When we were covering the 1998 World Cup in France, our last dispatch from Paris began, 'Outside my window all of Paris seems to be cheering in the streets,' or words to that effect. We were able to have the story online and being read around the planet while the cheering was still going on." Along with the first-person narratives, Salon Travel weaves in columns, including George's take on travel books.

What's a Zine?

John Labovitz, publisher of "John Labovitz's e-zine list," says, "Zines are generally produced by one person or a small group of people, done often for fun or personal reasons, and tend to be irreverent, bizarre, and/or esoteric. Zines are not mainstream publications—they generally do not contain advertisements (except, sometimes, ads for other zines), are not targeted toward a mass audience, and are generally not produced to make a profit."

National Geographic & National Geographic Traveler (www.nationalgeographic.com)

With its remarkable photographs and in-depth stories, *National Geographic* is certainly the most saved magazine in the country—it's just too beautiful to toss in the trash. The National Geographic Society has adapted well to the Web, where readers can tag along as explorers venture to the ends of the earth. **National Geographic Traveler (www.nationalgeographic.com/traveler)** combines current features from the print magazine of the same name with hints for family travel and an archive of past issues. Click on "Trips" to browse the library of past issues and get "timeless" information for more than 250 destinations. For stories aimed at kids, visit **National Geographic World (www.nationalgeographic.com/world/index.html).**

The Connected Traveler
(www.connectedtraveler.com)

Veteran travel writer Russ Johnson has collected some of his best stories and combined them with streaming audio and video. A recent feature on Fiji included a high-quality recording of one of that country's magnificent a capella choirs. With the **RealAudio** player (available for free download at **www.real.com**), you can listen to these lustrous sounds as you read the story. The old knock against reading online is that unlike a print publication, "You can't take it to the bathroom." True enough, but on the other hand, I've never had a newspaper sing to me. The Connected Traveler also includes dispatches from other terrific writers, including Jan Morris.

"For a writer, the Web is a great way to put your money where your mouth is," Johnson says. "That is, to discipline yourself to keep writing, to experiment and develop a voice that is uniquely your own without the scrutiny of editors trying to mold you into a form that fits their publication's branding. On my Web site, I can be whatever I want: a Wired pundit, a slice of New Yorker wry, one of the Three Stooges. If it is good, I sometimes get instant praise from readers. If it is bad, I can trash it or rewrite it almost instantly. I have thousands of copy editors to keep me straight.

"I think the Web is the ultimate storytelling medium," Johnson continues, "and will become more so as bandwidth increases. In past

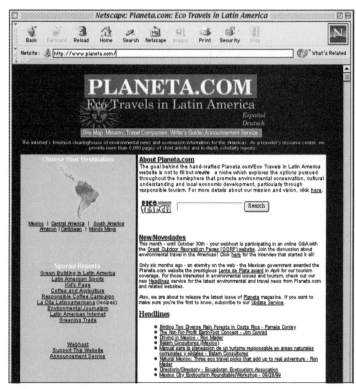

Planeta.com: Eco Travels in Latin America (www.planeta.com) shows that an individual can produce a respectable and widely read online magazine.

lives I have produced for print, radio, and television. On the Web I can now choose the best medium to tell the story. I can combine a complex description that only the written word can convey with the simple statement of a photograph and a video interview that reveals emotion and personality. I can Webcast the excitement of a live event from almost anywhere in the world."

Planeta.com (www.planeta.com)

The Internet revolution has made it much easier for one person with a mission to promote a worthy cause. Ron Mader does this with Planeta, which focuses on sustainable tourism in Latin America. Planeta is a deep resource (8,000 pages and growing) and includes a directory of ecologically aware tour operators and a listing of Internet cafes. A free e-mail newsletter keeps readers current on developments in the region.

The Web is home to dozens of other worthy e-zines too numerous to list here. To learn more about others, see the Web directories at the back of this book, consult the Yahoo listing of travel magazines, or see **John Labovitz's e-zine list (www.meer.net/ ~johnl/e-zine-list)**. Inserting the keyword *travel* yielded a list of 115 zines, including "Be There Now: A Zine of Budget Travel and Beating the Rat Race." Each listing includes a brief summary, publication frequency, and a link to its site.

Summing Up

Though this chapter lists some of the best of the Web, it's only the tip of the tip of the iceberg. Like every real-world journey, each excursion through the Wild Wild Web is unique. This chapter is simply a guide: Use the information here as a jumping-off point, dive in, and see what you find. The same, sage advice for traveling, "keep your mind open and let curiosity be your guide," is a good way to approach the Net as well.

Although lots of terrific destination resources are listed in this chapter, many sites listed in other chapters are also valuable for trip research. Some of the tools mentioned in chapter 10 (online maps, international advisories, and ATM locators, for example) have become indispensable for travelers who want to make their trips as convenient as possible.

Finally, remember there's more than one way to use these resources. Whether you print out a few sheets to supplement your guidebook, jot down some notes from your favorite sites, or simply browse to become more familiar with your destination, the Net can help you get the most from your travels.

Other Chapters to Check

Chapter 2: "Booking Flights Online"—Booking sites' travel guides, advice and travel news

Chapter 5: "On the Road"—Map sites and getting point-to-point trip directions

Chapter 11: "Taking Care of Business"—Business travel advice and sites for frequent fliers

Chapter 12: "A Traveler's Toolbox"— Essentials including official advisories, health tips, and language tutorials

Chapter 13: "Online Discussion Forums"—Getting advice from other travelers

---

BECOME YOUR OWN TRAVEL AGENT

A few years ago, I sat in a travel agent's office as she checked my flight options. She tapped the keys—I waited. Then, she tapped some more and offered me a couple of choices. I knew she was seeing all the options and wished there was some way I could turn the screen around and see for myself. Well, through the Web, millions of travelers have rotated the screen, as new booking services let them explore the same databases that agents use. The beauty of these services is they're open twenty-four hours a day, seven days a week. So if you want to sit down in your bathrobe on a Sunday morning and plan your trip to Tahiti, go right ahead.

The Online Booking Revolution

By providing access to airline timetables and other travel booking databases, online agencies, such as **Expedia.com** and **Travelocity (www.travelocity.com)**, are revolutionizing the travel industry. These sites offer one-stop shopping for flights, hotel rooms, and rental cars, without the arcane codes that travel agents must master. And they provide up-to-date travel news, advice from veteran experts, and incentives (such as bonus frequent flier miles) for booking online. You can even learn about cruises and package vacations and snag last-minute deals.

Airlines love these systems because they can go directly to consumers and sell some seats (at cut-rate prices!) that might have flown empty. Consumers enjoy new saving opportunities, unparalleled convenience, and the ability to research trips for themselves.

And online booking sites offer features that not even the best travel agents provide. Many sites, such as Expedia, have low-fare e-mail alerts: Each week **Expedia's Fare Tracker** will send an e-mail message with the lowest fare to your favorite destination. Online agents also provide timely news updates; special offers, such as $99 companion fares; and flight-tracking features that let you see when a flight is due or send a message to your pager if a departure is delayed.

Where to Book It

There are two primary types of online booking systems: online agents like Expedia that search the databases of hundreds of airlines, and airline booking sites (such as Delta's at **www.delta-air.com**) that typically sell tickets just for that airline. Of course, there are other places to book travel, such as online discounter **1travel.com.** Each has its advantages, though it makes sense to start with broad sites like Expedia because these are the best places to comparison shop.

After finding the airline with the best deal, try going to that airline's site because there may be incentives for booking there. If it appears that your best deal is on, say, American, then go to American's site (**aa.com**) because it may be worth buying directly from that site. American recently offered 4,000 bonus frequent flier miles for first-time buyers at its site—

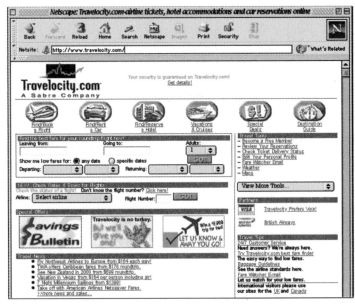

Travelocity (travelocity.com) is one of the Big Three online travel agencies.

returning users could receive 1,000 bonus miles. **Preview Travel (www.preview travel.com)** and other big booking sites are also offering some incentives, so compare and go with the site that has the most appealing deal.

Is My Credit Card Safe?

Probably the two questions travelers ask most frequently about booking on the Net are: "Can you get a better deal on the Net?" and "Is it safe to put your credit card online?" The answer to the first question is "sometimes," and the answer to the second is almost always "yes." As this book went to press, there have been no reports of credit card theft at major booking sites since they installed secure encryption technology in the mid-1990s.

Even if there's an unauthorized charge to your credit card (for anything, not just online purchases), you're only liable for $50, at least in the United States. And some online booking sites, including Expedia, are saying they'll pay the $50 if they are ever responsible for any illegal charges to your card. Ironically, after Expedia spends pages telling you how safe it is to book online, its site includes a banner ad for the American Express card, saying AmEx won't ever hold its customers liable for unauthorized charges.

Just as consumers were slow to warm to automated teller machines (ATMs) in the early 1980s, some are a bit hesitant about putting their credit card numbers online today. As airlines lure travelers with incentives for booking online, more people are giving it a shot and becoming increasingly comfortable with the process. As consumers get used to the convenience and ease of online booking, the Net will become an indispensable tool for millions of travelers.

Finding *the* Best Deals

The question of finding the best deal is trickier than just booking a flight. The Net wins hands down for last-minute specials. Airlines can send e-mail out a few days ahead of flights that aren't filling up and lure more passengers with cut-rate deals. Most of these offers are for weekend getaways, but some airlines are offering specials for flights weeks or months in advance.

Southwest (www.southwest. com) recently had an Internet special of $33 each way between Oakland and Burbank (near Los Angeles). Typically, these tickets must be purchased online—and for those with flexible schedules they're a great deal. (More on last-minute deals in chap. 7.)

When you have to plan ahead, human agents can help find deals you might not uncover on the Net. Recently, I was planning a trip from San Francisco to Chicago to New York and back to San Francisco. Because this wasn't a simple round-trip, I called an experienced agent who told me that if I was willing to leave New York an hour later than I originally had planned, I could save about $100.

For basic round-trips in North America, the Net is a fine tool for scanning timetables and booking trips. All the major online agencies have adopted technology that searches alternate flights to

Preview Travel (www.previewtravel.com) has one of the most inviting home pages on the Web.

see if you're getting the best deal. For example, if I request a flight on **Preview Travel (www.previewtravel.com)**, its **Best Fare Finder** will check flights that are a bit earlier or later to see if there are better deals out there. Of course, if you want to make sure you're getting a good deal, you could scan newspaper travel sections or call a travel agent and see if she or he can beat the prices you find online.

Information Is Power

Even if you use a travel agent, it's great to be able to check flight availability on the Net. Back in 1995, when booking systems were just coming online, I'd reserved a trip to Mexico (through a traditional agent) and wanted to change the date of my departure. So I called the agent who sold me the ticket, and she said she couldn't change it because there was no availability. The next day I used Preview Travel to check and found that not only were there open seats on the flight I wanted, but the fare was lower! I called the agent again, and she said sometimes these flights open up and rebooked me.

She may very well have been truthful, the flight might have been full when she checked,

Who Should Use Online Booking Agents?

Online booking agents are not for every traveler. Some might be better served using the Net simply to find interesting travel destinations and offers, and then turning to a professional to book the trip. So who should use online booking agents?

Use online booking engines if you

- travel primarily in North America. Although it's easy to book popular international routes (New York to London), you won't often get the best price.

- want to take advantage of last-minute deals, which must be purchased online.

- enjoy the convenience of booking anytime and anywhere. If you're too busy during the day to call a travel agent, log on after you put the kids to sleep and explore your options. Or if you use a computer at work, take a break and book a flight—you'll still appear to be working.

- would like to take advantage of Net-only specials. **Southwest (www.southwest.com)** is one of several airlines offering special Internet fares, available only to those who book online. These aren't just valid for last-minute travel but can be booked months in advance.

- want to earn incentives for booking online, such as bonus frequent flier miles.

- have strong loyalties to a particular airline. If you have a favorite airline or want to stick with a frequent flier program, you can go directly to that airline's site or set up a preference for that airline at an online agent.

or she simply may not have checked at all and told me it was full. This shows one of the advantages of online booking services: You can be your own travel agent. It's not fair to expect professional agents to keep checking flights for you, especially if they're only getting a $20 or $30 commission. But if you have time, you can check as often as you like and find a great fare or last-minute deal.

An End Run around Clogged Switchboards

A couple of years ago, Southwest triggered one of the most astounding fare wars in recent memory, offering $50 round-trip fares on most of its routes. Other airlines rushed to match these fares, and thousands of travelers clamored to get through to flooded reservation switchboards.

Don't rely on booking engines if you

■ have a complex itinerary with lots of stops. The more complex your itinerary, the more difficult it will be for you to find the best deal through an online agent. Although online sites are constantly evolving, they can't always do what a human can, which is suggest alternate routes or the cheapest days to fly.

■ travel to remote areas. If you're flying to Ecuador, Pakistan, or some other less-visited destination, consult a travel agent or consolidator (an agent who lists special unpublished fares) who specializes in that region. Some sites, including **1travel.com.** and **intelliTrip.com** are offering consolidator bargains online, but real-world consolidators tend to be specialists in certain regions, and they can often find the best deal.

■ are looking for the cheapest international flight. Although it's not hard to book standard international flights online, consolidators will often offer the best deals.

■ require follow-up services from travel agents. Though Expedia and the others are accredited travel agencies and employ agents to assist customers, they're aimed at the self-service consumer. It can be easier to enlist the services of a local agent if you feel it's likely you will have to change your ticket after it's issued.

tip

■ Look for a small image of a lock—in Netscape's browser it's in the lower left-hand corner, in Internet Explorer it's bottom right—to see whether you're in secure mode. If the lock is locked, you are; if it's open, you're not. If you're in secure mode, your credit card number and all other sensitive information will be coded before it's transmitted, making it almost impossible to pilfer.

Can Travel Agents Survive?

Are travel agents doomed? Of course not. As veteran travel writer Morris Dye has said for years, travel agents have traditionally sold two products: access to the computer reservation system (CRS) and expertise about the travel industry. Today, access is far less important, because anyone with a Net connection can log into these databases. (You don't even have to own a computer; you can get online for little or no cost at libraries, copy shops, and Net cafes.) But expertise is still essential, and good travel agents continue to help their clients save time and money. And no matter how useful the Net becomes, many busy people will still prefer the convenience of picking up the phone and calling a savvy agent.

Through the late 1990s, the number of travel agents declined slightly, though not markedly. Most of the decline was in small agencies, but in 1999 only 3 percent (according to projections by **Jupiter Communications**; see **jup.com**) of all travel was booked online. Though this number is relatively small, it was up from less than 1 percent in 1997 and projected to grow to 11 percent by 2003.

Systems engineer Keith Jarett of Oakland, California, turned to Travelocity after failing "in 500 or so autodial attempts" to get through to Southwest's phone reservation system. "I got three tickets from Travelocity. An Oakland to Phoenix round-trip for me, Oakland to Los Angeles round-trip (Disneyland) for the family, and Oakland to Seattle for my parents."

A Preview Travel spokesman said the big sale is "a perfect example" of why online booking is better than traditional ticketing systems. "We could handle the load. Southwest triggered a fare war the likes of which we hadn't seen in ten years." As other airlines matched Southwest's fares, the outpouring of demand swamped traditional ticketing systems. "We tripled our volume," he said, "We're open twenty-four hours a day, seven days a week. When all the travel agents closed and the airline reservations switchboards went to skeleton crews, we were open and ready to go. That's the real magic of online and scalable systems."

Asked if there's a battle brewing between electronic and human agents, the spokesman said that there's a war being fought, not between online agents and storefront agents but between travel suppliers and all agents. Travel suppliers, including airlines, hotel, cruise lines, and tour companies, are working to "cut the agent out of the loop

tip

■ Before you book, find out if you'll have to pay a fee to change the time or date of your flight. Most airlines now charge a fee of up to $75 to change a ticket after it's issued. Check the restrictions online or call an airline's toll-free number to find out. Some airlines, for example, Shuttle by United, will let you change times or dates for free in some cases, if you don't alter the route. So although a ticket on one carrier might be cheaper, it could cost you more in the end if you have to change your ticket.

and save the commission." If a travel supplier sells directly to a consumer, that supplier doesn't have to pay a commission to anyone.

In recent years, airlines have been successful at grabbing a bigger piece of the online booking pie, according to **Jupiter Communications (jup.com)**. In 1996 online agencies, such as Preview and Expedia, handled about four of five online bookings, with suppliers (United, Hilton, etc.) accounting for about 20 percent of bookings at their own sites. Just three years later, travel suppliers, mainly the airlines, had grabbed about half of all online bookings. That number is expected to rise to 60 percent by 2003.

Using Leading Online Travel Agencies

To book a flight through most online agencies, you must become a member. Don't worry—membership has its privileges, and it's free. All it takes is entering some basic information, such as your name, a user ID, and password. Online agencies can store this, so that each time you return, all you have to enter is your password. What's actually happening is that the booking site recognizes your computer, so if you log on from a different machine, you'll have to reenter you username as well as your password.

Remember you can do as much, or as little, as you want. If you'd like to price a ticket online, then call a real-world travel agent to see if that person can get a better price, go right ahead. For an introduction to online booking, we'll go through the steps at Expedia—the process is somewhat similar at most other booking sites. Finally, keep in mind that this is a snapshot of the online booking world as it exists at press time; some changes will undoubtedly occur as these sites evolve at a breakneck pace.

Expedia.com

When you first visit **Expedia.com**, which was created in 1996 by Microsoft, you'll be greeted by a screen, offering flight, hotel, and rental car booking, as well as a host of options to buy resort packages, travel books, and other merchandise. If you scroll down, you'll see links to Expedia's excellent magazine features, which include current travel news and columns from travel experts. But if you want to use the booking features, you first must become a member.

Start by clicking "Register with Expedia." Doing this leads to a page that requests your name and asks you to create a user ID and password. You can also sign up here for **Fare**

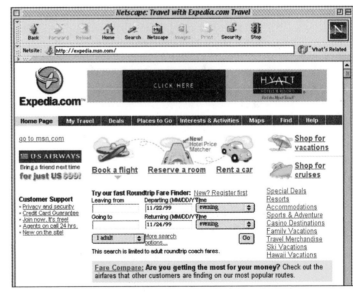

Expedia.com (expedia.com) offers online booking and lots of helpful travel planning features.

Tracker, which will send a weekly e-mail notice, listing the best deals to your favorite destination. Click "Continue" to reach a page that confirms your membership and has a lengthy list of conditions for using the service. If you're like most people, you probably won't wade through the legalese, and you'll just click "I Accept." As a member of TRUSTe, Expedia pledges not to sell or share your e-mail address or other personal information without your consent.

Like a good salesperson, Expedia's **Travel Agent** remembers your name and greets you when you walk through its virtual door. The Travel Agent page has what it calls the **Flight Wizard, Hotel Wizard,** and **Car Wizard.** You can start with any of these or fill out a profile with your flight preferences. The profile includes spaces for contact information, seat and meal preferences, and frequent flier numbers. You might feel that it's more trouble than it's worth, but keep in mind you'll only have to do this once, and it will make future booking faster and more convenient.

tip

■ **Pick one password and use it for all the sites you visit. I'd recommend selecting a six- to eight-digit password that's a mix of letters and numbers. Make it easy to remember but not obvious: It's not a good idea to use your name, birthdate, or other information that can be easily linked to you.**

Comparing Fares

A good way to get a sense of current prices is by clicking on Expedia's **"Fare Compare"** to scan the lowest current fares to your destination. (Other sites have similar services—Preview calls its service Farefinder.) Expedia is set to add another price comparison feature, enabling users to see the lowest fare that other travelers were able to purchase for the same route. At the bottom of the Fare Compare page are two boxes labeled "From" and "To"—simply enter your departure and arrival cities (or airport codes, if you know them) to see what the best deals are.

Remember, the lowest current fare might not be available for the dates or times you want to fly. To see if this fare is available for your itinerary, you'll have to try booking it through Expedia's Flight Wizard. Fares change daily—even hourly—so if you find a good deal grab it; if you don't, keep checking because you never know when it might change.

Booking a Flight

Cruising back over to the Flight Wizard, I notice that my departure airport is already set at San Francisco because that's the one I chose on the preference page. If I want to explore flight options from other nearby airports, such as Oakland or San Jose, I can just change the outgoing airport. To find a flight to New York, I fill in the boxes below: date, time, class, and number of people traveling, then I click "Continue." Expedia searches for a few seconds and comes up with a list of best-priced flights.

To see if there's a better deal, you could try another outlet, such as the discount ticketeer **Cheap Tickets (www.cheaptickets.com)**. Sometimes, these discounters have deals that aren't available through more mainstream channels. Registration at Cheap Tickets requires inputting a credit card number before getting started, which is one reason many people elect to call the company's toll-free number rather than booking online.

Back at Expedia, select a flight from the list of those that meet your itinerary, and you'll get a list of conditions, including the $75 fee to change. If you agree with these rules, click

booking flights online

"Reserve." On the next screen choose between purchasing the ticket now or reserving it. Airline fares are not guaranteed until purchased, so beware that a good deal could slip away if you wait to buy it.

Even if you just want to hold a reservation, Expedia asks for your credit card number, which might miff some people. If you're comfortable proceeding (and it's probably safer than giving your card to a waiter), enter this information, and you'll get to a confirmation screen. To buy a ticket, input your credit card number and choose whether you'd like a traditional paper ticket or if you're willing to fly ticketless. For most flights you can also choose your seat online. An image of the plane's interior shows which seats remain. Click on your preference.

When you've completed the booking process, don't forget to print out the confirmation page, which lists your flight information and confirmation number. This procedure is especially important if you're flying ticketless.

Express Booking and Other Reasons to Visit

The major online booking services have come under fire because it can take ten or more screens to get to the "Book It" button. Recently, however, Expedia and others have introduced a mini-booking screen on their home pages, meaning you can go from inputting your destination to purchasing a ticket in as few as three Web pages. At some sites this feature only works for domestic round-trips, but it's a lot nicer than having to wade through so many pages.

Another reason to visit Expedia, even if you're not buying a ticket, is for its fine magazine features, including its **Insider Advice (expedia.com/daily/experts)** section. These features range from Dr. Alan Spira's travel health tips to savvy suggestions from *Today Show* travel editor Peter Greenberg, whose column is called Travel Detective. Check the Insider Advice archive for a lengthy selection of past articles from such insiders as Douglas Ward, who writes a cruise column. You'll also find world news from MSNBC, the latest travel deals, and enticing destination features ("San Diego Springtime") in the magazine.

Expedia's Resources section includes weather reports, flight status (see if an incoming flight is on time), and destination information, but the destination guides are pretty generic and limited, and the navigation is tedious—you can do better at an online guidebook. Expedia recently introduced a vacation package finder, enabling users to input their interests and budget (windsurfing, Hawaii, under $1,000 a week) and see what trips meet their criteria.

Of course, Expedia isn't the only major booking site—the others are Preview Travel, Travelocity, and Internet Travel Network. Though the biggies are pretty similar, each has unique features. It's probably worth visiting each one to see which feels most comfortable.

tip

■ Expedia and other booking sites can search simultaneously for the best deals to several airports in a big city. If you enter "Chicago" in the destination box, the next screen will offer a choice of O'Hare (the leading airport), Midway, or all Chicago airports. By choosing all airports, you have a better chance of finding a bargain. Most likely, the best fare will be to Midway, as more budget airlines fly there. But because you never know where the deals are, it's best to check all airports.

Ticketless Travel: Lots of Pros, One Possible Con

Ticketless travel has become increasingly popular in recent years: Airlines like it because it saves them the expense of processing paper tickets (though most airlines still send a page of confirmation information), and travelers appreciate the convenience. There's no need to worry about losing the ticket—there's no ticket to lose. Just show a photo ID (and sometimes the credit card used for purchasing the ticket) at check-in.

There is one potential drawback to flying ticketless: If a flight is canceled, it can be harder to transfer your ticket to another airline. If your airline goes on strike, for example, you may have to get the airline to issue you a paper ticket before another carrier will accept it. And if hundreds of others are trying to do the same thing, it can be a major hassle. Though these problems don't occur often, they're something to consider before electing to go paperless.

In some cases, such as with American's weekend getaway Net SAAver fares, you have no option but to go ticketless. And many travelers find it's well worth the small risk to take advantage of these Net-only bargains.

Travelocity: Fast Booking

Like its competitors, **Travelocity (www.travelocity.com)** has become a travel portal, providing a wide range of travel tools and destination guides for its users. Travelocity uses the same SABRE computer reservation system employed by thousands of travel agents, and it has led the way in expediting the booking process. If you start booking on the home page, you can book a flight in less than a minute (assuming you've already filled out a profile with your address and credit card number).

In the left-hand column on the home page is a nice assortment of tools for travelers, including a currency converter, maps, and weather forecasts. One of the coolest tools is a feature called **Flight Paging.** If you own an alphanumeric pager with national access that can receive e-mail, this paging system will alert you if your flight is delayed. You can keep tabs on up to four flights on participating airlines. Most major North American airlines are part of the system.

With Travelocity's **Fare Watcher,** you can input up to five routes, and Fare Watcher will send you e-mail every time the fare jumps or drops by $25 or more. Fare Watcher also creates a custom Web page for each member who wants one, meaning you can go to that page anytime time and check the best rates on your preferred routes.

Preview Travel Makes It Easy

If **Preview Travel (www.previewtravel.com)** seems easy to use, that's no coincidence; it's the primary booking service for AOL and shares AOL's philosophy of making the Net as welcoming as possible. (Note: Though Preview is AOL's booking service, AOL members can use other online agencies by venturing out onto the Web.) Lots of features demonstrate Preview simplicity, such as **Farefinder,** which lists the best current rates from any airport you choose to dozens of domestic and international destinations.

With Preview's excellent **Fare Alert** feature, you can set fares for up to three routes, and you'll receive e-mail notices when the fare dips below your target amount. For example, I've asked Fare Alert to notify me when the round-trip fare between San Francisco and New York drops below $300. This way I don't have to constantly check for cheap fares—Preview will automatically keep me posted.

Preview Travel & Travelocity Set to Merge

As this book went to press in late 1999, Preview Travel and Travelocity announced a merger. The new company will be known as Travelocity.com, as the second- and third-ranked online agencies merge to take on the former number-one service, Expedia.com. The alliance makes the new Travelocity.com the top-ranked booking service in sales and members, though its combined membership of 17 million is misleading because many people had registered with both Preview and Travelocity.

Travelocity benefits by gaining Preview's well regarded content (which includes destination information from Fodor's). It should be a good match given that Preview had a knack for devising a user-friendly interface while Travelocity's strength is its technical know-how and reputation for fast booking. The combined company is expected to have more than $1 billion in annual sales, making the new Travelocity.com the third largest e-commerce company behind retailer Amazon.com and eBay, the online auction firm.

Although this appears to be a done deal, a Preview Travel spokesman cautioned that it still requires federal approval. If it goes through, and it's widely expected that it will, the new Travelocity.com will incorporate the best features from both sites. Around the same time, Travelocity should replace Preview Travel as AOL's travel booking service.

For AOL Users:

ONLINE BOOKING

Airline Center (keyword: *Airline*): AOL calls this a "one-stop shop" for booking flights, as well as finding info on bargains, frequent flier programs, and strategies for finding deals.

Internet Travel Network

Some months ago, I sent an e-mail message to a product manager at Internet Travel Network, asking some questions about **ITN (itn.com)**. He asked me to wait a few weeks until ITN completed its redesign, and went on to tell me how much leaner and more efficient ITN would be. Well, he wasn't exaggerating. The new ITN site is superb.

Gone are any extraneous graphics, lending the site a sleek, cutting-edge feel, and making it a pleasure to navigate. It's everything a site should be: clear, clean, and fast. And it gets the little things right—enter San Francisco, for example, and it doesn't ask you which airport you mean, it assumes SFO. (Though for regions where you can check multiple airports, such as New York or Chicago, this assumption can be a draw-back because it means ITN will check only one airport. Then, it's up to you to do further searches for the others.)

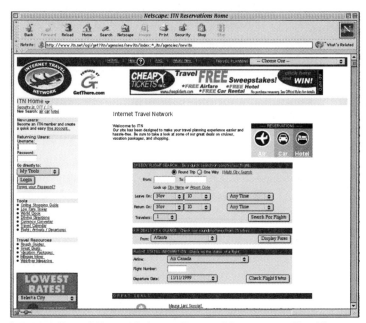

Internet Travel Network (www.itn.com) has streamlined its booking sites for quick loading.

Another little thing I love: Enter the date of your flight and ITN immediately shows what day of the week that is. And you can scroll the calendar so that if it's showing July and August and you want to see September, you just scroll down without having to go to another page.

If you want to go another step, set up a **Fare Mail** file. Here, you enter your home airport and up to five destinations, and ITN will alert you by e-mail if the price drops below the threshold you set. ITN can also let you know if the fare drops, or simply if it changes by an amount you specify (you could get updates whenever the fare goes up or down $40, for example). Other big booking sites have similar tools, but ITN has done an excellent job of letting users set their preferences. The only drawback is that you can't set different departure airports.

Like other services, ITN offers booking for hotels, rental cars, and vacation packages and has some specials on hotel rates, ski vacations, and more. ITN is also the booking technology behind many other major sites, such as **United Airlines (www.ual.com)** and **CNN.com**. So it's no surprise that ITN has lots of partner content enhancing its site, including travel news from **CNN**, guidebook information from **Rough Guides**, **WebFlyer** magazine, and **Mileage Miner,** which helps subscribers keep track of the frequent flier mileage accounts. (For more on Mileage Miner, see chap. 11, "Taking Care of Business.")

tip

■ The auction service Priceline.com, which encourages people to "name your price," can be a source of good deals but it has its drawbacks. (Priceline and other cut-rate ticket sellers are covered in chap. 7.)

Buying Directly *from* Airline Sites

With the major booking sites listing hundreds of airlines, some people might be wondering, "What's the point of visiting the airlines' own sites?" Well, there are many reasons, including the following:

■ Incentives, such as bonus miles, for buying at airline sites.

■ Last-minute deals that you have to purchase directly through an airline's site.

■ Some Internet-only discounts are offered solely through the airlines' Web sites. In other words, you may find a discount offered at Continental's site that's not available through Expedia.

■ Some airlines—typically, low-fare carriers—aren't listed at big booking sites. Southwest, which often has the best deal on a route, isn't affiliated with Expedia or Preview Travel, so you have to go to Southwest's site (or Travelocity) to get these deals.

The Battle for Bookings

During the winter of 1999, Delta Air Lines imposed a booking surcharge of $2.00 per domestic round-trip on all bookings except for those made through Delta's Web site. Though Delta blamed the surcharge on higher distribution costs, this was a blatant attempt to get customers to book directly through Delta's site, allowing the airline to avoid paying commissions to travel agents. Even those who booked with online agents, such as Travelocity, would have to pay the surcharge.

Customers and agents were outraged, and Delta eventually backed down. But Delta's move was the opening salvo in the latest battle for bookings. These are the realities of the war between airlines and agencies: Fact 1: Airlines spend billions of dollars annually on commissions. Fact 2: The Internet, particularly the World Wide Web, gives airlines the direct sales channel they've been dreaming about for decades. Fact 3: Airlines, like most businesses, seek to cut costs and boost profits in every possible way.

Delta's move was undoubtedly a blunder; though it was only a $2.00 fee, travelers were

Seven Tips for Finding Cheap Flights— Online or Off

■ **Stay over a Saturday night:** Most people who are unwilling to stay over Saturday night are business travelers; thus, airlines charge more for tickets that don't involve a Saturday night stay.

■ **Fly on the right days of the week:** Saturdays, Tuesdays, and Wednesdays are usually less busy than other days, many of the cheapest fares are available on these days.

■ **Book 14 to 21 days ahead:** The best deals are often for fourteen- or twenty-one-day advance purchase flights. If you can't book this far ahead, try to book at least seven days in advance or prepare to be gouged.

■ **Avoid holidays if possible:** Holiday fares are usually among the highest of the year, but that doesn't mean there aren't deals out there. You can often find very low fares if you're willing to fly on Christmas Day or a Sunday during a three-day weekend.

■ **Consider alternate airports:** If you can't find a cheap flight into New York's Kennedy, try La Guardia or Newark. Most major cities have secondary airports that can sometimes be more convenient.

■ **Use frequent flier miles:** If you can't plan ahead, try to cash in those frequent flier miles rather than pay a high fare.

■ **Choose flights with plenty of empty seats:** Not only are these typically cheaper, but you'll have more room to stretch out. But how do you know how many seats are left? Some online agencies, such as **ITN (itn.com)**, let you select "expert" or "advanced" in your profile. If you do this, you'll see how many seats are left. (*Note:* You won't see actual seat numbers but a single digit for each class, from 0 for sold out to 9 for plenty of availability.)

outraged by its punitive nature. The more intelligent approach is to lure ticket buyers with incentives and discounts, as many airlines are now doing.

With the development of the Web, airline sites can appeal to customers with weekend getaway deals, bonus miles, and other services. So it's no surprise that many are shopping at Expedia and Travelocity, then buying at United or American. Is this fair? Not in the eyes of booking sites, which provide a fine service for travelers. Airlines have drastically slashed commissions paid to these online agencies; it often costs more for these sites to process a ticket than they earn in commissions. This has led Expedia, Preview, and the rest to focus on other revenue streams, such as selling ad space.

Leading Airline Sites

In the mid-1990s, **American Airlines (aa.com)**, which introduced the first frequent flier program in 1981, saw a phenomenal opportunity: use e-mail and its Web site to sell empty seats at the last minute for deep discounts. These weekend getaway deals have taken off, and airlines now have millions of subscribers to their e-mail dispatches. If you don't want to subscribe, you can check e-fares at airline sites. But this is only one of several reasons to visit these sites. (It's something we'll cover in more depth in chap. 7.)

American and some of the other sites require travelers to join their frequent flier clubs before booking. It's no secret why—they're trying to get more members who will stick with

tip

■ Biztravel.com and Trip.com, which target business travelers, are good places to book flights, hotels, and rental cars. (They're covered in depth in chap. 11.)

the airline for the frequent flier benefits. That's all fine, but one thing they should do is remember your number. If online agencies like Expedia can remember your name, airline sites should be able to remember your frequent flier or ID number and just have you enter the password of your choice.

When you sign up at United, for example, you have to wait a couple of weeks for the airline to send you (through the U.S. mail, also known as "snailmail") a password that enables you log on. I hope that by the time you read this, UAL will have entered the new millennium and upgraded to online registration.

A Closer Look at United's Site

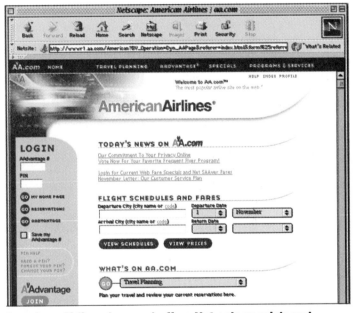

American Airlines (aa.com) offers Net-only specials and incentives for booking online.

Though they could do a better job, airlines' sites can be a good resource. At United's site **(ual.com)**, you can examine timetables, check flight status (is an incoming flight late?), and locate ticket offices. **United Vacations** describes its package deals, and under the **Special Services** category are tips for flying with children, pets, or "differently-abled" passengers.

siteseeing

Southwest Airlines' Home Gate (www.southwest.com)

As mentioned earlier, sometimes the best reason to visit an airline's home base is that you won't find that airline's flights on a big booking service, such as Expedia. The prime example is Southwest, which has become a Top Ten U.S. airline by offering bargain-basement fares on short-hop flights. Let's have a look at some of its features.

Reflecting its image as an airline of the people, Southwest's site makes it easy to find the best fares on the route of your choice. Click on departure and arrival cities, select the time frame (before 10:00 A.M., 10:00 A.M.–2:00 P.M., etc.), input how many people are flying, and you're off. The nice thing about Southwest's site is that it displays all the fares for a route, showing those that are available and those that aren't. You might spot a promotional fare of $50 from Houston to Dallas but see that it's not available Friday night (when a lot of weekend travelers take to the skies). So you can try Saturday morning and see the same fare with an open circle, indicating availability.

The best deals on Southwest are its Internet specials. These are still the early years of the Net, and airlines are doing their best to shift business to this new dis-

Click on **"At the Airport"** and then on "Airport Maps" to see the layout for about a dozen of UAL's most visited airports (Chicago's O'Hare, Denver, Frankfurt, Honolulu). You'll also find a list of airports where United has a Red Carpet Club.

In the Air discusses duty-free shopping, menus, even what movie you'll see, so if you can't wait till you get on board to find out, just click on **"Entertainment."** And if you really loved that endless loop of jazz standards you heard on your last flight, you can buy the CD through United's site. **Upon Arrival** includes an archive of features entitled "3 Perfect Days" from UAL's inflight magazine. So if you're off to Amsterdam, New Orleans, or Rome, see how they recommend spending seventy-two hours there.

Last but not least, you can check your frequent flier mileage account online. Just use the shortcut menu at the bottom of the page. Again, you'll have to enter your frequent flier

tribution channel. So they're willing to offer some amazing deals to get customers to try booking online, such as Southwest's recent Internet-only fare of $33 each way between Oakland and Los Angeles. By offering deals like this only on the Net, Southwest decreases the number of people calling its toll-free number. Not only does the company save a bit on phone charges, its reaps even more benefits by reducing staffing for its phone reservation centers. More people booking online means the company can hire fewer sales staff and pass the savings on to customers.

By clicking on the image on Southwest's main page, you can learn about the airline's unusual frequent flier program, peruse its route map and schedules, and even submit a resume online.

Though it can be slow to load, Southwest's site (www.southwest.com) is worth checking because this airline's flights are not listed by some of the major online agencies.

number and password, but it's worth the time. You can get much more current statements online than through the mail, and monitor airlines to make sure they credit your account properly.

Finding Airline Sites

With hundreds of airlines out there, it would be nice if there was one place you could go to find listings for them all. Thankfully, there is. Way back in 1994, Marc-David Seidel, then a University of California at Berkeley graduate student, created **Airlines of the Web (www.flyaow.com)**. A couple of years later AOW became part of ITN's network; today, it offers links to airline Web sites, toll-free numbers, airport codes, and a nice summary of cyberfares (aka last-minute deals).

Of course, you can find airline sites through Yahoo and other search engines, and major airlines are listed in this book's Web directories. But AOW is simpler than a search engine and more extensive than the directory, so it's a good place to poke around.

Featuring an airport motif, AOW's sections include **Terminal, Hangar** and **Tower.** In **Sky Lounge,** a section called Air Tips includes advice for senior travelers, ideas for overseas travel, and even suggestions for Hawaii vacations. If you really like to know all the details, click on "Aircraft Specs" to learn more about different planes.

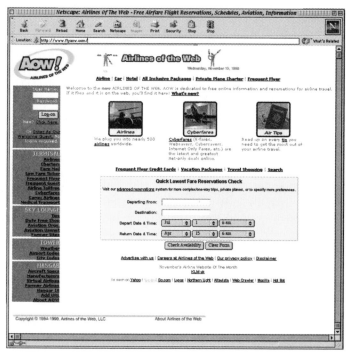

Airlines of the Web (flyaow.com) can help you locate airline Web sites and toll-free numbers.

How would you know what type of plane you're flying? If you book (or just look) at Travelocity, you'll find out while booking. Travelocity and several others also list on-time performance and number of stops, so you have a good idea of what you're getting—often more than a human travel agent will tell you—before you buy.

Not for Booking Only: More Online Tools

Though some people consider the Net to be just a way of streamlining airline bookings, it offers a much broader array of services for travelers. The Web is a great tool for finding fares at national discount ticket agencies as well as locating highly specialized travel agents.

If you want to know what to expect when you land, you can find airport maps online that include ATMs or restaurants in different terminals. Wondering if a flight will be on time? You can see how often a particular flight beats the clock and find out when a flight that's already taken off is due to touch down. You can even have a look at government sites that track airline accidents so you can judge an airline's safety record for yourself.

Discount Ticketers

Although buying directly from airline Web sites is your best bet for last-minute specials and Net-only deals, purchasing from discount agencies or consolidators can save you hundreds of dollars when you need to plan ahead and can't find ultralow prices online. This is one occasion when it's probably best to start with your local paper's Sunday travel section and browse through the ads to find the best fare. Scanning the Sunday paper is also a good way to see which agencies specialize in the destinations you plan to visit.

Most of the agencies have toll-free numbers, but if you want to do some research on your own, try searching online. Sometimes these agencies list their URLs in their ads—if they don't, you can use a search engine to look them up.

For those who don't live in a major metropolitan area, the Net is a superb tool for visiting discount agencies, such as **Council Travel (www.counciltravel.com)**, which specializes in discount airline tickets. More general sites, such as **Arthur Frommer's Budget Travel (frommers.com)** and **1travel.com (onetravel.com)** link to a database of consolidator fares and provide booking services. (We'll discuss consolidator fares and discount ticketing in more detail in chap. 7.)

■ **Another excellent source of airline information is Airline Information FAQ (www.iecc.com/airline).** This FAQ (frequently asked question) is a treasure trove of advice for the online traveler: "If you're looking for seats on a sold-out flight, an airline's home system is most likely to have that last, elusive seat."

tip

Finding the Right Travel Agent

The Net is also a terrific tool for finding the right travel agent. Because travel agents can reach a worldwide audience online, some have become specialists; for example, a Florida agent who sells Walt Disney World packages to an international clientele.

Nancy Zebrick of **All Destinations Travel (www.alltravel.com)** is a travel agent who specializes in spa vacations and serves clients from around the world. She says the majority of her business comes to her through the Net, and this figure is growing rapidly. "I don't consider us local anymore. I consider us global. Right now I'm working with a client from Oslo (Norway) arranging a trip to Club Med and Disney World here in Florida."

I found All Destinations Travel by visiting Yahoo's list of online travel agents at **(dir.yahoo.com/Business_and_Economy/Companies/Travel/Agents)**. This is a long list, but I took a few minutes to browse through the short descriptions of each agency. Another way to find specialists is to search for keywords, such as "spa vacations."

As we discussed in chapter 1, you can search within Yahoo categories, limiting your hunt to a few hundred sites. At the top of each category next to the search box is a pull-down menu. You can select "all of Yahoo" or "just this category."

Lycos (lycos.com) and others have similar features. So to refine your search for a specialist in spa vacations, go to Yahoo's listing of travel agents, put "spa vacations" in the search box, and then select "just this category."

Nancy's e-mail address was clearly listed on the site, so I sent her a note asking about her qualifications and received an e-mail reply in less than twenty-four hours. She described her background in diet and fitness and explained that she'd visited more than forty spas. I was impressed that her site didn't have any ads and felt secure that she wouldn't just recommend one of her sponsors. Through our e-mail interactions I could sense that she really knew her subject; the fact that her office is on the other side of the country became irrelevant.

tip

■ If you have a hard time finding agencies with generic names, try searching for their phone numbers at HotBot (hotbot.com) or any other search site; for example, put "800–555–1234" or "(800) 555–1234" in the search box, with the quotation marks.

For those who have an agent they like, the Net is still a fine tool because lots of questions can come up shortly before embarking on a big trip. For a recent trip to Guatemala, I arranged my trip through Kenneth Johnson at **Guatemala Unlimited (www.guatemala unlimited.com)**. Ken and I probably exchanged about a dozen e-mail messages prior to my

Your Guatemala Information Source

Guatemala Unlimited (guatemalaunlimited.com) is an example of a niche travel agency that's gone online to attract clients from around the world.

trip, on topics ranging from "What shots do I need?" to "How cold does it get at night in the highlands?" Using e-mail was much more convenient than playing phone tag, and it gave me a record of responses to review on the eve of my departure.

Another advantage of e-mail is that you can use it to contact a travel agent while you're on the road. Of course, you can call, but if you're in another country, this can be prohibitively expensive. And while you're awake in Sydney, Australia, your agent might be sleeping soundly in Boston. But if you can send e-mail (at a Net cafe or hotel business center) and check it a day or two later, you can get a question answered conveniently and pay only a fraction of what a phone call would have cost.

All about Airports

Arriving in an unfamiliar airport can be bewildering. You have to find the baggage carousel, figure out where to get a taxi or bus to your hotel, maybe even change money, get a bite, or check e-mail. Thankfully, the Web makes it easier to get your bearings before you take off.

Trip.com has an serviceable directory of airport maps. Point your browser to **trip.com** and click **"Guides & Tools"**; then select **"Airport Guides."** You'll see a listing of dozens of domestic airports—click the one you're headed to and then you have a choice below. Click **"Airport Map"** to get an overall view of the airport, or choose **"Regional Map"** to see where the airport is located relative to the city it serves.

After choosing Atlanta, I clicked on **"Terminal View"** for a list of services and shops. I found an ATM in the South Terminal Atrium and a post office at the west end of the South Terminal. I noticed a travel electronic shop in the North Terminal and a Ben & Jerry's ice-cream stand in Concourse A. Given that you often have an hour or two to spare in airports, this is good information to have at your fingertips. It may be worth printing out and adding to your custom guidebook. Trip.com also lists strategies for moving efficiently through airports **(trip.com/ strategies/airport)**.

Because Trip.com covers only domestic airports, you'll have to look elsewhere for international airport maps and directories. **QuickAID (www.quickaid.com)** has an extensive list of airports, offering links to airport home pages outside its site. So when you click on the link for the Oslo, Norway, airport, you'll get information from Oslo. Thus, the quality of the information depends on the airport site you link to. Most are quite good, but a few airport sites could be better organized. The only way to find out is to get online, select the airport link for your destination, and see for yourself.

Will Your Flight Be Late?

Though you can never predict with certainty whether an airline will be on time, you can get a good idea. Booking sites such as Preview Travel and airline sites like United include on-time information on their booking screens. Other sites track airlines overall on-time performance.

The **Office of Airline Information (www.faa.gov/asafety.htm)** has a searchable database, listing the on-time performance of major carriers. The database enables you to study airlines' punctuality on specific routes, for example, Dallas to Denver. A search on these routes for December 1998 showed 22 percent of United's flights touched down fifteen minutes or more after their scheduled arrival time (the standard definition of late), while 30 percent of Delta's arrivals were tardy. You can even see an average of how late each flight is— the typical United flight was 7.3 minutes late while Delta clocked in at 8.6 minutes.

This is probably more information than you want or need, but it can be fun, and if you see one airline has a much better (or worse) record than the rest, it may help you choose. Keep in mind that airline statistics can be misleading: Over the past few years many airlines have pushed back their arrival times to boost their on-time performance.

tips

■ **Know your rights. In Rules of the Air (www.onetravel.com/rules/ rules.cfm), consumer advocate Terry Trippler has posted sections of airlines' rule books. Use the pull-down menu to choose the airline and topic and see excerpts of rules pertaining to your issue.**

Flight Tracking

To see if a specific flight is on time, you can check an online flight tracker. The one at **Trip.com** is cool because you can see an image of where the plane is, in addition to arrival time, distance from arrival city, flight speed, and cruising altitude. If you don't have much computer memory, it's best to stick with the basic flight tracker. Remarkably, you can use this tool even if you don't know the flight number: Select "Find a Flight by City and Time" and enter departure and arrival cities as well as arrival time.

Airline Safety Records

At its root, the Internet is a government-created tool for finding information, and one of its best applications is accessing public databases. The **National Transportation Safety Board (www.ntsb.gov/aviation/aviation.htm)** enables you to search by airline, airport, type of aircraft, or any assortment of these and other factors. However, the agency cautions that the data can be misleading; for example, many of the accidents listed are relatively minor and not predictive of passenger safety.

Just to try it, I entered Delta and searched records from 1993–1997. NTSB's site came up with dozens of reports, but most of these were not midair collisions or life-threatening accidents. Here's a typical case, from May 26, 1997: "During an international flight, a flight attendant stepped on a salt shaker, breaking her left ankle and cutting her finger." The NTSB also lists the "probable cause" of the accident, in this case: "The failure of flight attendants to maintain control of loose cabin service equipment, a salt shaker, that resulted in an uncorrected tripping hazard." In other words, some-one forgot to put away the salt.

tip

■ **To get airline safety information from the FAA, see its Aviation Safety page at (www.faa.gov/asafety. htm). The latest press releases from the FAA are online at (www.faa.gov/ apa/pr/safety/index.cfm).**

At the **Cross System Search** page **(nasdac.faa.gov/asp/fw_crosssys.asp)**, you can search several federal safety databases simultaneously. These include NTSB and FAA data-bases, with their listings of near misses (though shouldn't this more accurately called "near hits"?).

If you don't speak bureaucratese, other sites try to make sense of the air safety picture, and most of these wisely warn against making hasty generalizations. **Airsafe (airsafe.com)** lists recent fatal accidents and has Q&A sections on topics such as "Bird Hazards to Aircraft." For one individual's critique of the FAA's management of airline safety, see **www.geocities.com/CapitolHill/9499/index.html**.

Summing Up

The Net has rocked the travel-planning world, shifting the balance of power toward consumers and airlines and away from travel agents. Yet even for those who prefer the convenience of calling a travel agent, the Net is a terrific way to get a sense of flight sched-ules, special deals, on-time performance, and airport information. Simply put, information is power. When travelers can see all the options, they can make better choices about when to go and how much they need spend.

COMPARISON SHOP & SEE HOTEL IMAGES ONLINE

Though many people don't give accommodations much thought, a successful trip depends largely on finding a place that's comfortable and affordable. No matter how beautiful the surroundings, it's pretty hard to have a good time if you find your beachfront hotel is a couple of miles from the ocean—or if you feel you're spending so much money on lodgings, that you have to economize on everything else. Though the Internet can't ensure your stay will be trouble-free, it can help you to select a place that's best suited to your needs. Whether it's a simple recommendation for a homey little inn in southern Spain or a directory of thousands of hotels throughout the world, the Net can help you find places that work for you.

Hotel Directories on the Web

This chapter will show you how to use the Net to take some of the uncertainties out of choosing hotel rooms, and how to find the amenities you want at a price you can afford. It also considers less typical lodging options, such as home exchanges, B&Bs, and hostels, and how to sort the good ones from those that are nightmare inspiring. Finally, it will show you how to get advice about off-the-beaten-path accommodations and describe strategies for finding places that suit you.

A key point to keep in mind when browsing through online directories is that not all the listings are editorially unbiased. At **InnSite (www.innsite.com)**, a popular B&B directory, innkeepers submit their own listings and typically describe their properties in glowing terms. There's nothing wrong with this—InnSite couldn't review thousands of B&Bs around the world without hiring a large staff—but it's best to be informed about what type of listing you're viewing. At other sites the lodgings that appear at the top of the list are those that have paid for prime placement. Because it's not easy to discern, this book tells you more about each directory, providing a better idea about how the listings are presented.

Any Room at the Inn?

Using Web hotel directories and newsgroups to find the right hotel room is a solid one-two punch for previewing and evaluating lodging options. Thousands of hotels around the world have gone online, either by putting up their own sites or by getting listed in one or more indexes. The largest directories, which include listings for thousands of hotels, are valuable for finding chain properties but not as useful for locating one-of-a-kind places. Fortunately,

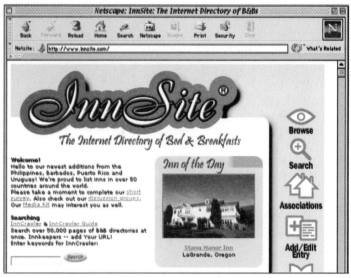

Innsite (www.innsite.com) is a popular site for fine bed and breakfast inns.

there are other options if you're looking for nonchain lodgings, such as **Places to Stay (www.placestostay.com)**, which specializes in resorts around the world.

Using the Net to choose a room has several advantages over a printed guidebook. By searching for lodgings online, you can

- get lots of information, such as pictures of the rooms, conference facilities, and restaurants.
- search for properties based on specific criteria, for example, a nonsmoking room in the $75–$150 range in downtown San Antonio.
- reserve a room online or get the information to make a decision, then book by phone or through a travel agent.
- find special weekend rates for last-minute getaways.
- use e-mail to get in touch with proprietors and ask questions about their facilities.
- restrict your search to the chain at which you have a frequent traveler bonus plan. If you earn points by staying at Hyatt, for example, you could search solely for Hyatt hotels.

Similar to airlines on the Net, hotel chains have staked their claim in cyberspace by creating their own sites, as well as by getting listed in directories, such as **TravelWeb (www.travelweb.com)**. Here, travelers can search for rooms by region, by hotel chain, or by a set of preferences tailored to their needs. You can, for example, choose a city and then search for rooms in a certain price range with the amenities (gym, conference facilities, laundry service, etc.) you want.

tip

It's always a good idea to print a confirmation page or at least a confirmation number when booking online. And be sure you're fully aware of cancellation policies before you fork over your credit card number.

Top Hotel Directories: An Introduction

To get a broad overview of what's available at your destination, directories are a good place to start. Input the specifications you require, and they'll come up with properties that fit your criteria. Hotel directories come in many forms: Some focus primarily on hotels (TravelWeb), while others (Preview Travel) are part of big booking sites that also let you book flights and rent cars. Then, there are those that cover a tightly defined niche, such as resorts and inns. And don't forget to check online guidebooks: Fodor's and Frommer's are excellent sources of hotel information. You can also use search sites like **Excite (www.excite.com)** to find regional hotel directories, like **San Francisco Reservations (www.hotelres.com)**. What follows is a review of some of the best from each category.

TravelWeb

Listing tens of thousands of hotels in the United States and abroad, **TravelWeb (www.travelweb.com)** is the online arm of Pegasus Systems, which provides a massive hotel database for travel professionals. Like other leading online agencies, it appears pretty objective in evaluating all the properties it lists, but it lists only those that pay the fee to be a part of Pegasus's database, which are primarily chain hotels.

With its thousands of listings, TravelWeb can help you compile a short list of suitable lodgings for destinations around the world. To find a hotel at TravelWeb, start by inputting the city, state or country, and then choose whether you want a list of all hotels or only those that offer online booking. One nice feature is that you can enter most of the relevant information on one page. So after entering the city, scroll down to select the chain you prefer (or all hotels) and the price range (or any price). Next, check the boxes for the amenities you can't live without: concierge, free locals calls, safe deposit box, or whatever else you find essential.

Keep in mind that if you're very demanding and select lots of amenities, you'll find fewer

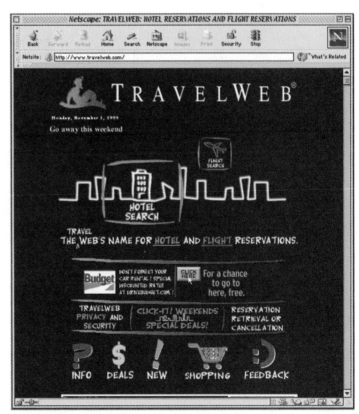

Travel Web (travelweb.com) enables you to access a hotel booking system that travel agents use.

hotels that meet all your criteria. Searching for a room in Cleveland for under $150 at a hotel with a business center, room service, and no-smoking rooms, I found that the Sheraton Cleveland City Centre had everything I was looking for. Other hotels were listed even if they only had some of the selected amenities, with a note saying "2 of 3 amenities matched." Nice to know, but it doesn't say which amenities—to find out, click the **Hotel Info** icon to learn more about each property.

To find out more about the Cleveland Sheraton, I clicked on "Hotel Info" and found the price of the least-expensive room ($144), the address, ratings (3 diamonds, 3 stars), and a phone number for reservations. I also learned it was built in 1975, renovated in 1996, has twenty-two stories and isn't far from Jacobs Field and the Rock and Roll Hall of Fame.

Through TravelWeb, I had a peek at the room photo, then clicked on the map feature, which showed that the hotel is near the waterfront and the convention center. However, the map didn't have any scale so I couldn't really judge distances. A click on the weather icon generated a five-day forecast for Cleveland. If you're going abroad, try the currency converter to see how much your dollar will buy.

Finally, if you're looking for a weekend bargain, hop over to **TravelWeb's Click-It Weekends (travel web.com/TravelWeb/clickit.html)**. These offers are similar to weekend air deals, and if you snag one of those, you'll need a place to stay. Click-It Weekends offers some terrific bargains because hotels that cater to business travelers

TravelWeb's Click-it Weekends (travelweb.com/TravelWeb/ clickit.html) offers last-minute deals at major chain hotels.

have low occupancy rates during the weekends. That means they're eager to offer great deals to fill as many of these rooms as possible. A recent sample: $79 a night at the Seattle Airport Hilton or £99 British at London's Grosvenor House.

Although some of these offers are bargains, others are actually more expensive than typical hotel discount rates. So contact the hotel directly to check its best weekend rate before booking through Click-It Weekends.

All Hotels on the Web

Including not quite all the hotels on the Web, **All Hotels (www.all-hotels.com)** does list tens of thousands throughout the world. Bear in mind that each hotel listed has paid a fee ($25 and up) for placement, so it's not an objective list, but more like a book of online brochures. The colorful world map on All Hotels' home page is the first sign that the focus of this site is international. Drill down to your destination by clicking first on the continent (Europe), then the country (France), region (Provence), and finally the city (Nice). About twenty Nice hotels were listed with their descriptions and star rankings. The following is the description of the three-star Hotel Massenet:

> The Massenet hotel is located at the beginning of the pedestrian precinct, a few meters from the Walk of the English and the sea. It offers to tourists all the advantages of hotels in the center of town without having the disadvantages of noise and ceaseless comings and goings of an intense circulation. Located on a residential street, the majority of the rooms are equipped with a kitchen.

To learn more, click on the name of the hotel and connect to a French hotel directory that offers booking. The trouble is that the site is in French, though it's easy enough to understand and offers online booking. This is a nice site for browsing, but beware that the imagemaps take a long time to load, especially if you have a slow modem (28.8 Kbps or less).

Two other worthy sites are **Hotels and Travel on the Net (www.hotelstravel.com)** and **Hotel Reservations Network (hoteldiscount.com)**, which both buy blocks of hotels rooms and sell them at up to 65 percent off rack (retail) rates. Like all the other sites, you can't count on these to always come up with the best deals, but they're certainly worth checking. An advantage of these sites is that because they book blocks of rooms, they sometimes have rooms for "sold-out" dates.

Fodor's Hotel Index

The great thing about **Fodor's (www.fodors.com)** is its editorial voice—the site includes reviews from Fodor's guidebooks. If you check the box for Fodor's picks, you get a little red star next to the places recommended by this guidebook publisher. Like the Custom Miniguides, the Hotel Index is based on the content in Fodor's guidebooks, so you get to hear how the author felt about each place.

The almost one hundred destinations covered include a wide range of international locales. Just select a city, say Barcelona, and choose whether you want to search by hotel name or by criteria. A search for Barcelona hotels endorsed by Fodor's turned up several

tips

■ **TravelWeb** often lists hotels that can be pretty far from the city center, or even outside city limits. Searching for a Cleveland hotel yielded properties in Richfield, Akron, even Elyria. So check maps or use other means to be sure the hotel you select is convenient for you.

■ **HotelView (www.hotelview.com)** is a terrific site for seeing images of hotel rooms. The site combines a slideshow with an audio tour, giving viewers a compelling presentation. Only a few hotels in major cities now have tours, but for those that do, this is a very cool resource.

hotels, ranging from the lowest price category to the highest. The one thing I didn't like was that room prices were given in Spanish *pesetas*, so I had to bop over to the **Universal Currency Converter (www.xe.net/currency)** to see how many pesetas my dollar would buy.

Places to Stay

Although the Radisson and Ramada are just fine for a business trip, you may want a more unique place to stay on your vacation. **Places to Stay (www.placestostay. com)** lists thousands of resorts and inns around the world, many of which don't appear on TravelWeb and other sites that focus on the big chains. (You will find some chain properties at Places to Stay, but it also lists many one-of-a-kind properties.)

"Only about 15 percent of hotels are listed in the global distribution system" (and thus available through sites such as TravelWeb), says Greg Jones, CEO of WorldRes, the parent company of Places to Stay. "We're hitting the other 85 percent."

Places to Stay doesn't charge properties to be listed but instead earns a commission on each booking—and, of course, the site is free to users. It's deepest in North America, but it does have substantial listings for independent lodgings around the world, though

these aren't all mom-and-pop operations. The Japan page, for example, includes mostly hotels with hundreds of rooms, with prices in yen.

In other cities, more small properties are listed, such as Rome's thirty-two-room Hotel Barocco, near the Spanish Steps and Trevi Fountain. Clicking on the Barocco link leads to Places to Stay's page for that property, with prices (in lira), photos, a message from the host, and amenities. Though the main listing said the cheapest room is 360,000 lira (about $200), clicking on the room descriptions shows basic rooms available for as little as 200,000 lira. And even if you see a listed price that's above what you're willing to pay, don't give up. You might find specials listed elsewhere or even try to negotiate a lower rate directly with the hotel.

Places to Stay is probably best for finding smaller-scale properties in nonurban locations throughout North America. Clicking on the page for Carmel/Monterey (on California's central coast) lists dozens of properties, from the upscale thirteen-room

> ## tip
> ■ Sometimes when you connect to sites in another country, download times can be painfully slow, even if you have a fast modem and high-speed connection. This is often due to the data "pipeline" into or out of the countries involved.

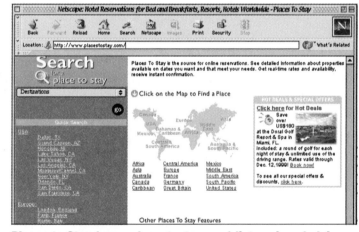

Places to Stay (www.placestostay.com) lists unique lodgings such as inns and resorts, as well as larger properties.

Carriage House Inn in downtown Carmel to the more affordable Spindrift Inn near the Monterey Bay Aquarium. Some properties list Hot Deals that package lodging with tickets to the aquarium or whale-watching tours. But do your homework: It may be cheaper to get a lower price on a room and buy the tickets yourself.

Think Globally, Surf Locally

There are hundreds of local hotel directories out there, and these can be among the best places to find lodgings. **Local Hotels (www.localhotels. com)** has done a terrific job aggregating all these disparate sites. Simply click the region (South America), then the country (Chile), and you'll get a page of online hotel directories for Chile, such as **Hotels & Lodging in Chilean Patagonia (www.chile austral.com/hotels.html)**.

San Francisco Reservations (hotelres.com) is one of many hotel sites that lets you see images of hotels and their rooms, such as this image of the Mark Hopkins in San Francisco.

I was concerned that this site might not be in English, but when I visited, I found it was. If you get to another site that isn't, look for a link to an English-language version. Even if you don't find this, you may be able to get by in another language. The Patagonia directory listed dozens of hotels in the region, with brief descriptions and links to their Web sites. Once at a hotel site, you can find more information and usually an e-mail address for getting in touch with the proprietors.

Local hotel sites are nice because they're typically more personal than the massive directories. **San Francisco Reservations (www.hotelres.com)**, another example of a local hotel directory, ranks the 175 hotels it lists based on value, service, and convenience.

There are two ways to search at SFR: by neighborhood (with Java maps taken from aerial views) or by criteria. Although it's cool to have an aerial view of the city, this feature is cumbersome, and I found it easier to use the more traditional method of inputting my date of arrival and other criteria to find a room.

After choosing a criteria-based search, I selected neighborhood (Nob Hill), price range ($150–220), and amenities (voice

tips

■ **Fodor's is not a booking site, but it does provide phone and fax numbers, or you can go to search engines and use them to find more about a property and get its e-mail address.**

■ **VacationSpot (vacationspot.com) is another excellent site for finding one-of-a-kind lodgings around the world.**

mail and modem hookup). Three hotels came up, with the Mark Hopkins at the top of the list because SF Reservations considered it the best value of the three properties that met my criteria.

Clicking on the Mark Hopkins link led to a photo of the hotel, its rates, and more detailed rankings by SFR, including the quality of service and the convenience of its location. Impressed by its high ratings, I clicked on the **"Guestroom"** icon and got the full list of amenities and an image of a typical (or more likely one of the nicest) rooms. To reserve the room, I clicked on **"Reserve,"** and filled in my name, address, and credit card number. Then, I was able to rest easy.

TravelBook (travelbook.com), another popular site, lists New York hotel rooms for under $100. The site also links to hotels in Washington, D.C., Boston, and San Francisco. Although a $100 room might not be such a good deal in most of the world, in New York, if it's clean and safe, it's a steal.

Expedia.com and Travelocity

If you're already booking air travel at Expedia or Travelocity, you may find it convenient to book a hotel at the same time. Some big booking sites offer incentives, such as Travelocity's recent deal of 1,500 bonus miles for those who book air and hotel at the same time. Yet each of these three sites has some drawbacks. **Travelocity (www.travelocity.com)** can be the most frustrating because its hotel directory is closely linked to airports. So if you enter a city name, it will ask you to select the appropriate airport, and after you do that, you go back to the original hotel page. If it sounds confusing, that's because it is. On the plus side, Travelocity makes it easy to input your frequent traveler program and number for hotel and airline programs.

Expedia.com is a little better. Though its directory is also linked to airports, you can input a city name, and Expedia can go from there. However, when searching for a Hilton in Denver, the only listing Expedia found was for the Hilton Denver in Englewood. Checking at Hilton's site **(www.hilton.com)**, I found the Hilton Garden Inn at Denver's airport, a new hotel that was just about to open.

In the fall of 1999, Expedia introduced a new feature called **Hotel Price Matcher**, which lets you select the price you're willing to pay for a hotel in fourteen U.S. cities. Select the city, dates, and price you're willing to pay, and Expedia will check its database to see if any hotels will accept your price.

If this sounds familiar, that's no surprise. This new brand of commerce is srikingly similar to Priceline.com's model (discussed in chap. 7). As expected, Priceline immediately sued Expedia, claiming Expedia was infringing on Priceline's patented e-commerce model.

tips

■ If you reserve online, be sure to print out the confirmation page so you have a record of your reservation.

■ If you're a member of an airline frequent flier program, you may be eligible for bonuses if you stay at certain hotels. A hotel may offer 500 miles valid in American's AAdvantage program, for example. Check an airline site (such as TWA's) to see a list of its hotel and rental car company partners.

Both companies have deep pockets and high-flying lawyers, so it could take a while to sort out the legal issues. But if Hotel Price Matcher is still around when you read this, you may want to try using it to find a cheap hotel room. Just be forewarned that you must enter your credit card before making a bid—and that if your bid is accepted your card will automatically be charged.

One Woman's Quest to Find the Right Hotel

Ami J. Claxton is an experienced traveler who knows what she wants. But she's learned that lodging descriptions in traditional travel guidebooks aren't always trustworthy. They can be dated and reflect only one reviewer's opinion. So for a weeklong vacation to Rome, Ami turned to the Internet.

By searching for "hotel AND Italy" in **Yahoo (yahoo.com)**, Ami, an epidemiologist, found dozens of sites with listings of Italian hotels. The most useful, she said, was **Italy Hotel Reservation (www.italyhotel. com/italy_us.html)**, which lists almost 10,000 Italian hotels and has a search engine that lets you select parameters, such as location and price. If you include your arrival and

Italy Hotel Reservation (www.italyhotel.com/italy_us.html) provides information and images for thousands of Italian hotels, such as Rome's Villa Delle Rose (www.italyhotel.com/ roma/villadellerose) pictured here.

departure dates, you can check availability. IHR links to the Web pages of hotels that have their own online presence and will even send a free fax to the hotel you choose.

First Person: Ami J. Claxton

I am quite particular about hotels (location, service, amenities), so I did not simply want to just reserve a place that was only very briefly described in a printed guidebook.

I scoured the Web looking for hotels in Rome and found an astonishing amount of information: Hundreds of Roman hotels had direct Web pages with photos, descriptions, and even e-mail addresses. I narrowed my choices down to a few hotels and then posted on rec.travel.europe (a newsgroup) asking for comments and/or suggestions.

I got about twenty e-mails from all over the United States and the world. Based on the information people provided, I made a reservation at a Hotel Julia, and I feel very confident that we will love it.

In addition, almost everyone gave me other great tips for visiting Rome, ranging from restaurant suggestions, to coffee-ordering etiquette, to bus information, to where to visit stray cats in Rome!

One caveat: I rarely, if ever, take advice off the Internet as gospel—I do check out the information. But most times it's quite obviously good info. For example, one hotel got consistent rave reviews from people in very disparate locations (New Zealand, Sweden, and Louisiana!), so I figured that it must be a pretty good hotel.

After selecting Hotel Julia, Ami used e-mail to negotiate a discount rate. Here's a copy of the message Ami sent to Hotel Julia:

I would like information on your rates for 2 persons arriving Nov. 21, departing Nov. 27. We require a room with a private shower, and prefer a queen bed if possible. Do you have any specials for us? Here are some reasons to give us a lower price: :-)

1. We found you on the Web.
2. We will stay for 6 nights during low tourist season.
3. We are staying over a weekend.
4. We are very nice! :)

Thank you, I hope to hear from you soon!

Aware that hotels frequently offer discounts during less busy seasons, Ami used this fact as a bargaining chip. Mentioning that she found the hotel online shows that the novelty of a Net connection hasn't worn off, especially outside North America. The proprietors may have felt that they and Ami are part of the same community (because they're all on the Net) and thus may have been more inclined to offer her a discount.

They wrote back and offered 190,000 (lira) per night (about $120 at the time) instead of the standard rate of 220,000. I then wrote back and said I'd guarantee with a credit card that day if they offered 170,000 per night. They did, I did, end of story. I was then in contact with them periodically before we left with little questions like "Do you have hair dryers in the rooms?" (answer yes), "Do you have irons available for guests to use?" (yes), etc. They were very responsive and helpful via e-mail. I found that *very* useful.

Another hotel that Ami had considered didn't have e-mail, which made it less desirable for her. In trying to make arrangements at this other hotel, "I had to call or fax, which was a real pain given the time zone differences."

Ami's account is typical of a pattern repeated by many Web travelers: First, they go to Local Hotels (**www.localhotels.com**) or another search engine and find a listing of hotel directories that apply to their destinations. Then, based on their criteria, they select a few strong possibilities. Once they have a short list, for example, five hotels in Paris, they go to the appropriate newsgroup (**rec.travel.europe** in this case) or an AOL forum and post a query, asking about these places. (Newsgroups and online forums are covered in greater detail in chap. 13.)

Other travelers use the conference areas of leading hotel and travel sites to get feedback about the hotels they're considering. Armed with helpful comments from travelers who participate in these online discussions, they make a selection and often finalize arrangements through e-mail.

Your Room Rate May Vary

Though it doesn't occur to most people, you can negotiate rates at hotels. They are especially willing to give discounts during times of low occupancy (for example, during weekends at hotels that cater to business travelers) or during the low season, such as February in London. So if you don't find the rate you want online, try calling a hotel reservations office.

And if you need to find a room the day of your stay, remember that walk-in rates can be higher than calling a central reservation system, because hotels figure that if you're already there, you probably won't look elsewhere. I once walked into a Las Vegas hotel and was quoted a rate of $69. I declined and then called the hotel's toll-free reservations line *from a pay phone in its lobby* and was offered a discount rate of $39.

Bed-and-Breakfast Inns: Homes Away from Home

These days more and more leisure travelers are seeking alternatives to the sterile predictability of major hotel chains and are discovering the charm of bed-and-breakfast inns. Unlike hotels, B&Bs don't have a fortune to spend on ad campaigns, so the Web is an effective—and affordable—way for them to reach consumers. If you're shopping around, the Net can be a good tool for evaluating B&Bs: You can have a peek at the inns and their rooms, and if you like what you see, you can usually follow up with an e-mail message to the proprietor.

Big B&B directories, such as **InnSite (www.innsite.com)**, are a good place to begin. At InnSite, which lists thousands of inns in the United States and abroad, you can browse by state or country or search for a specific city name or even the name of the B&B. (This would make sense if someone recommended a place, and you wanted to learn more about it online.) Clicking on the "Vermont" link; for example, leads to 172 listings, including six in Chester, a perfect spot to spend the night on a fall colors bicycle tour.

One of the six choices is the Chester House Inn, whose InnSite page includes a short description and rates, number of rooms, and what credit cards the inn accepts. Remember that innkeepers are writing the descriptions for their inns so approach

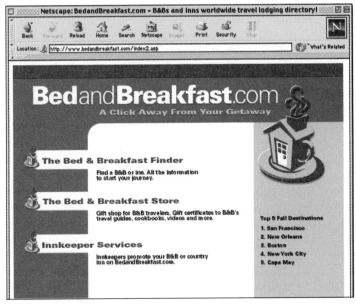

BedandBreakfast.com (bedandbreakfast.com) offers descriptions and images of inns as well as reviews from people who have recently stayed at these B&Bs.

these with a critical eye. Of course, the address, toll-free number, and fax are listed; best of all, there's a link to the **Chester House** site **(www.chesterhouseinn.com)**, making it easy to learn more.

What's really cool is that you can see images and check availability for each room (returning guests often have favorites) and learn more about the town of Chester. Any questions? Send e-mail to Randy Guy, the proprietor, who puts his e-mail address right on the site.

Some B&B sites, such as **BedAndBreakfast.com**, encourage people to submit reviews, similar to those at **Amazon.com**. These reviews enable you to see how others are evaluating a B&B you're considering, which can help you make a more informed choice. But be cautious about basing your choice on one review—look for several favorable comments that seem genuine, as opposed to one that appears scripted by a PR firm.

If the big national B&B directories aren't your cup of tea, try a regional directory, such as **Along the Way (www. bestinns.net/atway)**, a guide to B&Bs in the midwestern United States. Along the Way lists B&Bs by state and includes links to road maps of the Midwest and attractions in the region. You'll even find tasty recipes, such as Blueberry Stuffed French Toast from the Finnish Heritage Homestead in Embarrass, Minnesota. (Yes, there is a town in Minnesota called Embarrass—and while we're on the subject, there's also a very dull town in Oregon called Boring and a place in California called Cool, where summer temperatures often top 100 degrees Fahrenheit.)

Finding Homey Lodging around the World

Just about every country has some type of small-scale lodgings, such as French *gites*, Indonesian *losmen*, or Japan's *minshuku*. Finding these places can be more challenging than locating an international chain hotel, but the rewards can be far greater. You'll often have a much more personal and charming experience, and you may save a wad of cash.

To find small-scale lodgings, use search sites to find regional or single-country hotel directories, or visit the Web sites of national tourism offices, which often have links to lodging sites—some even provide online booking. To find links to international tourism offices, see **Tourism Offices Worldwide Directory (www. towd.com)**.

A search for "Japan" on Tourism Offices Worldwide turns up a link to the **Japan National Tourist Organization (www.jnto.go.jp)** which has a page called **Reasonable Accommodation (www.jnto.go.jp/03welcome/03frame.html)**. At the bottom of the page are links to descriptions of no-frills business hotels, *minshuku* (or family-style inns), and *ryokan* (traditional Japanese inns).

Finding a Perfect Place on the Other Side of the Planet

Nancy Thalman, a California computer programmer in her early 40s, spent some time poking around online before her recent trip to New Zealand. Here's her story.

First Person: Nancy Thalman

Deciding where to stay in a foreign country can often be a daunting experience, especially when you have little time and lots on your itinerary. In planning my trip to New Zealand, I started by browsing through a *Let's Go* book to get an idea of inexpensive places to stay. However, being in the prime of my life and a woman, hostels and bunk-bed places seemed less appealing to me than they did when I was in my twenties. Knowing I'd be flying for more than twenty-four hours and making several connections en route from San Francisco, I really wanted to find a quiet place to recharge for a couple of days. So I tossed the book aside and went surfing on the Net.

Using the Internet to plan this trip helped me break down the psychic distance and foreignness by providing some answers to my constant pre-trip mantra, "What is it like over there?" I started by typing "New Zealand" into a search engine, which took me to **NewZealand.com,** a commercial Web site. From there I explored several paths, which eventually led me to search "women's travel in New Zealand." Here's where I came across a listing of women's accommodations all over the country. This listing led me to the Hecate House site in Nelson. I was elated to see that it was a women's-only accommodation, because it seemed like a safe place to spend time resting and adjusting to New Zealand culture.

The Hecate House site **(www.brazen.co.nz/hecate)** contained pictures of the house and rooms, which looked very warm and cozy. I was also lured by the mention of the words *hot tub.* The idea of sitting in a Jacuzzi under the New Zealand sky after a long flight seemed very appealing. The price of $25 a night was affordable, and its central location in Nelson meant I didn't need a car and could walk everywhere. I used the site to book my reservations via e-mail, which required no deposit, just my word that I would show up for the reserved night.

After making the reservations, I wondered if Hecate House would be as nice as advertised. Well, it was even better. It felt like home almost immediately. Cynthia, the hostess, was very warm and friendly, and she provided info for local outings around town. It felt so comfortable that I ended up staying there another two nights at the tail end of the trip. Just before I left, Cynthia took a group on an evening picnic out to Cable Bay, where five of us shared a roasted chicken and wine from a beautiful overlook, followed by an evening swim in the ocean. Instead of being just another place to stay, it became one of the most memorable and fondest experiences of my trip to New Zealand.

Using Newsgroups for B&B Advice

Bed-and-breakfast directories and Web pages aren't the only places to get excellent advice. Newsgroups can also help refine a search by providing personal recommendations from other travelers. The most popular newsgroup for B&B listings is **rec.travel.bed+breakfast** (*Note:* Use the plus sign not an ampersand), but other groups related to a destination can be useful as well. You can access newsgroups through the Web at **Deja.com**. (We'll discuss newsgroups in detail in chap. 13.)

And don't forget online forums: At InnSite you can participate in one of its discussion groups or pore over the archives of the **rec.travel.bed+breakfast** newsgroup. A newsgroup search for "Oregon" produced a list of several messages, ranked by how closely they matched the search term. Here's an example of a reply to someone asking for a recommendation for a nice B&B on the northern Oregon coast:

> We have stayed at the Gilbert Inn in Seaside, about 30 miles south of Astoria. The Inn is a turn-of-the century Victorian. It is very well kept: clean, comfortable, roomy. The room we stayed in plus a few that we saw were furnished in wicker. The prices were from about $60 to $100 per night. Kids are allowed. You can see the ocean from some of the rooms. It is a couple of blocks from the boardwalk, where you will find restaurants, arcades, bike rentals. That can be fun; they have these four- and six-person "surreys" that you can pedal around town. They have beach tricycles . . . definitely worth a try.
>
> The owners were very friendly. I believe they have a cat that is allowed in the common areas (in case you happen to be allergic). They will send you a brochure describing each of the rooms if you call to request one. The original rooms are probably more "Victorian," with the wood paneling instead of drywall.

Newsgroup posts can nicely complement the information found at Web sites, and sometimes you'll get tips (such as the cat in the common area) that you might never have considered. In most cases the e-mail address of the person who posted will be listed, so you can send a note asking follow-up questions. Or you can visit **Deja.com** to join the discussion and ask the entire group. Then check back in a couple of days to see who has answered your questions—you may find that your post has led the discussion in a new direction.

Innkeepers Join the Discussion

B&B-related newsgroups represent a wonderful marketing opportunity for B&B owners. Though it is considered very bad form for proprietors to overtly advertise in newsgroups, it is perfectly acceptable to monitor them and answer direct queries. Say you operate a B&B in Nevada's gold country, and someone posts a query asking for B&B recommendations in your area. Go ahead and introduce yourself as an innkeeper and describe your establishment. If you do so, offer other recommendations, including places to dine and sights to see in the area. And be honest about who you are.

tip

■ Yahoo (yahoo.com) lists about one hundred B&B directories: Go to Yahoo and click on "Travel," then "Lodging," "Bed and Breakfasts," and "Directories," or search for "bed and breakfast directories."

Stay for Free with Home Swaps

Instead of staying in a $100 hotel room on your next vacation, why not try a place with three bedrooms, a living room, a kitchen, and maybe even your own pool. Too expensive—how about if it's free? By swapping homes with other vacationers, this dream can become a reality. The concept is simple: If you're willing to allow others to stay at your place while you travel, you can stay in their home. Of course, this takes some planning, not just arranging dates of exchange, but communicating and checking references until you feel comfortable with those with whom you plan to swap.

Although home exchanges have been around for decades, the Net, with online directories of available homes and instantaneous communication via e-mail, has made it much easier to arrange a home swap. Over the Net, travelers can exchange images of their homes, discuss terms, and seal a deal in just a few days, giving new life to what had been a relatively small niche travel market.

At most home exchange sites, it's free to browse through listings of places around the world, though some charge to place your home in their directory. When you find one you like, you can send an e-mail message indicating your interest. Of course, it helps if you live in a desirable location, but you don't have to live in Maui or Orlando to arrange a swap. To someone living in a crowded European city, a ranch in New Mexico might be ground zero for a dream vacation.

Ed Bello used the **International Home Exchange Network (www.homexchange.com)** to trade his place in Maui for a house in Atlanta during the 1996 Olympic Games. Because he lived in Maui, a desirable destination, he figured he could find a place for trade in Atlanta, even during the Olympics. But he didn't want just any place—he wanted a clean, comfortable, spacious house.

The International Home Exchange Network (www. homexchange.com) helps travelers arrange vacation home swaps, which can help save a bundle on lodgings.

While searching for information about home exchanges, Ed "just stumbled" on IHEN. "I listed my place and began browsing through the listings for Atlanta. I saw about ten places. Some home listings included photos. I picked four or five that looked interesting and sent e-mail to those people asking them to respond. After hearing back from them, I narrowed it down to two," Ed said. "Turns out that one of the two also requested my place in Maui. Once we got a link established, we communicated three or four times through e-mail. By the time we picked up the phone, the deal was almost done.

He's busy—I'm busy. Using e-mail was efficient; I was pretty impressed. So I got to see the Olympics, and he got to escape the madness."

Before the advent of the Net, most home exchangers subscribed to thick books that listed homes available for exchange, said Linda Allen, IHEN's creator. To reach potential home exchangers overseas, "they'd spend over $50 in postage and would have to wait weeks for an answer." Following up on the phone would cost a lot more money, she added.

With IHEN, users can browse the listings, and if they see something they like, they can send e-mail and sometimes get a response the same day. Another advantage is that IHEN is much more current than a book that's published annually, and if you need to make a change, such as saying your home will be available in July instead of August, you can do that quickly and easily.

tip
It's free to browse listings on the International Home Exchange Network (www.homexchange.com). It costs $29.95 a year to list your home.

Carl Bauer has been using online home exchange services for years and says the advantages of swapping homes online go beyond saving time and money. "Mutual screening can take place by interested parties . . . and a potential exchanger has a computer, knows how to write well . . . and can be checked if desired through directory sources." Reading between the lines, Carl is saying that most online home exchangers are professionals, and therefore he has more confidence that they'll respect his home. Computer ownership, however, doesn't guarantee that the person on the other end is reputable. So, as in other areas of Net-initiated agreements, be sure to thoroughly investigate prospective home exchangers before giving them the keys to your castle.

If you list your home on IHEN and send along a photo or two, IHEN will scan them and place them with your listing for free. Or you can scan them yourself and attach them to an e-mail message. You can include links to your personal home page and insert an e-mail link, so anyone who's interested can contact you directly. IHEN also lists a hospitality exchange, which enables travelers to stay with you while you're at home in exchange for your staying with them in the future.

If you can't work out a home exchange, you can use IHEN to list your place as a vacation rental to earn some money rather than leave your house vacant. This arrangement can be helpful if you have pets that need feeding or a garden that needs tending. Or you can host travelers in your home for a mutually agreeable fee.

Specialty Homestays

Specialty home exchange listing services, such as the **Jewish Travel Network (www.jewish-travel-net.com)**, are springing up on the Web. Through this online agency, a young Jewish woman from South Africa traveling through South America found kosher homes in Lima and Buenos Aires. A businessman who had to travel during Yom Kippur, the most important Jewish holiday of the year, sought a Jewish home in Lisbon to observe the holiday. Through these specialty services, travelers with common backgrounds or interests can connect through the Net and make arrangements to meet one another. (For more home exchange sites, see **Yahoo [yahoo.com]** and click on "Travel" > "Lodging" > "Home Exchange.")

Hostels: Wired Travelers' Picks & Pans

In the old days, budget travelers got recommendations for hostels from one another, as they sat in the common rooms of their $10-a-night hostels. Or they followed—often in sheeplike fashion—the gospel of Lonely Planet's immensely popular guidebooks. Today, the common room is larger; in fact, it encompasses the entire globe. Through the Net, budget travelers can evaluate different hostels by using sites that index and rate hostels, and then drop in to those sites' conference areas (also called forums) or hostel-related newsgroups to find good, cheap lodgings.

Hostels.com (hostels.com), a vast directory of affordable lodgings, also includes budget travel advice and travelers' tales.

Hostels.com

If you're planning to stay at hostels or simply want to learn more about them, a good place to start is **Hostels.com**. In addition to listing thousands of hostels around the world, the site includes a lengthy Q&A area, a forum where you can ask questions or share your experiences, and exchange reviews of budget guidebooks.

Hostels.com also includes sage advice from budget travel gurus Paul Otteson and Lucy Izon. In Hostels.com's **Guide to Budget Travel**, Otteson offers some excerpts from his insightful book, *The World Awaits,* which covers extended backpack travel. The excerpts range from big-picture philosophy ("You can't see it all.") to nuts-and-bolts tips ("Take less stuff and more money. If you don't have more money, take less stuff.").

Another link on Hostels.com's home page leads to **Izon's Backpacker News Wire**, with late-breaking news for budget travelers. Izon, whose column appears in the *Los Angeles Times* and other newspapers, informs her readers about such items as a new student ID card that also can serve as an ATM card. Another Izon story talked about making ski vacations affordable by staying at hostels.

tip

■ **Although Hostels.com is an excellent site, it doesn't monitor all the hostels listed—hostels submit their own listings, so they're certain to sound good. Remember, just because a hostel appears on the site doesn't mean it's endorsed by anyone. Use this directory the same way you'd use a phone book or a sheaf of brochures, following up to see if a place is up to par.**

Official Hostel Sites

Although Hostels.com includes thousands of hostels, it is by no means comprehensive; for instance, it includes only a fraction of the official **Hostelling International** (HI) youth hostels. For official HI locations around the globe, see HI's multilingual site **(www.iyhf.org)**, listing more than 5,000 hostels in seventy-seven countries.

HI's international site has a primer on what to expect at hostels, information on joining (members receive discounts at hostels), and listings for hostels around the globe, from Alaska to China. To find a hostel in Peru, for example, click on the link for "Worldwide Hostels," then select "Peru." You'll find a listing for a place in Lima with phone, fax, and e-mail. To find a hostel in Canada, click on the "Canada" link and see the address and phone of HI-Canada. To get listings, click on the "more info" link, which leads to the **HI-Canada** page **(www.hostellingintl.ca)**, where you can continue your search.

For U.S. hostels, start your search at **American Youth Hostels (www.hiayh.org)**, where you can locate hostels on maps and reserve a bed online. Clicking on the "Hostels" icon leads to a page with a primer called **What Are Hostels,** which shows that these hostel accommodations are a far cry from the big noisy dorm rooms that many expect. There are private rooms for families and couples, and most urban hostels have twenty-four-hour access.

Clicking on the "Utah" link shows a hostel in Salt Lake City. Choosing this hostel leads to a page with all the key information: cost ($12–$14), office hours (twenty-four-hour check-in), facilities (laundry, bike rentals), contact information (including e-mail), and a map with the hostel indicated by a solid triangle. The page also includes directions to the hostel, proximity to bus and train stations, and distance to nearby ski resorts (less than an hour drive!). The picture of the hostel is less than inspiring, but for a cheap sleep, who needs stunning architecture.

The Common Room Expands

Searching hostel directories and following up with a phone call (some U.S. hostels have toll-free numbers) is often enough to nail down the best place to stay. But sometimes, especially if you're traveling in unfamiliar lands, it helps tremendously to seek suggestions from fellow travelers.

Johns Hopkins grad student Sandeep Gupta was planning a trip to Switzerland for a weeklong conference and scheduled a few days afterward to explore the famed Alpine countryside. In an index of European hostels (an index that just went belly up), he found dozens of listings for Swiss hostels. But Gupta said the most valuable tips came from the eight people who responded to a query he posted with the newsgroup **rec.travel.europe**.

These direct e-mail responses were "extremely useful," he said, because they provided him with names and phone numbers for places recommended by travelers who had recently stayed at the hostels. "Like me, most were students on a limited budget." For a place to stay in Interlaken "everyone recommended Balmer's" **(Balmer's Herberge:**

tip

■ Remember that Hostelling International lists only members of its network, and that there are lots of fine hostels—such as Banana Bungalow (www.bananabungalow. com)—that offer lodgings in places like Santa Barbara, California, where there isn't an official HI hostel.

www.hostelwatch.com/hostels/balmers.html). Others went beyond recommending hostels and suggested activities Gupta could enjoy while visiting, like parasailing near Interlaken.

Of course, not every hostel is sweetness and light—some can be downright nasty. **Eurotrip.com** includes a section where readers can review hostels: From the home page click on "Accommodation," then "Hostel Reviews," then select a country. Most critiques are laudatory, but some warn travelers about places to avoid.

Apparently, the Agios Nikolaos on the Greek island of Crete is one such place. A visitor who reviewed this place wrote about: "bugs in the beds, no windows, no working plumbing, inhospitable owner/employees, and strange policies (i.e., taking your passport if you want to stay, etc.)." Another added: "The thing about the passport is entirely accurate. When I refused to hand it over, instead of just asking me to leave, this crazy Irishman who works for George punched me in the head. While the place may be cheap, I was back in Canada about two months before I got rid of the rash from the bedbug bites."

Hostel sites aren't the only places where Net surfers evaluate hostels. General budget travel sites can also offer good leads. The hostel forum on **Traveloco (www. traveloco.com)** consists mostly of travelers asking for advice ("Going to Brazil in January—can someone suggest a good hostel in Rio?"), but some people post recommendations, such as the following from "Rodent":

> Having extensively hoofed it around South Africa, I must mention a hostel in Plettenberg Bay on the Cape coast. A new establishment situated on a magnificent farm five minutes from town. It's called Loafers and is spotlessly clean and has a great vibe. Prices are good and the place is well organized and managed. They go out of their way to assist. Also Internet, TV and so on. Met a fellow traveler who has been there four months and is having trouble tying on his boots and resuming his journey. If you visit the Cape coast, you gotta visit this place.

Ultimately, you can never be sure how good a place is until you visit. What's paradise to one traveler (all-night hallway festivities), may be hell to another. However, by using directories and scanning reviews, you can get a pretty good idea of what to expect. And if it's not up to snuff, you can use the Internet access terminal in the common area to find another place to stay for the following night.

Camping: Where to Pitch a Tent *or* Park the RV

The ever-increasing cost of room and board has led more travelers to consider camping, anything from pitching a tent in a national park to rolling across the United States in a self-contained mobile home. Even without financial necessity, camping is often the best way to gain a true appreciation of a place—to sleep out under the stars, fill your lungs with fresh mountain air, and warm up in the morning to a pot of cowboy coffee simmering over a campfire. It's not for everybody, but those who prefer camping or choose it as a cheap way to travel will find the Net a powerful planning tool.

Millions of people camp in U.S. national parks each year. If you're planning to be one of them, take a look at the **National Park Service (www.nps.gov)** site. A section called **Visit Your Parks (www.nps.gov/parks.html)** enables you to locate parks on maps or by name. The parks area has links including **Select by State Map** and **Campground Reservation Information.**

You can also reserve a campsite online at **reservations.nps.gov.** Booking is available for dozens (though not all) national parks and is easy and straightforward. Select a park by name or click on the U.S. map, then choose a campground and the date you want to go. If you're not sure where to camp, have a look at the park maps—the campsites are indicated in blue. Keep clicking to find out about availability (including specifics, such as how many sites are reserved and how many are still free), rules, and fees. Overall, this site is very nicely done, letting you explore the park online before choosing where to camp.

For more detailed descriptions and features, visit the Great Outdoor Recreation Pages section on parks (**www.gorp.com/gorp/ resource/US_National_Park/ main.htm**). As one of the leading outdoors sites on the Web, **GORP (www.gorp.com)** is a superb resource for anyone interested in hiking information,

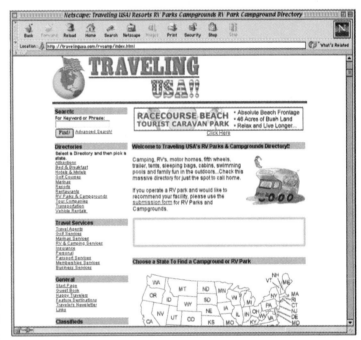

Traveling USA (travelingusa.com) can help you find a campsite in some U.S. states and Canadian provinces.

adventure stories, or outdoor gear. The GORP park area includes a locator map, parks listed by region, international parks, and related links.

For private campgrounds, see **Go Camping America (www.gocampingamerica. com/main.html)**, which lists thousands of U.S. campgrounds, many with links to Web pages. Use the clickable U.S. map and select a state to find campground listings. When you see one that might work, click on it to learn about its size, fees, hookups, even whether modems are available for your computer Another campground site is **Traveling USA (travelingusa.com)**.

Another site worth checking is **ParkNet (www.park-net.com)**, which includes campground listings for about a dozen U.S. states and Manitoba, Canada. Some states accept online bookings; for others reserve by phone. You can check availability for each particular camp site and see their locations on maps for some campgrounds.

Summing Up

Where you stay has a big impact on your trip. By employing the Net, you can consider more options, get a better sense of what to expect, and get feedback from other travelers to help you make your decisions.

Other Chapters to Check

Chapter 2: "Booking Flights Online"—Tips on using online agents

Chapter 7: "Budget Travel"—Last-minute deals on hotel rooms

Chapter 11: "Taking Care of Business"—Advice about using biztravel sites to find lodgings

Chapter 13: "Online Discussion Forums"—Tips on seeking advice from fellow travelers

tips

■ Travelscape (www.travelscape.com) has a no-risk guarantee. Book a hotel room with Travelscape, and if you find a better deal anywhere, the company will match that price. Also, if you cancel at least three days in advance you get a full refund.

■ USA Hotel Guides (www.usahotelguides.com) offers detailed information and booking for more than 30,000 hotels. Featured hotels have lots of images, which can be informative but slow to load.

a room with a view

FIND REVIEWS, MENUS & MORE on THE NET

Everyone has a different opinion about what makes a good restaurant. Some people love California cuisine, with its delicate little portions presented as if the plate were a canvas and the food was the paint. Others want plenty to eat, a massive burrito or a plateful of spaghetti, and they care more about value than presentation. So a tip from one person or guidebook may provide enough information to make an informed decision. By using the tools available on the Net, however, you can get opinions from lots of sources and many people. Examine online dining guides to see what a restaurant offers, seek recommendations in newsgroups, or visit a restaurant's home page to get a better idea of what it serves and at what price.

Restaurant Guides *on* the Web

Online dining guides come in all shapes and sizes. Some, such as **Fodor's Restaurant Index (www.fodors.com)**, are international in scope; others, like the **Gumbo Pages (www.gumbopages.com)**, are focused on a region or city. Then there are specialty guides, some for people with dietary restrictions (vegetarians, kosher), and others, such as **The Sushi World Guide (sushi.to)**, for those who just love a certain type of food. Finally—and these sources should not be overlooked—online city guides, newspapers, and magazines offer insightful reviews and commentary. In the following pages we'll have a look at some of the Web's finest dining guides and show how to use them.

Top Restaurant Guides

So why should anyone bother with online restaurant directories when they can get advice from print guides. Simply put:

- **Online databases** make it easy to find restaurants that meet your needs. At some of the better directories, you can input your preferences—cuisine type, price, neighborhood, etc.—and learn which restaurants match your criteria.
- **You can browse** a city's listings by type of food; for example, you may wish to look for Spanish restaurants in Philadelphia.

■ **The Web is a great place** to store voluminous archives. In other words, these databases contain thousands of listings, many with detailed information, including reviews, menus, and comments from others who have recently dined at particular restaurants.

Let's explore some of the best sites (for more detailed listings see this book's Web directories).

Reviews and Personal Opinions from CuisineNet

Covering sixteen U.S. cities, **CuisineNet (www.cuisinenet.com)** does a nice job of making it easy to find dining establishments that offer what you want, though not all listings are up to date. Select a city and browse among CuisineNet's top picks or scan the listings by type of cuisine. Choosing "Washington, D.C." and then "seafood" led me to a list of seven fish restaurants, each with a detailed description, including price, contact information, and ratings from other CuisineNet readers. The Grill from Ipanema, for example, which specializes in Brazilian seafood, received pretty high ratings (7.5 of 10 overall with higher ratings for food than ambience), and costs an average of $22 for dinner.

This is a nice overview, but CuisineNet offers more. Clicking on the link for The Grill from Ipanema led to a page with more detailed information, including hours, how many people the restaurant seats, how one should dress (a jacket for men, tie optional), and where to park. Perhaps, most valuable are the comments from those who have recently dined there. Click on "What They Are Saying" for recent capsule reviews from other diners. Here are a couple for The Grill from Ipanema:

Submitted on 02 Mar 99
The restaurant is quite small and very charming. It is best to have a reservation, however, my group did not, but the bartender was very kind and took care of us. The food was incredibly tasty and the portions were substantial.

Submitted on 23 Jun 98
The food is excellent, as is the Brazilian atmosphere. The only problem is the lack of space. My dining companion and I had to "scoot" around the table to sit down and move our table out of the way when the hostess wanted to seat the table next to us. Aside from that, the dinner experience was good.

This is just like having a couple of friends give you the straight dope. In just a few sentences, you learn how the restaurant handled an unexpected party, that portions are generous, and space can be a bit tight. A word of caution, though: If a review looks too good, it may have been written by the restaurant's owner or her good friend. So look for patterns, such as several diners recommending a place.

To further refine a CuisineNet search, go back to a city's main page, set your criteria (cuisine, price, neighborhood), and then search that city's database. This can be a good way to search for neighborhoods with lots of restaurants, such as San Francisco's North Beach, but it can be too limiting in other cases. My search for moderately priced ($21–$35) French restaurants on Capitol Hill, for example, didn't turn up any listings.

In this case a better way to go is to peruse CuisineNet's top picks for Washington D.C. Click on "Top Picks," then select from dozens of categories. Under **Top French Picks** is Gerard's Place, described by CuisineNet as "the perfect place to get away for an important, high-powered lunch meeting. The French menu offers some of the most flavorful and rich fish dishes in the downtown area." Some categories are based on cuisine type, while others focus on themes, such as **Top Date Picks** and **Top Under $25 Picks.**

Zagat's: The People's Choice

In 1979, Tim and Nina Zagat introduced their first restaurant guide, a survey of New York City's dining establishments. Unlike other critics, the Zagats didn't visit a restaurant a couple of times and review it; instead, they enlisted dozens of their friends to rank restaurants based on food, service, and decor. The guide became a bible for diners wanting to be in the know, and the survey grew to encompass many more U.S. cities.

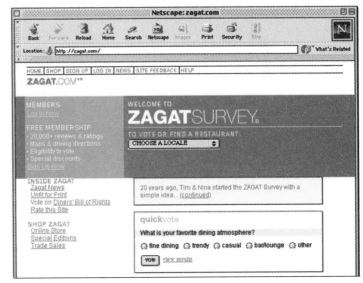

Little did they know it, but a decade before the advent of the Web, the Zagats came up with a system that would shine brightly in the online firmament. Today, diners from all over the world evaluate restaurants (and Zagat plans to rank hotels, too) at **Zagat.com**, enabling fellow food lovers to make better choices about where to eat.

To get started at Zagat.com, use the prominent pull-down menu labeled "Choose a Locale" and select a city. Next

The popular Zagat Survey has expanded its print guides to include hundreds of restaurant reviews for major cities at Zagat.com (zagat.com).

select a list of favorites in categories such as **Food, Decor, Service, Cuisine,** and **Neighborhood.** Or, take a look at all the listings (657 currently for San Francisco alone) and click on any that look appealing. *Note:* Listings for each city include restaurants for the region as a whole. I found a listing in the San Francisco category for a place in Mendocino, more than 100 miles from the city.

When you click on a restaurant, you get a brief description of the restaurant and its scores in each category. You can also click "Show Me More Like This" for a listing of restaurants that meet similar criteria. It would be nice if Zagat.com included comments from other diners, as these can be more insightful than a quickie description. Still, because it's based on such a large sample, the Zagat guide is a valuable resource for finding the best restaurants in the cities covered, which are mostly in North America, with a few exceptions, such as Paris, London, and Tokyo. (*Note:* Zagat.com is considering imposing fees for some content, but Nina Zagat said she is leaning toward a free model for the foreseeable future.)

Unprintable Reviews from Zagat

Tim and Nina Zagat, creators of the Zagat dining surveys, were both trained as lawyers and thus are very careful about what they print. So they've never printed some of the most clever, and most cutting, reviews. But they list seventy-six of them—without mentioning the restaurants—on a **Zagat.com** page called **Looking for a Laugh (www.zagat.com/help/outtakes.asp)**. Here are eleven of the best unprintable restaurant descriptions from readers:

- Suffers from delusions of adequacy.
- Also known as Ebola Cafe.
- Be sure to sit in the no-shooting section.
- Saves fuel bills—the heartburn will keep you warm all winter.
- "Hi, I'm obviously underage. Margarita please."
- Like a skunk, it's small, it's cute, and it stinks.
- A petri dish experiment gone horribly, horribly wrong.
- Where's the health department?
- The cockroaches are more energetic than the management.
- Gives health and food both bad names.
- I get sick from the food every time. At least it has consistency.

Online Guidebooks Show the Way

Taking a very selective approach, **Fodor's Restaurant Index (www.fodors.com)** compiles a short list of better-known places, rather than trying to cover all the restaurants in a city. Start by choosing one of the hundred or so domestic and international cities listed and search by name or criteria. These listings come from Fodor's guidebooks, so they are critical reviews, not paid listings.

Searching by name for Cancun led me to all twenty-seven listings for this resort town—with red stars next to places that Fodor's recommends. Because it has a red star, I clicked on "El Pescador" for a short description of the place, including price, decor, contact information, and specialties.

For larger cities, such as Sydney, Australia, it makes sense to search by criteria. You can go straight to Fodor's recommended restaurants or see what's available by neighborhood, cuisine type, and price. You can select more than one choice in each category; for example, you can look for places under $20 as well as in the $20 to $40 range. Just check both boxes.

A search for an Italian restaurant under $40 turned up two places, one for under $20 and another in the $20 to $40 range. (*Note:* These are Aussie dollars, so you might want to visit an online currency converter; see chap. 10.) Neither is recommended, so I tried another category: Australian food. Though I didn't really know what that meant, I figured a search for Aussie restaurants should give me a clue. Well, restaurants in the "Australian" category range from upscale pizza parlors to bistros, so I still don't really know what Australian food is. But I have a better idea of where to get rabbit stew next time I visit Sydney.

Fodor's doesn't have links to customer comments or menus, so you can check other restaurant directories or try searching for a restaurant's name and city on a search site

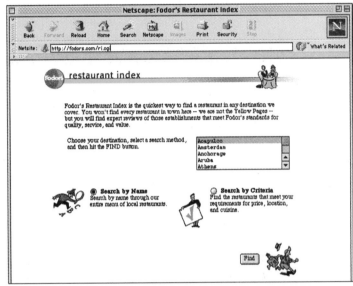

Fodor's Restaurant Index (www.fodors.com/ri.cgi) includes savvy advice from Fodor's guidebooks.

like Yahoo. It's quite likely that better restaurants will have Web pages, where you can learn more. Finally, remember that although online guides can be current, it doesn't mean they always are. If you want to be sure a restaurant is still open, give a call or check with the concierge before you shell out for a cab ride.

Another guidebook site that lists restaurants is **Rough Guides (travel. roughguides.com)**. Rough Guides puts the full text of most of its books online, so just search for a city, go to its main page, and click the dining icon at the top. The dining section starts with a nice introduction to a city restaurants, such as the following for Paris:

> Contrary to what you might expect, eating out in Paris need not be an enormous extravagance. There are numerous fixed price menus under Fr80, providing simple but well-cooked fare; paying a little more than this gives you the chance to try out a greater range of dishes, and once over Fr150, you should be getting some gourmet satisfaction.

City Guides & Online Newspapers Go Deep

In chapter 1 we discussed how city guides, such as **CitySearch (www.city search.com)**, can be valuable for getting a handle on a region with which you're unfamiliar. And one of their greatest strengths is restaurant reviews. These reviews are typically written by connoisseurs who have a keen sense for what makes a restaurant worth visiting. Their expertise makes the reviews quite credible; however, when you continue clicking to a restaurant's page on most city guides; you are seeing a paid listing so you need to view comments there with a more critical eye. Finally, city sites complement restaurant reviews with tools that include maps, parking tips, even ways to find the nearest cinema for an after-dinner movie.

Cut to the Chase at CitySearch

To find restaurants at **CitySearch (www.citysearch.com)**, start at the main page, select a city, and you're off and running. Click on "Restaurants" (in **Food and Drink**) and on the right will be categories with the number of listings, for example, "Chinese (105)" in Austin, Texas.

You can get a sense of what type of food predominates in a town: Austin has seventy-nine listings in the "Country Cooking" category, compared with five for French restaurants. The categories aren't all by cuisine type, some are by theme, such as "Child-Friendly." They're also broken down by price, and whether they deliver (112 restaurants) or are open twenty-four hours (33).

To home in on exactly what you want, search by neighborhood, price, and cuisine type, simultaneously, for example, a Thai restaurant in the $6–$10 range in downtown

The CitySearch online city guides have restaurant sections for many cities, each listing recommended places for kids, romance, and special occasions.

Austin. Because this search was so specific, it yielded only one listing: Big Bowl Noodle House on Guadelupe Street. To expand the search, try listing all neighborhoods, or all prices, whatever you feel most flexible about. Or just search for the type of cuisine you want and see listings for the entire city.

Clicking on "Mexican" led me to several pages of listings, and almost every restaurant mentioned had an "editorial profile"—an impartial evaluation. Some restaurants also had paid listings. The links to these are clearly marked "advertiser's Web site." Click on the profile for "El Gallo" for a couple of paragraphs of detailed description, including specialties, hours, prices, and a picture. Locate El Gallo with the map link; another link will lead to the more detailed information provided by the restaurant.

In the bottom left corner is a very cool feature called, "What else is nearby?" Using the pull-down menu, you can locate nearby movie theaters, clubs, bookstores, and more. You can even set the distance; for example, search for cinemas within a mile of the restaurant or bookstores within a half mile. These are the type of tools that make the Web shine.

Newspaper City Guides

Established newspapers view online city guides as invaders on their turf. In response, many leading newspapers have launched their own city guides, and some are excellent outposts for dining advice. **NYToday (www.nytoday.com)**, an online production of the *New York Times,* offers reviews of restaurants and bars and has extensive listings with commentary.

For a city with as many restaurants as New York, it's wise to be very specific about what you want. You can select type of restaurant (or NYToday top picks) and neighborhood; then click "Go." A search for a Russian place in Midtown yielded nine listings, including Firebird, ranked with two stars (very good) and three dollar signs (expensive). Clicking on the Firebird link led to a page devoted to it, including a synopsis of, and a link to, the *New York Times*'s review, a map locating the restaurant, and links to nearby bars and parking. One feature that's very helpful is that the review is dated, so you know how long it's been since this appraisal.

On the left coast of the United States, the *San Francisco Examiner* and *Chronicle* have teamed up to produce a site called **SF Gate (sfgate.com)**, which features a guide called **Bay Area Traveler (www.sfgate.com/traveler)**. Like NYToday, this is a special production for the Web, not merely recycled content from the newspapers. Clicking on "Restaurants" leads to a page dominated by a search box with links to reviews and features, such as **Top 100 Restaurants** and **Best Bargains**. You can even send e-mail to the restaurant critics and scroll through their answers to others' questions. Dozen of questions are already answered (with topics ranging from "Best Views" to "Cooking Like Mom's"), so have a look at these before posing a question of your own.

tips

■ Online versions of food magazines often contain reputable restaurant advice. On Epicurious (www.epicurious.com) are features and archives from *Bon Appétit* and *Gourmet.*

■ NewCityNet (www.newcitynet.com) lists dozens of alternative weeklies, from Syracuse to Santa Cruz. These weekly papers are good sources of dining advice.

Using Local Newspapers to Find Restaurants

Just because newspaper city guides have become valuable doesn't mean newspapers' own sites aren't worth checking. Many online newspapers have extensive restaurant sections, and alternative weeklies, which focus on entertainment, can be incisive. To find local newspapers, try **Newspapers Online (www.newspapers.com)** or **AJR Newslink** (**www.newslink.org**), which have links to thousands of newspapers throughout the world.

To find an Italian restaurant in Los Angeles, I visited Newspapers Online and scrolled down to California, where I found a link to the **L.A. Weekly (www. laweekly.com)**. Going to the Weekly, I clicked on "Dining" and selected "Italian" from the **Cuisines** menu. I then clicked on "View Restaurants" and got a list of about fifteen choices from all over L.A. Each listing included a capsule review by a Weekly critic. Keep in mind this is a relatively small selection; you won't find the majority of L.A.'s Italian places here. Other alt-weeklies have more extensive restaurant listings.

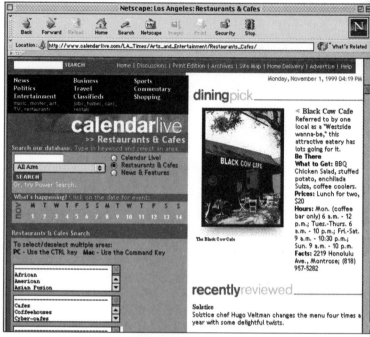

Like most major metro newspapers the Los Angeles Times (latimes.com) maintains a lively restaurant section. The easiest way to find it is to go to the home page and use the Calendar Live pull-down menu to select "Restaurants/Cafes."

Specialty Dining Guides

The Net is a valuable tool for those with particular dining interests. People who crave a vegetarian feast or kosher Chinese food can, in many cases, use the Net to find places where they can get what they want.

Even if your diet is not restricted, you probably have a favorite type of food. On your home turf, you know where to find your faves, but it can be harder when you travel. Hundreds of foodies have created tightly focused, highly personal guides to different types of cuisines. And these directories—such as The Gumbo Pages or The Sushi World Guide—are infused with their creators' passion for the foods they love. Many of the directories rely on contributions from the ever-growing online community to compile listings and keep them up-to-date, which can make them extensive, though not always reliable.

Vegetarian and Kosher Restaurants

Travel for those with special dietary needs can sometimes be intimidating—no one wants to get caught someplace where they can't find a restaurant that meets their dietary requirements. Fortunately, the Web can help, with guides for vegetarians, those who keep kosher, and others.

The **World Guide to Vegetarianism (www.veg.org)** has sections on Europe, the United States, Canada, and Australia. To find veggie restaurants in, say, Boulder, simply click on "World Guide," then continue on to the "U.S.," "Colorado," and finally "Boulder." Listings are divided into three categories: vegan (no animal products of any kind), vegetarian (dairy products allowed), and vegetarian-friendly restaurants (where the restaurant isn't vegetarian, but it's easy to get a good meat-free meal). Although this isn't the prettiest site on the Net, the listings are extensive, and it's easy to find your way around.

tip

■ In addition to the World Guide to Vegetarianism (www.veg.org), vegetarians seeking travel and dining advice can check The Vegetarian Resource Group travel section (www.vrg.org/travel).

For those who require strictly kosher dining, the Net is—pardon the pun—a Godsend. Finding a kosher restaurant while traveling can be difficult, but checking the Net beforehand will give you some options. A good place to start is the **Kosher Restaurant Database (www.shamash.org/kosher/krestquery.html)**. It's best to keep your search broad to get the most results.

A general search for kosher restaurants in Los Angeles spawned a list of dozens of options, from Pico Kosher Deli to Shalom Hunan (now that's a perfect place for Sunday night dinner). Each listing included prices, category (meat or dairy), the date of the entry, and a capsule review. Here's an excerpt from the evaluation of Shalom Hunan: "The best Kosher Chinese west of New York. Beautiful dining room, good service, and excellent food."

For kosher restaurants in New York, try **KosherLink (www.kosherlink.com)**. It has more than eighty listings for Manhattan, and many more for the rest of the city. For a trip to Chicago, you could visit **Kosher Eating in Chicago (condor.depaul.edu/~scohn/NTJC-Fd.html)**, though at last check this site hadn't been updated recently. For other cities, try a search engine, such as Yahoo, and search for "kosher restaurant" and the name of the city.

The Sushi World Guide

Some types of food are so beloved that they have their own international databases. Sushi is one of these specialties, as **The Sushi World Guide (sushi.to)** links to about 2,000 raw fish restaurants in some 600 cities. This database is the result of another remarkable community effort, as sushi lovers from around the world write in (via e-mail of course) to recommend their favorite places. The philosophy of the site's authors is simple:

The creators of The Sushi World Guide provide a forum for Sushi Lovers and Japanese Food Addicts around the globe so that neither connoisseurs nor newcomers are lost wherever they look for their favorite food. As we need your participation, please feel free to mail us whatever restaurant or specialty you might find worth recommending to keep this site alive and well.

Searching for a place in Santa Cruz, California, leads to several listings, all recommendations from people just like you and me. Here's an excerpt for Sukeroku:

I have been going to Sukeroku for over twenty years and this husband/wife team never fails. The fish is always amazingly fresh and the service great. The tempura is light and will not leave a pile of oil behind. The udon is superb with its light and colorful broth.

—Jenna [e-mail address would be listed here] (March 21st 1999)

A couple of things to notice about this review: It's dated so you can see how current it is, and it includes the writer's e-mail address so you can send her a note and ask a follow-up question, such as, "What are their specialties?" Like other sites where reviews are contributed by its visitors, you need to be cautious because you never know who's writing the review—that person might not have a very discerning palate or could even be the restaurant's owner. But the vast majority of the reviews are credible; relying on their advice can be a fine way to make informed dining choices

The Sushi World Guide (sushi.to) lets sushi lovers around the globe recommend sushi restaurants in hundreds of cities.

the next time you travel. (If you're looking for good road food, see the section on diners in chap. 5, "On the Road.")

Advice from Experts: Going Straight to the Source

For a trip to New Orleans, traveler Robert Buxbaum stuck his virtual spoon into **The Gumbo Pages (www.gumbopages.com)**, written by New Orleans native and culinary expert Chuck Taggart. Welcoming people to his site, Chuck tells people just what they want to hear: "Remember that in Louisiana . . . alcohol, butter, cream, and big piles of fried seafood are still good for you."

After perusing the restaurant recommendations page, Buxbaum followed up by sending e-mail to Taggart, asking for some specific advice. Chuck's e-mail address is printed in large type near the top of the page, making it easy to connect with him.

Their exchange highlights another advantage of using the Net for travel: Authors and "experts" are much more accessible. If Robert had bought a printed guide to dining in New Orleans, he probably would have had a tougher time connecting with the author and getting responses to his questions. Another huge advantage is that online guides can link to related sites, such as Gumbo's link to pages on Mardi Gras, a lesson in Yat speak (the local tongue), and weather forecasts.

Using Search Sites *to* Find Dining Guides

Many cities have dining guides devoted to them that can be worth a visit. The question is how to find these. Personally, I like to start with a directory like Yahoo or **LookSmart (www.looksmart.com)**, and then try a search engine, such as **HotBot (www.hot bot.com)**. What's the difference? At a directory, a selective list of sites is hand-picked by its producers so you can drill down from broad to specific categories. To find a Dallas restaurant guide at LookSmart, I followed a path from a category on the home page called **Entertainment to Dining** to "Restaurant Guides," and finally to "US States T-V" (T for Texas). The search yielded a manageable list of sites, and I found **Dallas Dines Out (www.dallasdinesout.com)**, with dozens of listings and reviews.

To find a place to eat in Maui, I tried HotBot, searched for "maui restaurant," and came up with eighty Web site matches. Near the top of the list was the **Maui Dining and Restaurants Page (mauionline.com/dining.html)**. Here, I found hundreds of listings with phone numbers, some with links to their own pages. One of these was Roy's Kahana Bar & Grill, created by famed chef Roy Yamaguchi—the page for this restaurant included Roy's dining philosophy, a sample menu with prices, and even recipes.

Using Search Sites to Find Specific Restaurants

Search sites can also lead directly to restaurant Web sites. One of the best techniques for accomplishing this is to search for a city name and type of restaurant and then narrow the search. At **Lycos (www.lycos.com)**, for example, after searching for "vancouver AND restaurants" (which yields a very long list), you can go back to search box, enter a more specific term, such as "chinese," and then click "Search These Results." The ensuing query won't search through Lycos's entire database; rather, it will search for "chinese" in the among the sites generated by the "vancouver AND restaurants" search. Though this might sound a bit confusing, it's quite simple; in essence you're just searching through a much smaller selection of sites.

> **tip**
>
> When an e-mail address is underlined, that almost always means it's a "mailto" link, enabling you to simply click on the e-mail address to send a message.

The first search—"vancouver AND restaurants"—yielded more than ten pages of results (one thing I dislike about Lycos is that it doesn't tell you the total number of results). Searching the first batch of results for "chinese" led to a smaller list, though most of the links still led to directories, rather than to specific restaurants. Although searching this way can sometimes turn up interesting restaurant sites, I find it's usually best to visit a restaurant directory and peruse the options there.

First Person: Morris Dye

Once I've narrowed down my choices using some kind of guide or newsgroup, I'll use a search engine to find other opinions about a place that looks promising. For example, say I found a favorable review of Thirsty Bear in CitySearch, but I'd like to hear what other reviewers say before deciding where to go for some tapas and a beer.

By doing a search for "thirsty bear san francisco" on **HotBot (hot bot.com)**, I come up with 910 listings, which is a bit overwhelming, but in the first ten results, there are links to Thirsty Bear's own site, to several other reviews (including **CuisineNet, sftravel.com, trippinout. com**) and some beer/brew-pub sites (like the **American Brewers Guild**), where Thirsty Bear is reviewed along with other similar places. This kind of search serves two purposes: It helps you find other opinions about the original place, and it leads you to other resources for finding more places to consider.

Online Yellow Pages

Another technique for finding restaurants is to use online yellow pages, such as **BigYellow (www.bigyellow.com)** or **BigBook (www.bigbook.com)**. I typically use these services to get contact information and maps for places that have already been recommended. You won't find the editorial advice you get at dining guides, but if you already know where you want to go, these services can be useful.

Simply enter "restaurants" in BigYellow's category box and then select city and state. A search for restaurants in Savannah, Georgia, yields 395 listings at both BigBook and BigYellow. That tells me that both these sites access the same database because they cough up the same results. To hone your query, click on "Detailed Search," where you can search for specific types of cuisine, such as Chinese restaurants.

Another cool feature is that you can look for places near your hotel or wherever you're staying. Say you're spending some time in New York: Click on "Search By Distance," enter the hotel's address, then select how far you want your search to range. You can look for Thai restaurants within a 1-mile radius, for example. Then if you want more information, you can see what a local city guide (such as NYToday) says about the restaurants you've turned up.

To locate a restaurant, just click on its name (which is underlined so you know it's a live link). This leads to a map that allows you to zoom in or out to get a sense of where a restaurant is. Then, there's nothing left to do except shut down the computer and go to dinner.

Using Map Sites to Find Restaurants

MapQuest (www.mapquest.com), a mapping site launched in the mid-1990s, has added new features over the years, such as **Travel Guide,** which lists more than 20,000 U.S. hotels and restaurants. From MapQuest's home page, click on "Travel Guide," which includes rankings by Mobil Travel Guides. Enter a city name or specific address, such as Kansas City, Missouri, and then click "Dining." On the next page, you can search for a specific place by name or enter some search parameters: how far you're willing to go, price range, food category, and credit cards accepted. You can even search for highly ranked places by selecting a required star ranking (has to be three stars or above, for example).

To take Travel Guide for a test drive, I tried to find a steak house or continental restaurant within 5 miles of downtown Kansas City in the under $15 or $15–$24 categories. I left the star ranking blank because MapQuest will list the number of stars when it serves up the results. This search spawned a list of seven places, all located on a city map. If I saw a restaurant that looked good, I clicked on it, and a new map with this restaurant at the center was generated. Below the map was contact information, accepted credit cards, and a short editorial description from Mobil, listing specialties, prices, and hours.

tip

■ **Yellow page listings are also available at major search engines, such as Yahoo and Snap (www.snap.com).**

MapQuest will also give you driving directions from any address to the restaurant. Simply return to the home page, click on "Driving Directions," and enter your starting point and the address of the restaurant. MapQuest will then generate turn-by-turn directions, with maps, to help you get there on time for your reservations. (We'll discuss using map sites at greater length in chap. 5, "On the Road.")

Word *of* Mouth: Online Forums

Sometimes the most reliable restaurant advice comes through personal recommendations, and the Net has made it easy for people in one region to advise restaurant-goers around the world. First-hand restaurant recommendations can be ferreted out in chat rooms or conference areas in online services, such as AOL or CompuServe, or through Usenet newsgroups.

Using Online Forums

Paul and Kay Henderson, proprietors of Gidleigh Park Hotel and Restaurant, in Devon, England, were planning to visit Charleston, South Carolina, and wanted some suggestions for fine restaurants there. So Paul posted his questions in CompuServe forums on wine, food, and cooks, as well as in the **rec.food.restaurant** Usenet newsgroup.

In three days I had about fifteen replies, including one invitation to dine with people which I have accepted because they mentioned that we have mutual friends. Most of the other respondents mentioned three specific restaurants, so I have made reservations at two of them. I've already booked Magnolia's and Louis's by phone, because they were in the top five of almost everyone who replied.

An Excellent Place Off the Beaten Path

When searching for restaurants, don't overlook the online discussion groups. Although some of these areas have become more crowded recently, they can still be good sources of recommendations.

When Rob Lake and his wife were planning a fifteen-hour drive from their home in Cleveland Heights, Ohio, to visit their daughter at a camp in Maine, they turned to Usenet's restaurant newsgroups for advice. "I found an excellent place off the beaten track in Syracuse, just right for both parents and kid. Going back up to pick up the daughter a month later, we took the other two kids. We detoured to a recommended clam shack on Cape Ann north of Boston."

Rob has used newsgroups ranging from **nyc.food** to **alt.food.barbeque.** If you're not sure which newsgroups might have the restaurant advice you're seeking, try searching for keywords at **Deja.com.** For example, entering "Los Angeles restaurant" will turn up the newsgroup **la.eats.** Then, you can browse through this online bulletin board and post a question if you like. It's free to browse and to post.

Summing Up

Though the Net isn't a perfect resource for finding restaurants, it is a good way to get ideas about places to eat. Many online directories contain reviews and round them out with customer comments, online menus, even nearby cinemas—features you typically won't find in print guidebooks or traditional newspaper reviews. Finally, you can get recommendations from other Net users by posing questions in (or simply combing through) online discussion groups, from AOL forums to Usenet newsgroups. Bon appétit!

Another Chapter to Check:

Chapter 13: "Online Discussion Forums"—Tips on using Internet discussion groups

---

RENT *a* CAR ONLINE *&* MAP YOUR ROUTE

Renting *a* Car Online

In an early episode of the TV sitcom *Seinfeld*, Jerry arrives at the rent-a-car counter to pick up the car he has reserved. Unfortunately, it's not there waiting for him. He chides the clerk at the counter, saying that she doesn't understand the concept of reservations. When she protests, "I know why we have reservations," Jerry interrupts, "I don't think you do. If you did, I'd have a car here for me. See, you know how to take the reservation, you just don't know how to *hold* the reservation."

Well, thanks to the Net, travelers can have a bit more assurance that when they get to the reservation counter, the car they want will be waiting for them. By employing the Web, anyone can peruse a car company's fleet, compare prices (including special deals for Net users), and reserve a car. And if you book online rather than over the phone, you can print out your reservation and confirmation. So if the clerk at the other end says you didn't request an economy car and offers you a Buick Le Sabre, you can stick to your guns.

Starting at Online Agencies

Just as it's best to scan the whole field when shopping for airline tickets, it's smart to start with online agencies, such as **Travelocity.com**, when looking for a rental car. Travelocity's database contains the major car rental companies, including those that focus on budget rentals, such as Alamo. And it's a lot easier to do one search at Travelocity than it is to call a bunch of different car companies or look up each company's Web page. Of course, you could just call a travel agent, but you might prefer to search online. This method lets you get specific information about a car's specs, find the best prices, and select a car that meets your needs.

Here is the procedure for renting a car at Travelocity:

1. Enter the airport code or city name for the location where you want to pick up the car and input the dates and times you'll need it. Then, select what type of car you want (compact, midsize, etc.) and, if you choose, select the car rental company.

2. Travelocity will come up with a list of rates from different companies. A search for a pickup at New York's La Guardia airport showed the best deal was at Dollar, but

National was only a couple of dollars more. (Hertz was $9.00 higher.) The listing includes pickup location (inside the terminal) and car details (economy two- or four-door, unlimited mileage, automatic transmission, and air conditioning).

3. Choose to save this itinerary or reserve the car. Clicking on "Reserve" leads to more details about the car (Dodge Neon or similar) and the hours of the rental counter (5:30 A.M. to 1:00 A.M.)

4. The next page is called **Renter Information** and this is where you input your address and account numbers for frequent renter or frequent flier programs (many car companies are allied with airline programs). Click "Continue" when finished.

5. This brings you to the Reserve Car page. Here you can enter your credit card number and special requests (no smoking, mobile phone, infant seat). There's also a space to enter a number for a discount coupon. If you're ready to commit, click "Reserve Car."

6. Next, you'll see your confirmation page—be sure to print this out and save it as proof of your reservation. At the very least, jot down the confirmation number for your records.

The procedure is similar at **Expedia.com** and a bit more efficient, as you'll need fewer pages to get your results. The one thing I don't like about Travelocity is that it offers only one listing per rental car company. So if the two cheapest cars come from Alamo, say an economy car for $190 a week and a compact for $193, you'll see only the economy car listed.

ITN (www.itn.com), another large agency, also offers rental cars, but when I took it for a test drive, searching for an eight-day rental on Hawaii's Big Island, ITN offered an expensive daily rate, which was far higher than the low weekly rate available for the same dates.

Rent Direct: Bonuses for Booking Online

Just as the airlines are offering incentives to those who buy directly through their Web sites, rental car companies are trying to lure you to do business directly with them. Rental car companies save money if you book on their sites because they don't have to pay a commission to a travel agent or employ a sales rep to take your call. The incentives for booking online range from Net-only discounts to special rates on one-way rentals (where the car is dropped off far from its pickup location).

A recent visit to Hertz's site **(www.hertz.com)** revealed several discounts, some specifically for online renters and others available to all customers, regardless of how they reserve. Here's a sampler:

■ 20 percent off when you book through Hertz's site on all rentals in North America (This shows how eager Hertz is to get its customers in the habit of booking online.)

tips

■ Leave the company category set at "All" to see who has the best rate for your itinerary. If you prefer a specific company, check at an agency like Travelocity and then compare this price with what's offered at a company's Web site (such as www.avis.com).

■ Online agencies are best for rental cars that you plan to pick up at airport locations. If you want to get your car in a city center, go directly to a rental car company's site, such as www.hertz.com.

- Special deals for members of Hertz's #1 Club Gold, such as double upgrades in some European countries
- "Freedom Rates" (discounts for those who keep their cars over a Saturday night)

Now these deals—except the discount for booking at Hertz's site—are available to all customers, whether or not they book online. But checking rental car companies' sites is a good way to find out about different promotions. Combining this with a search at an online agency such as Travelocity lets you weigh all the options. Travelocity showed that a Hertz rental at La Guardia airport cost about $9.00 more than the cheapest option, but if you can get an upgrade or bonus miles, or if you simply prefer Hertz, you may decide it's worthwhile to pay $9.00 more a day.

And remember, it's wise to compare prices because the rate Travelocity offers for a Hertz car might not be the same you find at Hertz's site. For an identical spring weekend rental from La Guardia, Hertz charged exactly $50 per day more than Travelocity ($123.99 versus $73.99). Even with Hertz's 20 percent discount for booking direct, Travelocity's rate was still much cheaper. It's hard to say why different databases yield different results, but sometimes they do. If the search becomes confusing, you can always call a car company's toll-free number and seek clarification.

Hertz's site does have some other features that make it worth visiting. One of the most useful features is the **Vehicle Guide (hertz.com/fleet/index.html)**, where you can learn about Hertz's fleet. Sure you may know what to expect when you rent a compact in Phoenix, but if you're curious about a convertible in Italy, take the Vehicle Guide for a spin. After choosing Italy, select convertible and up comes an image of Fiat Punto with some specs (manual transmission, airbag, AM/FM cassette, room for four adults, etc.). Now that sounds like a nice way to breeze through the Riviera.

Other Leading Rental Car Sites

Just about all the leading rental car companies have gone online and are worth visiting for the same reason Hertz's site is: special offers for online customers, visual information about cars, and a better sense of what each company offers throughout the world. What follows are addresses and some features of top car rental sites. (Remember, these offers were in place in mid-1999—by the time you read this, the sites may have evolved and the offers changed.)

- **Alamo (www.goalamo.com):** Don't be scared off by the goofy pictures of inanely happy Alamo salespeople and "customers." Its ad campaign notwithstanding, Alamo, offering rentals in North America, Central America, and Europe, is one of the leading discount car rental companies. Alamo offers up to 20 percent off for bookings through its Web site, along with other specials, such as discounts on ski packages or Hawaii rentals.
- **Avis (www.avis.com):** Avis offers domestic and international booking, discounts on weekend or weeklong rentals (though no Net-only offers at this time), fleet information, special deals on ski packages, and maps and directions.
- **Budget (www.budget.com):** Budget offers domestic booking (providing a toll-free number for international reservations), 20 percent off for online booking, fleet information, and special offers, such as deals on one-way rentals.

- **Dollar (www. dollar.com):** Dollar offers domestic and international reservations and special deals, such as free upgrade coupons, fleet information, and vehicle sales.
- **Enterprise (enterprise.com):** Enterprise recently unveiled a zippy reservation system that enables you to search by airport locations in North America or to find cars in your local neighborhood. To find cars at nonairport locations, search by zip code, city, or telephone number. To use the latter method, enter the phone number for where you'll be and Enterprise will come up with its nearby facility.

Alamo offers discounts for booking online and a simple procedure for reserving at its Web site (goalamo.com).

- **National (www.nationalcar.com):** National sure doesn't make it easy for those who don't know the airport code. You have to go through a ponderous process to search for the code before you can make a reservation—better to use an online agency like Travelocity or just call National's toll-free number.

Finally, there are lots of smaller car rental agencies out there that may have lower prices than the international chains. To find these, you can use a search site and look for something like " car rental AND chicago," or you can use yellow page listings, available on search sites, such as **Snap.com**, or through yellow page sites, such as **BigBook (bigbook.com)**.

For AOL Users

CAR RENTAL

AOL's **Car Renter Center** (keyword: *car rental*), links directly to special AOL sites for Hertz and Avis, with special deals for AOL members, such as free upgrades or $25 off a weekly rental. Whether these deals are better than those published elsewhere is debatable.

Using Online Classifieds *to* Buy
Cars *for* Long Trips

For journeys longer than a couple of weeks, it sometimes makes more sense to buy a relatively inexpensive car and sell it at the end of your sojourn. Considering that rental cars cost at least a few hundred dollars a month, you can save a bundle by buying a used car or truck when you get to your destination. In the old days (before the mid-90s), buying a car while traveling usually meant getting a newspaper on arrival and trying to quickly find a suitable used car. Today, there's a better way: using the Net to connect with used car sellers through online classifieds sites, Net newspapers, and virtual bulletin boards, also called newsgroups.

Though you can't really kick the tires on the Net, you can find potential sellers at your destination. There are several ways to do this:

- Use international classifieds, such as **Classifieds 2000 (www.classifieds2000. com)**, where you can find listings for most of the world's larger countries.
- Visit search engines or online newspapers that cover your destination and check their classifieds.
- Use online discussion groups that cover your destination and post a message detailing your arrival dates, what type of car you're seeking, and what you're willing to spend.

The cool thing about using the Net is that you can get these transactions in motion before leaving the ground. When you arrive you can meet the seller, check under the hood (or have a mechanic give the car a once over), and negotiate an acceptable price. You may even strike up a friendship and end up having someone give you a tour of his or her home city. So let's see what cars we can find online for someone who wants to buy a car for a long trip through New Zealand.

Classifieds 2000: A Shopper for the Planet

At the very bottom of the Classifieds 2000 site is a search

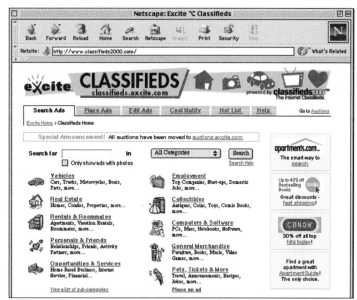

Classifieds 2000 (classifieds2000.com), part of the Excite network, can help you buy a car in another country, which, for long trips, can be a good alternative to renting.

box. Input "new zealand" in the search box, select the category "Vehicles" from the pull-down menu, and then click "Search." When I did this, in a few seconds Classifieds 2000 produced a manageable list of twenty-three offerings, including some vehicles that looked appealing, such as a 1986 Honda Civic, for $2,200. Because this is New Zealand currency, I visited the **Universal Currency Converter (www.xe.com/ currency)** and found that this is about US$1,150. Considering the car has a cassette player and air-conditioning, this would be an ideal car for a trip—if it runs well.

Classifieds 2000 showed the owner to be a private party (as opposed to a dealer), based in Tauranga, a mid-size town about 150 kilometers from Auckland. It also listed the date the car was put up for sale. If I wished to get in touch with the owner, I'd click "Send Message" and ask some questions about the car, how to get to Tauranga, and why he's selling it.

I could also ask if he might be willing to rent the car for a couple of months. For example, I could offer $300 dollars a month and return it at the end of my trip. Then he could still sell the car for close to what he's asking. Everyone wins: The owner should ultimately get more for his car, and I wouldn't have to worry about selling it at the end of my trip. Of course, I may have to provide some kind of collateral so that the owner has some assurance I'll return the car at the end of the rental period.

> ## tip
> ▪ **See the bottom of Yahoo's main page (yahoo.com) to link to its country and regional guides.**

Renting or buying this way may not be as secure as renting from Hertz. If you choose to go this way, it's sensible to have a car inspected before handing over the cash. You'll also need to inquire about licenses, registration, and insurance. Searching online for national auto clubs is one way to find this information. To find one, you could try going to the World Yahoos section at the bottom of Yahoo's home page **(yahoo.com)**. In this case, click on "Australia & NZ" and search the directory for an auto association in New Zealand. Using this method, I found **New Zealand Automobile Association Inc. (www.nzaa.co.nz)**, which covered insurance, registration, and other topics.

If you take these precautions, you'll likely end up with a serviceable vehicle at a fraction of the cost it would take to rent from a typical agency. You may not have considered renting a car because you assumed the cost was prohibitive, so this technique could give you the freedom and flexibility of having your own car rather than having to schlepp around on public buses.

Going Local with Regional Search Sites

The earlier example shows just one technique for trying to arrange a used car purchase before your trip. You could also use search engines, such as Yahoo, to track down the right car for your wanderings. Yahoo has more than a dozen regional guides for domestic and international destinations, such as Yahoo Australia & NZ, mentioned in the previous section.

Clicking on the "Australia & NZ" link leads to a page with categories much like any other Yahoo home page. A search for "auto AND classified" yields several categories, including one called "Automotive Classifieds." Clicking on "New Zealand Only" produces a list of four sites, including **New Zealand's Auto Web (www.autoweb.co.nz)**, which has used cars for sale. When you find one of interest, you can follow the same steps to get in touch with the owner as I did in the Classifieds 2000 example or search by criteria, such as price. Unfortunately, not all the listings have e-mail addresses, but you can follow up with a phone call.

Posting to Online Forums

Finally, don't overlook newsgroups, mailing lists, and forums. In short, these are electronic bulletin boards on which you can post a message, such as one with the subject line reading "Seeking used car," saying that you're looking to buy or rent a used car. To find newsgroups that would be right for your post, go to **Deja.com**. If you're not sure what groups would be appropriate for your message, click on "Travel" and check the list of forums.

When I did this search, it revealed two promising groups: **soc.culture. newzealand** and **rec.travel.australia+nz**. You can post to either or both groups and ask anyone interested to send you e-mail. Or you could keep checking these forums to see if anyone has answered your message. Remember, sometimes newsgroup users don't appreciate people who swoop in to make a request and don't keep checking the group. So if you request direct e-mail responses, say why, and mention that you'll keep visiting the forum from time to time.

Motorcycle Rentals

Renting a motorcycle is more challenging than renting a car. Because it's a much smaller market, in most places you can't just arrive at the airport, stroll up to the counter, and get the keys to your dream machine. In many vacation spots around the globe, however, you can find motorcycle rentals, and the Net can help you locate these.

Riding a Hog in Hawaii

Just to see what's out there, I cruised over to Yahoo and entered the search string "motorcycle AND rent AND hawaii." (I know I often use Yahoo, but there are good reasons—it's simple, fast, well organized, and if it doesn't have what you're seeking, it rolls over to the much larger Inktomi database.) Among the sites listed was one called **Hawaiian Riders (hawaiianriders.com/harley. htm)**, which specializes in Harley Davidsons. "You haven't seen Hawaii if you haven't seen it on a Harley," proclaims the home page. Hawaiian Riders says there's no helmet law in Hawaii, a very alluring proposition for those of us who like the wind in our hair.

Scrolling down the page are thumbnail images of each of the bikes for rent (click on the thumbnail to see the larger image) and prices. They're not cheap (nothing in Hawaii is,

tip

■ Rentals Across the Globe has its own Web address, but it's long and complex. The easiest way to get there is by pointing your browser to harleys.com and then clicking on the link to "Rentals Across the Globe." In sum, there's no comprehensive central database for renting motorcycles, but with a little legwork (or, more accurately, mousework), you might find a place to rent one for your next vacation.

except maybe coconuts) but what the heck, if you're on vacation, why not spend a few bucks for a ride you'll remember for years.

Hawaiian Riders isn't the only choice for renting a motorcycle in Hawaii. Another site, **DJ's Rentals (harleys.com)**, rents motorcycles and scooters on the Big Island's Kona coast. The site has images of the bikes, prices (starting at $90 for a half-day rental), and an e-mail address. And for those interested in renting elsewhere, there is a link called **Rentals Across the Globe**, which has listings for more than half the fifty states, Europe, and South America.

Customized Maps *and* Trip Directions

As mentioned briefly in the previous chapter, online mapping services are one of the Internet's most remarkable developments. Although these maps are no substitute for a well-crafted paper map, those found on **MapQuest (www. mapquest.com)**—and others of its ilk—can do things that no paper map can, such as give turn-by-turn trip directions between any two addresses in the United States.

But MapQuest offers much more: It can help you locate your destination on

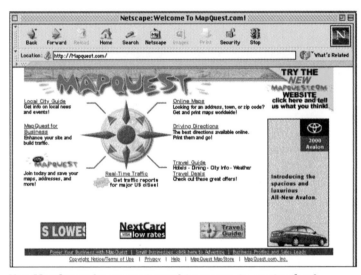

Use MapQuest (mapquest.com) to generate customized maps including places of interest you select.

a "zoomable" map, meaning you can zoom in and out to get a broader or more focused view. And it can enable you to find nearby attractions, from restaurants to golf courses to Internet cafes.

Creating a Personalized Map

From the home page, click on "Maps" to go to **Quick Maps**, where you can get an overview of U.S. cities and international metropolises. For U.S. cities, you'll probably find it more efficient to use the **Map Search** feature, where you can input an address and get a map for the region around it. Say you're heading to the Westin Michigan Avenue hotel in Chicago—enter the hotel's address and click "Get Map," which will produce a map you can customize.

Below the map is a section called **Places of Interest**. Here, you can add places of interest (POIs) to the maps. To show how it works, let's try adding automatic teller machines.

To search for ATMs near the Westin, click on "Banks and ATMs" and select "ATMs" from the following page. Then click "Update Map." In a few seconds the site will produce the same map with the addition of "dollar signs" to indicate ATM locations. In this case these are more than two dozen ATMs within a few blocks of the hotel.

To narrow the search click on "Show 5 Closest Selected POIs," which, in this case, assigns a number to each of the five closest ATMs. Below the map each ATM is identified by name and address, such as "Cirrus, 900 Michigan Avenue, Chicago." If you choose, you can then get directions from your starting point (the Westin) to the ATM. Because it's only a block or so away, you probably won't need directions, but for smaller towns where services are farther apart, it might be advantageous to use this feature.

ATMs are just one of the many POI categories offered by MapQuest. Click on **"Recreation"** to identify health clubs, swimming pools, or ski areas near your destination. Through the **"Transportation"** category you can add icons for airports, train stations, or bus depots; or use **"Attractions"** to add museums, parks, or tourist information booths. And if you're looking for an Internet cafe (the perfect place for checking e-mail while on the road; see chap. 14, "The Connected Traveler"), click on **"Dining"** where you can check the box for Net cafes or Chinese restaurants—or both!

Say you clicked on several categories, such as Net cafes, Chinese restaurants, and Thai restaurants. You can get information about any POI by clicking on the radio button at left, called the "Identify Icon," and then by clicking on the icon for the POI you're interested in. A new map will materialize with that icon highlighted and the name, address, and phone of the places at the top. However, MapQuest doesn't tell you what category the icon is from (though when I tried it, the restaurant identified was called Nanjing, which probably means it's a Chinese place).

To print this map, click on "Large Map," which will produce a map that's easier to read, and then select "Printable Map." This will regenerate the map without lots of extraneous options, making for a nicer printout. Of course, you can print maps of any size by simply hitting the Print button on your browser.

You can also e-mail the map to anyone with an e-mail address. If you were planning to fly to Chicago, you could create a map with your hotel marked by a star in the center (as described earlier) or send the same map customized with the restaurant where you plan to meet for dinner. Click "Email Map" and insert the recipient's address—there's even a box where you can type a short

tips

■ You only can add Places of Interest (POIs) to maps that are on a city scale or lower. Even on a city level, there are often too many places to make it worthwhile, so try zooming in closer to street level, where you'll get a more manageable and easier-to-view number of POIs.

■ A radio button is a circle that works like a check box. Click on it to fill it in. In the earlier example, clicking on it tells MapQuest you want to identify the next icon you select.

■ Don't rely on e-mail messages generated through Web sites. Though these usually work fine, it's more secure to send important messages from your e-mail program. So if you send a message via MapQuest or some other site, it's wise to follow up with a second e-mail message from your e-mail program (such as Eudora), to see if the first message arrived and to confirm any details, such as where and when to meet.

message, such as, "Here's the map for my hotel and the restaurant, it's called Nanjing, see you there Saturday at 7:30." And if you join MapQuest, which is free, you can store personalized maps at the site and refer to them in the future.

Finally, whenever you generate a map, you'll see a category at the bottom reading "Quick Places of Interest" for companies such as Kinko's and Borders. These are paid links (advertisements) and can be useful for finding a nearby copy shop or bookstore, but only if it's a Kinko's or Borders—other similar businesses (such as Barnes & Noble) won't show up on these searches.

Getting Directions from Map Sites

For whatever reason, some people just don't like to stop and ask directions. And other people, when asked for directions, will give them even if they're not quite sure. Fortunately, MapQuest and other leading map sites have found a way to generate turn-by-turn directions between any two addresses in the continental United States. Though these directions aren't always perfect, they are usually reliable. I've used MapQuest dozens of times and the vast majority of the time the routes were fine. Once MapQuest suggested a route I hadn't considered that turned out to be faster than the way I'd usually gone. Still, take these directions with a grain of salt—sometimes there is a faster way.

From the home page, click on **Driving Directions,** then choose between door-to-door or city-to-city. The first option is better for short trips; the second makes sense for long road trips, say from Boston to Orlando. MapQuest offers three display options for directions: overview map with text (one map at top with printed directions), text only, or turn-by-turn maps with text. This last option offers small maps for each turn.

After selecting the options you want, click on "Calculate Directions," and in a few seconds your directions come up. To test drive this feature, I inserted an address in Sebastopol (an hour north of San Francisco) and another in San Francisco and asked for turn-by-turn maps with text. MapQuest produced a relatively large image at top, mapping out the entire route. Below this map were the turn-by-turn directions with a small map at each turn.

MapQuest states the driving distance between each turn and lists the total distance of the trip as well as the estimated time. Even after using these features for years, I'm still amazed that I can enter a pair of addresses and get such complete driving directions in just a few seconds. All that's left to do is print them out and hit the road.

tip

■ You can also get maps and directions at other map sites, such as MapBlast (www.mapblast.com) and Maps On Us (www.mapsonus.com), or from search sites like Excite (www.excite.com).

For AOL Users

MAPS

In AOL's aptly named **Maps and Directions** (keyword: *mapping*), you can get driving directions between any two U.S. addresses or locate a place on a map. You can also generate maps for cities, regions, states, and countries.

The Great American Road Trip

There's nothing like throwing some clothes into a bag, loading up the cooler, and heading out onto the highway. Writers and musicians from Jack Kerouac to B.B. King have long sung of the joys and hardships of the road, inspiring others to follow. Although part of the fun of a road trip is spontaneity, you can enhance your journey by having a look at some Web sites before hitting the road. There are plenty of Web pages that can enliven your journey—from those that check for speed traps to others that find bizarre roadside attractions.

Road Trip USA

Author Jamie Jensen has driven more than 100,000 miles searching for "the perfect stretch of road" and the result is a richly detailed book called *Road Trip USA*. His publisher has put most of *Road Trip USA* online, so you can take a virtual tour of the eleven routes that Jensen describes, such as Route 66 or the Great River Road which parallels the Mississippi. Moon Publications' willingness to share the book online has paid off, as Road Trip USA has become the company's top seller.

Road Trip USA (www.moon.com/road_trip) avoids interstates and focuses on America's blue highways, seeking a connection with local people and their shops and restaurants, a closeness that's lost on the superhighway. In a note from Jensen on the site, he says, "The simple act of avoiding the soulless interstates, with their soggy franchises and identikit chains, opens up a vast, and much friendlier, two-lane world. You'll chance upon monuments marking the actual sites of things you last thought about in high school history classes, or kitschy little souvenir stands flaunting giant dinosaurs outside their doors, and inside still selling the same postcards as they have for decades."

Clicking on the **Road to Nowhere** trip, which covers US 83 from North Dakota through Texas, leads to a split screen, with a map of the route on the left and some highlights described on the right. To get more detailed information, select a state by clicking on the map, which produces a detailed list of attractions. After choosing the Road to Nowhere trip, select "South Dakota," where you'll find information about the Sitting Bull Memorial and the Pioneer Auto Museum in Murdo.

Throughout Road Trip USA, you'll see little yellow flags, labeled by month, next to descriptions for attractions: These are for events that happen during that month. Click on the flag saying "Aug." next to the heading for the Rosebud Indian Reservation to learn about an August event, in this case a big powwow. You'll also find homey, affordable restaurants, call letters for cool radio stations, and lots more.

Get Your Kicks . . .

A section on road trips wouldn't be complete without mentioning Route 66, that road of dreams that stretches from America's heartland to the Pacific coast. While Road Trip

tip

■ If you tend to push the pedal to the metal, you may want to check WWW Speedtrap Registry (www.speedtrap.com), which lists speed traps for the United States and many other countries, including Germany (didn't know they had a speed limit) and Israel (by the time you break the speed limit, you're at the Jordanian border). Speed traps are submitted by the online community, so if you happen to know of a particularly heinous one, let your fellow drivers know.

siteseeing

Roadside America
(www.roadsideamerica.com)

After childhoods spent as "unwilling captives" on trips to Walt Disney World, the Grand Canyon, and other tourist meccas, Doug Kirby, Mike Wilkins, and Ken Smith have spent the past two decades crisscrossing the country seeking out truly odd and offbeat attractions. Gigantic Paul Bunyans, alligator farms, even the world's largest ball of twine (17,400 pounds and 12 feet in diameter) inspire them to hit the road. Though others have put some weird tidbits of Americana online, no one has documented—in such an extensive and professional way—the truly bizarre roadside attractions that make America great. "We try to have a payoff on every page, a reward for every click," says Wilkins.

Visitors who enter through the home page are greeted by a clickable postcard. Emulating an actual roadside attraction, the site offers a **Welcome Center,** a good place for the first-time visitor to get oriented. From here, the world's biggest buffalo, a patriotic pig, and Salem Sue (the world's largest cow) are just a click away. The **Electric Map** offers a clickable map of the United States, so visitors who are planning a trip through a particular state can find some attractions there.

For a trip to Nebraska, use the Electric Map to find Carhenge, a Stonehenge-inspired series of monoliths, in Alliance, Nebraska. And the blurbs that go with the images are always informative, irreverent, and lively. Exhibit A: Only 40 percent of those who visit Carhenge, have heard of Stonehenge. In Roadside America's **Pet Cemetery,** which catalogs the remains of celebrity animals, one learns that Smokey Bear was a cub rescued from a forest fire. When his successor, the little-known Smokey II, died, the Park Service didn't know what to do with his body, so they burned it.

Thanks to e-mail feedback from users, the Roadside team has learned of new places to visit and received updates about some of their favorite attractions. "Several visitors let us know that the Tragedy in U.S. History Museum in St. Augustine, Fla., which featured Lee Harvey Oswald's bedroom furniture, has closed, its contents auctioned off." Kirby calls this "a great loss" but in the same breath he perks up and says, "But a new conspiracy museum in Dallas thrives!"

If there's one criticism of the site, it's that it doesn't make it too easy to find a series of attractions for a given stretch of highway. Yet this is by design, Kirby says. "To plot a tour, people have to get out a paper map and draw dots on it." Roadside doesn't aim to be overpackaged or hyperefficient, Kirby says. And it's not. It's akin to a meandering journey along a scenic blue highway, rather than a see-nothing blur along an eight-lane interstate.

Roadside America (www.roadsideamerica.com) is an unparalleled guide to offbeat attractions.

USA does a fine job covering the Chicago-to-Los Angeles highway, other sites are devoted solely to the Mother Road.

One of the best, called simply **Route 66 (route66.netvision.be)**, does a nice job chronicling the history of this storied highway and listing upcoming events. It has state-by-state descriptions of the attractions along the route, and it recommends hotels and restaurants along the way. You'll also find detailed directions, which is terrific because some segments of the old route are poorly marked—or not marked at all.

Another really enjoyable ride down Route 66 is provided by a couple of *Houston Chronicle* staffers who spent a few weeks filing dispatches during a summer road trip. Their virtual journey, called **Get Your Kicks (www.chron.com/voyager/66)**, includes stories from the road; profiles of memorable characters; tours of roadside attractions, such as the Route 66 Hall of Fame; and a trivia quiz. For more on Route 66, see Yahoo's listing at **dir.yahoo.com/Recreation/Travel/Automotive/Route_66** or look up "route 66" on a search engine.

Finding Diners & Other Cool Places to Stop for a Bite

The classic American diner is alive and well, though you might not know this if you always travel along interstates. Stopping at a diner can be one of the highlights of a road trip, and Web sites can help you find the good ones and avoid the pretenders. Next are some sites that can help you find diners before you set out.

Diner City (www.dinercity.com)

Making it easy to find diners in most of the fifty states, Diner City lists diners with photos, addresses, and phones. You'll also find a guestbook with diner reviews written by the site's visitors. Site creator Ron Saari has traveled through much of the country, propelled by his passion for diners. In his mission statement, Saari writes, "In the early 1980s, there were plenty of stainless steel and enamel diners to be found in my home state of New Jersey. Many have since been demolished. Over the past few years, I have photographed hundreds of diners, with the hope that my images might foster some appreciation for these historical treasures."

EatHere: The Online Guide to Road Food (www.eathere.com)

Listing hundreds of diners and other homey restaurants across the country, this site includes a search engine that will cull listings by state, city, or name. Just enter the search term and see what comes up. Searching for "new jersey" yields more than two dozens listings, with the city for most of them mentioned in the results. See the latest additions to the EatHere's menu in categories ranging from "barbecue" to "truck stops."

Roadside Magazine (www.roadsidemagazine.com)

More a tribute than a directory, Roadside can still help you find some of the best diners around the country. Click on "Diner to Diner" to get Roadside's recommendations. This isn't a comprehensive list, but it does highlight dozens of worthy places. (You can get more thorough listings at Roadside's Diner Finder, but it costs $5.00; you can order online.) Click on "Links" to see other sites devoted to diners, some of which have listings such as **NJDiners (www.njdiners.com)**. And if you just can't wait to visit a diner, click on DinerCam, where you'll get an indoor view of a New Jersey diner updated every thirty seconds.

RV Travel *on the* Information Superhighway

Traveling in a self-contained mobile home seems to grow more popular every year, which is no surprise because when you travel in an RV, you have a vehicle, a place to stay, and a little kitchen, meaning you can see a lot without breaking the bank. And in a country as vast as the United States, there's a lot to see and plenty of places to park for the night.

Planning Ahead

A little planning can ease your journey, and once again the Net steps up with campground guides, advice, forums, and travelogues. What follows are a few sites to get you started. For more, visit **Snap.com** (or any other search site) and drill down through categories, such as Travel > By Road > RVs. (*Note:* Snap's directory can be confusing: You'd expect to find a "road" category alphabetically under the *R*'s, but at Snap it's under *B* for "By Road.")

RV Zone (www.rvzone.com)

Listing everything from campsites to service centers, RV Zone is not a bad place to get your bearings. But don't expect lengthy lists of campsites; these listings are pretty thin.

RV America (www.rvamerica.com)

If you like KOA campgrounds, this is the place for you. While RV America has some fine independent areas, such as its well-trafficked interactive forum (where anyone can post a message), as of now the campground directory is sponsored by KOA and lists only KOA "Kampgrounds."

For AOL Users

RVing

Part of the AOL Travel network, **Recreational Vehicles** (keyword: *RV*) includes RV advice, a checklist of essentials, family camping tips, and AOL's lively format and chat areas, where you can swap ideas with other RV lovers. Other sections target disabled RV travelers, cross-country tips, and provide weather reports.

Go Camping America (www.gocampingamerica.com/main.html)

Listings for thousands of U.S. campgrounds, many with links to Web pages. Campground listings include information about size, fees, hookups, even whether modems are available for your computer.

Often the most beautiful place to stop for the night is a national park. As mentioned in chapter 3, the **National Park Service (www.nps.gov)** has a section called **Visit Your Parks (www.nps.gov/parks.html)**. The parks area has such links as "Select by State Map" and "Campground Reservation Information." You can also reserve a campsite online at **(reservations.nps.gov)**. Booking is available for dozens of national parks (though not all) and is relatively easy. You could also try **ParkNet (www.park-net.com)**, which includes campground listings for about a dozen U.S. states and Manitoba, Canada. Some states accept online bookings, for others reserve by phone.

Finally, there's a wealth of listings for RV travelers at search sites. Many of these specialize in a region or state, so don't hesitate to try a search such as "arizona AND rv" or "rv AND southwest." Many of these sites have forums where you can get tips from other RV enthusiasts or share your wisdom. Happy trails!

Summing Up

No matter how you get around when you travel, you can almost certainly employ the Net to learn more before you go. Whether you're renting a Land Rover in Namibia or looking for a place to park the RV in Montana, rev up your Net connection to see what's out there. And even though you can get door-to-door trip directions online, remember that when it comes to road trips, it's the journey that counts, not just the destination.

HOW *to* FIND SCHEDULES, FARES *&* RAIL PASSES

While riding the rails in Italy during a summer backpacking tour, I probably spent more time leafing through my Italian rail timetable book than reading my guidebook. I was fascinated by the number of options available and dreamed about the seemingly limitless possibilities. After getting home, I kept that timetable as a souvenir for several years because it held so many memories. Today, with online rail sites, you can start planning your journey from home by checking timetables, fares, and Eurail plans. Or you can just log on and start dreaming about the possibilities.

Finding Fares *and* Schedules

Although there are no worldwide databases for train travel (as there are for airlines), many regional and national rail sites offer route maps, timetables, and fare information. At some, you can book tickets and have them mailed to you or pick them up on arrival. The trick is finding these sites.

One way is to simply use a search engine and search for a term, for example, "italy AND train." However, this can turn up sites for training courses and others unrelated to travel. The best bet is to start with an online rail agency, such as **RailEurope (www.rail europe.com)** or **Amtrak (www.amtrak.com)**. At both these sites, you can select two cities and, in seconds, get a timetable and fares. RailEurope is especially remarkable—it covers more than a dozen national rail systems throughout Europe.

Another good site for finding links to national and other rail sites is **RailServe (www.railserve.com)**, which has a Yahoo-style directory, including links to major rail sites around the world. To find timetables for the French rail system, for example, click on "Switchyard" or scroll down and then click on "Passenger and Urban Transit–Europe." RailServe is especially good for digging up rail information in less traveled regions, such as Africa.

European Rail Sites

The most popular region for rail travel is probably Europe, which makes sense. The cities are close together, the rail system is highly evolved, and for many people it's more efficient and less expensive to travel by rail than by air or car. This is especially true for travelers, most of whom are on a budget, who can get around just fine without renting a car.

RailEurope and Other Good Starting Points

To find a fare on **RailEurope (www.raileurope.com)** from, say, Milan to Rome, pick those two cities from the pull-down menu, choose a date, and select a currency for the price quote. Then click "Get Fares & Schedules," and in seconds you'll have a page listing prices for first- and second-class tickets, average travel time, distance in miles and kilometers, and a timetable for this specific route. Below it is an order form that allows you to choose first or second class and buy tickets with a credit card. For the busy summer travel season, it's often a good idea to book ahead, and this site makes it a breeze to do it yourself. RailEurope also has a rudimentary interactive map you can use to see the major rail lines in each country.

However, RailEurope doesn't necessarily show all the options, simply those it considers the best. To find a national rail site, try a rail database like **The European Railway Server (mercurio. iet.unipi.it)**, which rounds up the best links for rail travel and organizes them by country, city, or region. Although this organization helps immensely, finding useful rail information is more challenging here than at a site such as RailEurope. Some national sites are available only in a language you may not speak, while others are poorly organized and leave you at dead ends. The best advice is to give it a shot, following the site's instructions, and, if you can't quickly find what you want, go back to RailEurope or turn to a travel agent.

tips

■ Sometimes, tourist office Web sites can be helpful, especially if you can't find a site specifically devoted to a country's rail system. For example, the Korean National Tourism Organization (www.knto.or.kr) has general rail information and timetables in English.

■ Reservations are required for some European trains, such as France's high-speed TGV; some sleepers in overnight trains; and the Eurostar link between Britain and France.

A couple of Web pages are good starting points for planning a European rail journey. I like the European Railway Server primarily because of its single page listing of rail sites by country. The page, simply titled **Links (mercurio.iet.unipi.it/misc/links.html)**, has listings for thirty-six countries, each represented by its flag, as well as a link to some general sites for Europe.

Back at the Railway Server, click on the country you're planning to visit, and you should see a few links, ranging from train photos to timetables. Clicking on the Italian flag leads to a page with several categories, including official servers, timetable pages, and rail museums. Start with the official sites, which are generally the most authoritative, most likely to offer online booking, and have pages in English.

Clicking on the link to the official Italian rail site, **Ferrovie Dello Stato (www. fs-on-line.com)**, leads to a home page, where you click on the British flag for information in English. When the English home page comes up, click on **"Timetables"** and enter "Milano" in the outbound box and "Roma" for arrivals. But this isn't enough for this site —it wants specific station names. If you don't know what the stations are called, go back to the home page and find a link called "Stations," which lists the main stations; then, return to the **Timetables**

RailEurope (www.raileurope.com) makes it easy to find schedules and fares for European trains.

page and enter "Milano Centrale" and "Roma Termini," the primary stations for these cities. As you can see, this is much more complicated than the simple procedure at RailEurope.

Going back to the Timetables page and inputting these stations yielded a listing of nine trains leaving Milan within three hours of my planned 10:00 A.M. departure. I also learned how long the trip would take (4 hours and 25 minutes). One train left right at 10:00 A.M., so I click on the train number to learn more, including services available (a restaurant and smoking area), what route it takes (stops in Bologna, Florence, etc.), and classes of service (first and second). Notably absent is price information—reservations can't be made through the site. My options are to try another site, such as RailEurope; call a travel agent; or just booking on arrival.

This example shows some of the quirks you can expect to find at national rail sites. Ideally, you should be able to enter city names (not specific stations) like you can at RailEurope and get a custom timetable and fares. But it's not really fair to expect a uniform approach from dozens of different systems, so it's better to approach these sites as informative resources rather than as state-of-the-art booking systems. If booking is essential, it's probably best to use RailEurope.

Finally, consider that you might enjoy your trip more if you don't book ahead, as one of the joys of taking trains, rather than flights, is that you can be more flexible. And if you find a

tip

■ Listings on the European Railway Server's Links page (mercurio.iet.unipi.it/ misc/links.html) won't always appear to be alphabetized to English speakers. For example, though the text page is in English, the link for Germany is under *D* for "Deutschland." The site uses the same international abbreviations you see on those oval bumper stickers on the backs of cars, such as *CH* for "Switzerland."

place you especially like, you'll be free to stay a couple of extra days and get a ticket when you're ready to leave. Just don't get caught without a ticket on busy routes in the middle of the summer, because you may end up staying longer than you like.

Using Rail Sites to Plan a Scottish Adventure

Like other online booking tools, rail sites enable travelers to see their options before booking their travel. Rob McIvor, a bank PR manager in his late 30s, recently used the Web to plan a cycling adventure in the Scottish highlands. Here's Rob's story.

First Person: Rob McIvor

I had two weeks' vacation time that I had to use or else lose it. I had read in a newspaper that there were some very good deals available on trains to Scotland, so I decided to head off for a two-week cycling holiday there.

I began by using **Railtrack (www.railtrack.co.uk)**, a timetable for UK trains, to establish where I could get to and at what time. I then linked from there in to the **Virgin Trains** site **(www.virgintrains.co.uk)**. This enabled me to play around with a variety of time-of-travel options until [the site] came up with a combination of travel times and price that I was happy with. The site also indicates availability, so I was then able to order my ticket over the Web, and it arrived in the post two days later.

Next came route planning. I didn't want to book all of my accommodation before I went as I wanted to retain as much flexibility as possible, but as I would be in Scotland over a public holiday weekend, I wanted to make sure that I didn't find myself with nowhere to stay on the busy nights!

The **Scottish Youth Hostels Association (www.syha.org.uk)** has an excellent site, which includes a map of the country. Clicking on the locations took me straight into the details for each hostel. They haven't got online bookings yet, but it only took a phone call to their central booking service. In one of the places I fancied staying, the hostel was full, so I used the **Scottish Tourist Board (www.holiday.scotland.net)** to find a pub to stay in. I linked straight from [the Tourist Board site] to the pub's own Web site and made my booking by e-mail.

I had also identified one part of the trip where a short rail journey across an area not served by roads could save me about a day's cycling. Again, using the Railtrack site, I was able to check on the times of trains (only three a day) and plan accordingly. I also collected a few e-mail addresses on my travels, so my full report will, eventually, be winging its way around the world.

Choosing *the* Right Eurail Pass

Speaking of flexibility, it's hard to imagine a more spontaneous way to travel around Europe than with a Eurail pass. The basic idea is simple: Buy a pass that allows multiple train trips within a certain number of countries for the length of time you'll be traveling. The number of types of Eurail passes have proliferated in recent years, but, thankfully, so has online information about them.

Rick Steves' Eurail Guide

There aren't too many people on this planet who know as much as Rick Steves knows about traveling in Europe. Best known for his pioneering *Europe Through the Back Door* guidebook, Steves has developed an extensive online resource center called **Rick Steves' Guide to European Railpasses (www.ricksteves.com/rail).** Steves offers common-sense advice for prospective rail pass buyers, such as suggesting you add up the cost of individual tickets and compare this figure to the cost of a Eurail pass. Sometimes, it's cheaper just to buy the point-to-point tickets you need. You can use Steves' rail guide to calculate the costs of both options.

Steves' site is also a good place to learn about the various types of rail passes. He discusses, for example, the variations between a Flexipass and a Consecutive-Day Pass, and explains the difference between first class and second class. Here's what he has to say:

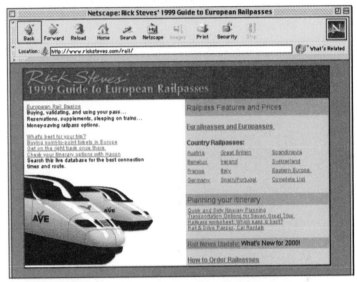

Rick Steves' Europe Through the Back Door includes an informative Eurail guide (www.ricksteves.com/rail).

Remember that nearly every train has both first- and second-class cars, each going precisely the same speed. If you're rugged and on a budget, go second class. In much of Europe, the new second-class cars are quite nice. And Back Door travelers know that nuns and soldiers are partying in second class. First class is filled with Eurail and Europass travelers age 26+ who had no choice, and business travelers who paid 50% extra in hopes that they wouldn't have to sit with the likes of you and me.

Steves' site also includes guides to single-country rail passes, a primer on differences between Eurail passes and Europasses, and tips on discounts. You'll also find a section entitled **Quick and Dirty Itinerary Planning** and transport options for seven great trips.

Steves does a nice job in this section comparing the cost of individual tickets, rail passes, and renting a car.

If you feel ready to order a Eurail pass, Steves' ETBD includes an order form, but as of mid-1999, there was no way to order online: You had to print the form and then fax or mail it in. For each rail pass ordered, you can choose one of Steves' guidebooks as a free bonus.

If you'd like to buy online, you can do so at RailEurope or other Eurail agencies, such as **RailPass Express (www.railpass.com)**. RailEurope lists options for multicountry or single-country passes, but doesn't have close to the depth of information you'll find on Steves' site. Just don't buy a pass too far in advance—you have to start using most Eurail passes within three months of purchase.

North American Rail Travel

When it comes to riding the rails in the United States, there's only one choice for long-haul trips between major cities: **Amtrak (www.amtrak.com)**. In recent years Amtrak has tried to buff its image by adding new high-speed trains (primarily in the Northeast); however, its Web site won't do much to enhance this image. Sure, you can get timetables, and there are even a couple of cool features, such as **Arrival Status,** which can tell you when a train in progress is due in (which certainly beats calling 800–USA–RAIL and waiting on hold).

But the navigation here isn't as seamless as what you'll find on RailEurope. Here's one example: To get a timetable for a trip from New York to Boston, I entered the names of these two cities, chose the date, and clicked "Get Schedule." This produced an "Error Page" with the following message:

> The Amtrak Internet System has found three station names for Boston. The stations found are Boston-Back Bay (BBY) , Boston South Station (BOS), and Boston Route 128(RTE). Please return to the previous page, enter the station code (shown in parenthesis) and then press the continue button again. Thank you.

Not too user friendly. If someone is not familiar with the area, how would they know which is the major station? I took a stab at Boston South because the code name BOS seemed most likely to have trains coming in from New York. This turned out to be correct, but if I'd been wrong, I'd have had to go back and try a different code. Contrast this to RailEurope where the timetable search automatically goes to the major stations.

Another unfortunate aspect of Amtrak's site is that you have to register to get fare information. Although this is free and doesn't require more than entering a username name and password, it's just one more unnec-

> **tip**
>
> ■ For rail journeys in Canada see the bilingual VIA Rail Canada site (www.viarail.ca), where it's easy to quickly find schedules, fares, and route maps.

essary step. After registering, you're set to get fare information, and this can go pretty quickly. To book online, click "Book This Fare" and enter your credit card information. Or simply call Amtrak's toll-free number, which, given the complexities of this site, you may have already decided to do.

Like many airlines, Amtrak offers some specials available solely through its Web site. Once you're registered, you can click on **"Special Offers,"** then scroll down to **Rail Sale**. When I checked, the offerings here were quite thin, but if your route is included, you might find a good deal. There are also discounts (available to all, not just Web users) for seniors, kids, and groups. You'll find the North America Rail Pass listed under Special Offers, which is akin to a Eurail pass and valid for unlimited travel in the United States and Canada (through an agreement with the Canadian rail service VIA).

Navigating Subways

When most of us consider foreign rail journeys, we usually think about romantic and lengthy trips from one major city to another. But the reality is we're more likely to hop on and off the local metro, underground, el or "T," more often than we take long rail journeys. These labyrinthine subway systems can be daunting, but figuring them out is often one of the small victories of a trip.

Subway Navigator

The **Subway Navigator (metro.ratp.fr:10001/bin/cities/english)** is one of those amazing little sites that can help you make sense of a mystery, providing maps, routes, and estimated trip times for more than sixty metropolitan subway systems around the world. Though not perfect, the Navigator is an excellent guide, another project from a hobbyist who doesn't appear to be motivated by profit. The Navigator covers transit systems in North and South America, Europe, and Asia. If you visit a city (or live in one) that's not covered, you can send the local subway map to creator of the Subway Navigator, and he'll add it to the site. Or you can search the Web to see if that transit system has its own Web site.

You start by choosing a city. Then, you'll be asked for depar-

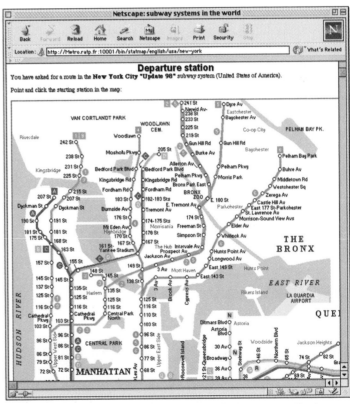

Subway Navigator (metro.ratp.fr:10001/bin/cities/english) puts subway maps online, such as the New York map shown here.

ture and arrival stations. In most cases you'll have no idea what the stations are called— that's probably why you're turning to the Subway Navigator in the first place! But don't panic, there are two other methods for finding your way: by choosing from a text list of station names, or, better yet, looking at the transit map and clicking on your stations. In most cases, you'll find it easiest to go with the map. Let's go through the procedure for an imaginary trip under Manhattan.

Start by clicking on "New York City," where you'll learn that the Navigator covers the city subway system, as well as suburban rail lines to Long Island and Westchester. Then, you'll see boxes where you are to enter departure and arrival stations. Keep scrolling down to where you can click on the link to the map. This transit map covers New York City—for the suburban lines you'll have click on the "List of Stations" link. Now, let's plan a trip from New York University to 96th Street on the Upper West Side. First click on "NYU 8 St." The same map will come up again and ask you to pick an arrival station. Your imaginary friend lives on 96th Street, so click on this station and, voilà, you get the following directions on where to get on, what stops are along the way, where to transfer, and how long the trips will take:

Result of the route search from "8 Street/New-York
University/Broadway" to "96 Street/Broadway."
   Estimated time-25 minutes
      Line "N," Direction "Ditmars Boulevard/Astoria/31 Street"
         8 Street/New-York University/Broadway
         14 Street/Union Square/Broadway
         23 Street/Broadway
         28 Street/Broadway
         34 Street/Herald Square/Broadway
         42 Street/Times Square/Broadway
      Line "2," Direction "241 Street/White Plains Road"
         42 Street/Times Square/Broadway
         72 Street/Broadway
         96 Street/Broadway

It's very simple, yet almost magical. Even if you're not planning a trip to these cities, it can be fun to just see how people get around and how long it takes. Of course, the site is not precise; trips can take much longer than estimated at peak commute times. And Subway Navigator doesn't always come up with the most direct route, especially if your trip includes several transit systems.

An example: I tried planning a trip from Scarsdale in Westchester County to Great Neck on Long Island. I know from real-world experience that the best way to go about this is to take the train from Scarsdale into Grand Central Station, walk over to Penn Station, and the hop on a train bound for Great Neck. But the Navigator offered a more convoluted route that ignored Penn Station and would have taken longer than necessary. For trips within a city's metro subway system, Subway Navigator seems much more reliable.

City Subway Sites

While the Subway Navigator is a good place to start, it's certainly not the only place to find urban train information. Many city transit systems have their own Web sites, which can be excellent sources of information. The following are sites for some major cities:

- **London Transport (www.londontransport.co.uk):** A guide to the Underground as well as to bus service in the city. Click on "Underground" to find fares, maps, stations, and information on the different lines.

- **Paris Metro (www.paris.org/Metro):** Hosted by an extensive site called The Paris Pages, Paris Metro offers a map, prices, an image of a ticket, and a bit of history.

- **MBTA Boston (www.mbta.com):** This well-designed site includes a maps for the "T," ticket information, links to commuter rail and bus advice, even a guide to art in the subway stations.

- **San Francisco Bay Area Rapid Transit (www.bart.org):** Check schedules and fares, learn about accommodations for the disabled, and find out how to get your bike on BART. Though its service within San Francisco is limited to one main line, BART is useful for traveling between Bay Area cities, for example, a trip from San Francisco to Berkeley.

These examples offer a general idea of what you can expect from regional transit sites. For more, consult the Web directories at the back of this book or use a search engine to search for a city's transit sites.

Rail Tours *for* Train Lovers

Not everyone who hops on a train does so because it's the quickest, cheapest, or easiest way to get from Point A to Point B. Sometimes train lovers seek out trains for the sheer joy of riding the rails—from the Orient Express to the narrow-gauge trains of Wales. The Web is the perfect place to take a virtual journey on some of the lines to get a sense about whether you'd like to sign up for the real thing. Here are a few sites to explore these rail journeys. Some are for individual train lines, but most offer links to many different trips.

The Great Little Trains of Wales (www1.roke.co.uk/WHR/gltw.html)

"The Great Little Trains of Wales are narrow gauge railways built through the beautiful scenery of north and west Wales. Built in a time less hasty than our own, most originally served to carry Welsh slate from hill to harbour. Now tourists have replaced slate as the main traffic, and dedicated volunteers have joined the paid staff in the work of restoring and running these pretty little railways." So reads the introduction from the home page. If that's not enough to make you want to hop on the next flight to Cardiff, this site includes links to eleven Welsh narrow-gauge rail sites, with names like Talyllyn Railway and Ffestiniog Railway.

Orient-Express (www.orient-expresstrains.com)

The Orient-Express site, from a booking agency, offers images and information about what is perhaps the world's most famous train journey. The Orient Express passes through some of Europe's most beautiful areas and offers private sleeping compartments with burnished wood furnishings. Click on **"Travel Planner"** for departure dates, timetables, and prices, which are rather steep. Or have a look at the pictures in the

Photo Gallery to get a sense of the scenery, dining car, and sleeping compartments.

Eastern & Oriental Express
(www.orient-expresstrains.com/pages/eomenu.html)

Not to be confused with the Orient Express, this elegant train runs along the Malay Peninsula between Singapore and Bangkok. Another line meanders from Bangkok to Chiang Mai in northern Thailand. Use the site to study the route, see images of the dining car, or learn about schedules, fares, and specials.

Grand Canyon Railway
(www.thetrain.com)

After rolling through 65 miles of high desert and Ponderosa forests, the Grand Canyon Railway stops near the canyon's rim. Passengers have a "layover" of three and one-half hours so they can have time to explore the canyon and then hop back on for the return trip. The site offers fares, timetables, a map, and even weather reports.

Trans-Siberian Railroad
(www.iaito.com/transtour.html)

Ever wonder what it would be like to travel by train across eastern Russia? You can get an idea here though images, itineraries, and fascinating pages on the history of the various regions. The nuts-and-bolts information is all here. If you want more, there's an e-mail link and phone number for an office in Seattle.

More Sites *for* Finding Terrific Train Trips

Though much of this chapter has focused on train travel in North America and Europe, trains are essential vehicles for getting around throughout the world. To learn more about rail systems in Asia, Africa, South America, and other locations, consult the following sites:

NMRA Directory of World Wide Rail Sites
(www.ribbonrail.com/nmra)

Offering more than 3,600 different rail sites in categories such as "Narrow Gauge," this site can help you find the train trip you're looking for. Scroll down to find international links under the headings **Traveling by Rail** and **Tourist Sites.**

RailServe (www.railserve.com)

As mentioned earlier in this chapter, Railserve is a directory with hundreds of rail links. Click on "Switchyard" or simply scroll down to get to the directory to find links to passenger and tourist trains all over the world. Clicking on "Passenger and Urban Transit—Australia and New Zealand" leads to twenty-one rail links for these countries, such as the Great South Pacific Express, a luxury rail journey between Sydney and Cairns, along Australia's Great Barrier Reef.

Rail Travel Center (www.railtvl.com)

This site comes from an agency offering mostly high-end train tours, ranging from "Springtime in the Alps" to "Vietnam by Rail" to lots in between. You can find itinerary dates, prices, some stunning images, and a form to request a printed catalog. You can also sign up for occasional e-mail updates and offers.

Yahoo Train Travel (dir.yahoo.com/Recreation/Travel/Train_Travel)

The Yahoo site includes all sorts of trains, from passenger rails to trips for tourists. If you're interested in tourist trips, click on "Tourism Trains" for Yahoo's listings in this category.

Virtual Train Trips

Many of the sites listed earlier have travelogues that enable you to take a virtual ride on the rails, either in preparation for the real thing or just for the fun of it. Many travelers read through these accounts to get a better sense of what to expect from different rail journeys. A good place to find travelers' rail stories is the **Cyperspace World Railroad Lounge Car (www.mcs.com/~dsdawdy/Parlor/parlor.html)**. The accounts range from a ride on a Polish steam train to a trip from the across the Sierra Nevada range (Roseville, California, to Sparks, Nevada).

There are some types of train trips you'll probably never take, such as hopping a freight. Sure, Kerouac made it sound romantic, but in reality it is grimy and dangerous. However, it can be fun to read about such journeys, and Yahoo has a category devoted to train hopping. To learn more about train hopping, visit **Train Hoppers Space (www.cat alog.com/hop)**, where you can read firsthand accounts. Some of the accounts may surprise you. Here's a brief excerpt from someone named Mark about his first hop:

> About 45 minutes after rolling out of Stockton, we pulled off at a siding and stopped. I poked my head out and looked forward, and saw someone else's head sticking out of a car just ahead of mine! Turns out he had hopped on the train at Stockton too, but had been waiting deep in the yard for it. Anyways I moved to the other side of the car where I had a lot more room to sit down without the brake stuff in the way. We sat there for about 30 minutes waiting for another train to pass, so I called up a few friends on my cellphone to tell them about the trip so far!

Finally, don't forget to check rail newsgroups and forums, where you can interact with other rail buffs, asking questions or simply scanning the topics that have already been discussed. Here are a couple of newsgroups to investigate: **misc.transport. rail.americas, misc.transport.rail.australia-nz, misc.transport.rail.europe, misc.transport. rail.misc** or **rec.railroad.** (For more on how to participate in newsgroups and forums, see chap. 13.)

Summing Up

For some people, a rail journey is simply a way to get from here to there; for others, it's a romantic way to see a new place. Whichever camp you fall in, the Net can help plan a trip, with links to fares and schedules, advice if you're considering a rail pass, tips for navigating subways, and information on train trips, such as a ride on the Orient Express, that are destinations in their own right. And if you're a train buff, planning your trip online can become part of the journey.

CASHING IN
on the NET'S
BEST DEALS

Can You Get *the* Best Deal Online?

It seems the first question people ask about online travel services is, "Can you get the best deal booking on the Net?" The only definitive answer is, "Sometimes." However, this question may miss the point. Part of the reason the Net is such a valuable tool is that it can make you a more informed consumer. And if you have a better sense of what really is a good deal, you'll be in a better position to seize good values when you find them.

Though last-minute deals get the most ink, all sorts of travel bargains lurk in the Net's virtual alleyways. And the sources for finding these bargains are almost as diverse as the bargains themselves. There are last-minute deals through e-mail alerts, hotel bargains listed on Web sites, cruise bargains that become available ten days prior to sailing, and a whole range of eleventh-hour bargains consolidated in one place, such as those available at **LastMinuteTravel.com**.

Because weekend airline deals have garnered so much interest, let's start with them. If you can be spontaneous, you can find some terrific deals (like a round-trip fare between New York and Paris for $229). And these offers have expanded so you often get more than three to five days to plan ahead. **American Airlines (aa.com)**, which pioneered e-mail newsletters for last-minute weekend getaways, recently made its Net SAAver fares good for not just the upcoming weekend, but also for the weekend after that, so travelers now have ten to twelve days to plan for domestic and international getaways.

And a few airlines, such as **Southwest (www.southwest.com)**, sometimes let you plan several months ahead and still cash in on bargain-basement fares through their Net-only specials. Southwest and other airlines are eager to get passengers in the habit of booking online because when people book directly, airlines don't have to pay a commission to a travel agent or pay a reservation agent to handle phone reservations. Because direct booking saves the airlines money, they're sometimes willing to offer lower fares for purchases made through their Web sites.

If You Have to Plan Ahead

Last-minute Net bargains won't always come through. Most of the time, you can't roll the dice—you'll have to plan further ahead. If so, it pays to shop around, on the Net and off. But be forewarned: Thousands of travel booking sites are trying to lure your business, and it seems they all claim to have the best deals. Of course, that doesn't mean they do. Studies by newspapers and consumer groups have found that sometimes Web sites live up to their hype, and sometimes travel agents dig up the best deals. In many cases the deals are virtually the same, so if you're pressed for time, you can just hand your business over to a reliable travel agent, and let the agent do the digging.

In terms of strategy, I'd recommend first checking with a broad booking site, such as **Expedia.com**, which lists hundreds of airlines and millions of fares (see chap. 2, "Booking Flights Online"). Then see which airlines are offering the best deals and check with those airlines' sites—lots of airlines offer deals exclusive to their own Web sites. In other words British Airways might have a deal that's only available if purchased through BA's site **(www.british-airways.com)**. Finally, check the budget sites, such as **1travel.com** and **Bestfares.com**, which list consolidator fares and other bargains. After finding the best deal, call a travel agent or consolidator, see if he or she can do better, and, if so, then buy the ticket through the agent.

Another recent phenomenon is the emergence of auction sites (or, in some cases, reverse-auction sites) such as **Priceline.com**, where you "name your price," as the ad campaign says. In some situations, for example, if you can't plan far ahead and can't find any last-minute bargains, Priceline may offer the best deal. But in many situations, it's no bargain. We'll discuss Priceline and other auction sites later in the chapter.

Net-Only Airfares & Weekend Deals

Though you can't always be sure you'll find the best deal online, there is one area where the Net clearly has the best fares going: last-minute getaways. If you have to fly from Los Angeles to Chicago on short notice, you might pay $1,000 or more for a round-trip; fares are especially high if you're unable to stay over a Saturday night. But if you can find a special Net-only fare, you might pay $250 or even less for the same flight. Why the huge disparity? Airline pricing structures are designed to squeeze business travelers (whose companies typically pay for their tickets) and offer lower prices to leisure travelers.

Most Net-only fares are for weekend getaways. The typical routine is that you sign up to receive e-mail dispatches offering low fares based on availability, as the airlines aim to fill unsold seats. These deals—typically valid for Saturday departures and Monday or Tuesday returns—are usually offered at prices considerably lower than the twenty-one-day advance purchase fare.

If you see one you like, move quickly because these deals are often snapped up in a matter of hours. These tickets must be booked online and generally are issued ticketless. This means you show a picture ID at the airport instead of a paper ticket. Be sure to keep all records and confirmations so you have something to refer to if there's a mix-up.

Finding Last-Minute Airfare Deals

There's more than one way to find out about weekend deals: The most popular is signing up directly with airline sites to receive weekly e-mail dispatches of current fares. Of course, each airline sends only its own fares, so you have to subscribe to several airlines' alerts to stay posted about the cheapest flights from your area.

Another way to stay abreast of current deals is to subscribe to e-mail alerts from companies that aggregate last-minute deals from many carriers and send them to you in one e-mail. A site called **1travel.com** compiles deals from nineteen airlines and sends the ones that are relevant to your departure points. In other words you can choose up to five airports, and 1travel.com will send you a list of late-breaking deals from those airports. This system is convenient, but it has a serious drawback: Some of the best deals may be gone by the time you get the dispatch. Typically, 1travel.com and other sites that provide these e-mail alerts wait until all the airlines post their deals for the week—by the time the last deals are posted some of the first deals are already gone.

Here's an example: Southwest Airlines makes its specials available each week just after midnight on Tuesday mornings. Most other airlines make their deals public on Wednesday morning, so by the time you get a dispatch listing deals from multiple carriers, the Southwest bargains are more than twenty-four hours old and some—especially those for the most popular travel times—will undoubtedly be gone.

A useful strategy is to learn which carriers have the best specials on certain routes and to check those airlines' sites as soon as they announce their weekly deals. For example, living near the Oakland airport, I've followed fares and have learned that **Southwest (www.southwest.com)** usually offers the best late-breaking deals on short-hop flights to the Los Angeles area.

So if I'm planning a trip to L.A., I check Southwest's site on Monday night just after midnight central time (Southwest is based in Dallas). At this time the new deals come online, and I can be one of the first to see what's available. Most other people don't find out about these deals until Tuesday morning, when their Southwest e-mail alert reminds them to check the airline's site for bargains. You can employ similar strategies to check for last-minute deals on United, American, and other airlines.

Airlines have recently begun to expand their last-minute deals beyond weekends. For example, American Airlines introduced "Daily FAAres" with a maximum fare of $298. Unlike the weekend fares, Daily FAAres can be used for travel during the week: Monday through Thursday and on Saturday. Another difference is that you can plan several weeks ahead with Daily FAAres; the e-mail specials are valid for travel beginning within twelve days. Like the popular weekend specials, these fares have some restrictions, including:

- All tickets must be purchased through American's Web site.
- A Saturday night stay is required.
- Fares are nonrefundable, nonchangeable, and nonreusable.

Will other airlines follow suit? Most likely they will; the Net has proved to a fine tool for the airlines to sell seats that would most likely have remained empty. As inventory management systems become more sophisticated, the airlines will be able to offer more deals.

Leading Last-Minute Bargains

What follows is a round-up of leading airlines that offer last-minute bargains. Visit their home pages and then click on the links for these deals to get the latest information on what each airline is currently offering. The only way to buy these specials is on the Web or through the toll-free phone number provided by the airline.

American Airlines Net SAAver Fares (www.aa.com)

You can sign up for e-mail alerts about domestic fares, sent each Wednesday, and international fares, sent each Monday. These fares are valid for the weekend that starts ten to twelve days hence. To check fares for the upcoming weekend, go directly to the Web site to see what's available. American requires you to sign up for its frequent flier program before booking tickets.

America West Airlines Surf 'n Go Specials (www.americawest.com)

Each Wednesday through Friday AWA publishes its specials online. AWA doesn't send out an e-mail newsletter, so you have to check its Web site for weekend deals.

Continental Airlines CO.O.L. Specials (www.continental.com)

Cobbling together a weird acronym for Continental Online, Continental calls its specials CO.O.L. and sends domestic and international e-mail alerts each Wednesday. Those who have signed up for the e-mail alert can check Continental's site on Tuesday evenings and get a sneak preview of fares for the coming week.

Northwest Airlines CyberSavers (www.nwa.com)

Each Wednesday, Northwest sends a lists of special deals for the upcoming weekend. You can also sign up for occasional updates on Northwest's vacation packages and frequent flier mileage offers.

Southwest Airlines Click 'n Save Specials (www.southwest.com)

Southwest sends out its specials just after midnight central time on Tuesday morning. Many of these deals are good for several weeks or even months in advance.

United Airlines E-Fares (www.ual.com)

Like many other airlines, United will send you e-mail dispatches on Wednesday for domestic flights and Monday for international flights (sign up at **www.ual.com**), or you can simply check the site when these fares are announced. However, you do have to register, and United, which has one of the most poorly designed sites of any major airline, makes you jump through a lot of hoops instead of providing what should be a very simple process.

US Airways E-Savers (www.usairways.com)

US Airways does what all these other programs should do (and probably eventually will do): It lets you specify what cities you're interested in. So rather than get a lengthy e-mail listing all its specials, US Airways sends a short note that lists departures from airports you select. You can use the sign-up form to select any departure you like, or if you prefer, you can choose to see the full list of all special fares.

tip

■ Several sites aggregate domestic and international last-minute deals from various carriers, and some send e-mail dispatches to anyone who subscribes, which is free. In addition to 1travel.com, Smarter Living (www.smarterliving.com) has an e-mail alert feature and also lists deals at its Web site. WebFlyer.com, which specializes in frequent flier advice, also lists last-minute domestic and international deals. Travelzoo (www.travelzoo.com) aggregates deals on flights and vacation packages

Last-Minute Deals for Hotels, Cruises, and Rental Cars

Most Internet successes are quickly emulated, so it's no surprise that airlines' success at selling excess inventory is being copied by hotel chains, cruise lines, and rental car companies. It just makes good business sense: Rather than get stuck with empty rooms, cruise cabins, and slots on package tours, these perishable products are sold online at a discount.

TravelWeb (www.travelweb.com) was one of the first sites to offer last-minute discounts on hotel rooms and remains a leader in aggregating deals from various chain hotels. Here's an example: On short-notice I recently needed to find a room in Albuquerque, New Mexico. So I visited TravelWeb, clicked on **"Click-It Weekends,"** and then selected "Locations" from the menu at the bottom of the page. You could also click on "Hotels" to get listings organized by hotel chain.

For my needs it made sense to get listings for all chains, so after choosing "Cities," I scrolled down to "New Mexico," saw a price of $87 for the Albuquerque Hilton, a nice break compared with the regular $109 rate. Do keep in mind, however, that last-minute deals aren't always the lowest rates—you may want to call the hotel's toll-free number or a good travel agent to see if there's a better deal out there.

If you want to get the online rate, a simple form enables you to input your dates of travel—remember, these deals are usually just for Friday, Saturday, and Sunday nights—and see if the room is available. If it is, you can input your preferences, including what size bed you want, smoking or nonsmoking, etc. Then, you can book the room with a credit card; and shortly afterward you'll receive a confirmation message sent via e-mail.

You can also go directly to a hotel chain's Web site to find special offers and last-minute deals. For example, **Hyatt (hyatt.com)** has a feature that lets you search for deals by destination, or you can sign up for a weekly newsletter, similar to those sent by airlines, listing weekend deals at properties around the country. And remember that e-mail dispatches from airlines often include specials on hotels and rental cars. These companies have recognized that once travelers sign up for a weekend escape, they often need a place to stay and a way to get around. The American Net SAAver e-mail alert, for example, includes weekend offers from Holiday Inn and Budget Rent a Car.

Not too many cruise lines offer the type of last-minute deals available on flights, hotels, and cars. But that's likely to change soon—as the world's big cruise companies continue to add megaliners to their armadas, they will be eager to find a way to fill unsold cabins. Though a senior executive of Royal Caribbean recently said that his company has no intention of selling "distressed inventory" at discounts through the Net, other companies have already begun using this method.

tips

■ Some lodgings, such as hostels, are always cheap, and you don't have to wait until the last minute to book them. For more on hostels, see Hostels.com or Hostelling International (www.iyhf.org). (These and other cheap sleeps are covered in chap. 3, "A Room with a View.")

■ To find weekend deals and other late-breaking specials on hotel rooms and rental cars, go directly to those companies' sites and see what's being offered. At many sites you can sign up for e-mail alerts. The URLs for most major chain hotels are simply the hotel name followed by ".com"—such as sheraton.com.

Windjammer Barefoot Cruises (www.windjammer.com), known for its tall-masted sailing ships, recently introduced a program called **CyberSailors.** Sign up online for e-mail alerts, and ten days before departures, you'll receive an update on any available cabins, which can be booked at half-price. Of course, these reservations are valid only for new bookings. You can't cancel an existing reservation and then book one of these deals.

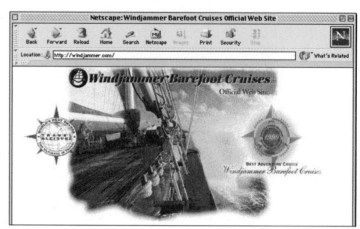

Other sites, such as **1travel.com**, collect cruise deals, and in addition to putting these specials on their sites, they send notice of them via e-mail to subscribers. You can also find cruise deals at major booking sites, such as **Expedia. com**, by visiting the cruise sections of these sites and

Windjammer Barefoot Cruises (www.windjammer.com) has a program called CyberSailors offering deals on cruiese that don't fill up.

checking specials there. Keep in mind, however, that just because a price is listed online as a special bargain, it doesn't mean it's the best deal. Sometimes, travel agencies that book a lot of cruises can get you a better price because they're rewarded for volume.

For AOL Users

TRAVEL BARGAINS

AOL's **Travel Bargains** (keyword: *travel bargains*) lists a wide range of deals on flights, lodging, car rentals, and cruises. There are also deals for seniors, students, and families. You'll also find the Daily Bargain, such as a free companion ticket for those purchasing a full-fare ticket. Other specials are targeted by region, for example, a $49 deal on flights from San Jose to Lake Tahoe.

Traveler's Advantage (keyword: *travelers advantage*) This program promises 5 to 25 percent off the regular advertised price on over one hundred quality vacation packages, but take a close look before you sign up. Many vacation packages are generally sold below "the regular advertised price," so this might not be such a great deal. And after a three-month free trial, this program costs $59.95 per year.

Eleven Top Budget Travel Sites

The Internet has come a long way since the early days (the mid-1990s) when it was primarily a means of accessing the same databases that travel agents use. Today, it's a way for travel suppliers to connect directly with buyers, which enables suppliers to offer flights, cruises, hotel rooms, rental cars, and package vacations at substantial discounts. We've already discussed some of ways this direct connection has been employed. Now, let's take a look at some leading budget travel sites, illustrating how the Net has become a force for delivering deals to travelers.

1travel.com (www.onetravel.com)

One of the pioneering budget travel sites, 1travel.com offers deals on domestic and international flights, cruises, hotels, and all-inclusive resorts, such as Club Med. For example, 1travel.com's Saving Alert aggregates last-minute air deals, so you don't have to scroll through multiple e-mail alerts. But as mentioned earlier, remember that by the time you receive these alerts, some of the best deals may be gone. A feature called "Drive a little using low-fare airlines" helps map out strategies for using alternate airports to find lower fares. **Farebeater** searches a database that includes published fares, consolidator bargains, and special deals exclusive to 1travel.com.

Airtech.com (www.airtech.com)

Remember years ago when the airlines had deep discounts for standby passengers. Well, those fares have been abolished, but Airtech uses a similar concept to offer rock-bottom deals to its clients. Here's how it works: Choose a four-day window when you can travel, and Airtech promises to get you on a flight during those dates. You pick a region, not a single airport. For example, if you want to

1travel.com (onetravel.com) offers lots of ways to save on flights, hotels, package vacations and more.

fly from New York to London, you say you're available to leave between July 23 and July 26, and you may depart via JFK, La Guardia, or Newark. Airtech is also a great source for one-way tickets, which can be very expensive elsewhere. When I checked, I found a one-way deal from New York to Amsterdam for $169. I had to give a four-day range of departure dates, but for deals like this, it can be worth being flexible.

Arthur Frommer's Budget Travel Online (frommers.com)

Frommer's site gives you something you don't see too often on most other travel sites: testy yet informed opinions on everything from hotel quality to whether a destination is generally a good deal. The highlights of the site include a daily e-mail newsletter that show-cases up to six great deals each day. You'll also find travel features, some from the print version of *Arthur Frommer's Budget Travel* magazine, such as a **Hot Spot of the Month** and **Tip of the Day**.

Other sections reveal insider secrets for finding cut-rate prices on flights and cruises, as well as listings for deeply discounted cruises and vacation packages. A section called **Research Destinations** covers more than 200 of the world's most popular vacation spots; it is especially strong in evaluating hotels. You can also book travel through this site. One of my favorite sections, though it doesn't directly relate to saving money, is called **Testy Opinions (www.frommers.com/philosophy)**. Here, Mr. Frommer rails on everything from the state of travel journalism to "slave labor on the love boats." In sum, a visit to Frommer's site is a quick course in how to uncover travel bargains, and whether you buy online or through a travel agent, these tips will likely save you money in the end.

Bestfares.com (www.bestfares.com)

Bestfares.com is one of the best sites for catching those briefly offered deals, such as a recent four-day sale from Chicago to London for $438 round-trip. But there's often a catch: For some offers, you must be a member of Bestfares.com to cash in. And, unlike many other sites, membership is not free, but the $60 fee can be a sound investment if you save more than that on a flight you find here. Besides the membership requirement for many fares, there's another major drawback: The site is poorly organized. To find a good deal, you have to scroll through hundreds of fares from all different destinations, rather than checking, for example, all deals originating in the Miami area. If you have time and don't mind poring over all these offers, Bestfares.com might help you find a bargain.

Cheap Tickets (www.cheaptickets.com)

Cheap Tickets offers discounted fares on domestic and international airline tickets and hotel rooms, negotiating deals with airlines that aren't necessarily available through more mainstream channels. Registration at Cheap Tickets requires inputting a credit card number before getting started, which is one reason many people elect to call the company's toll-free number rather than booking online. However, Cheap Tickets can be worth the effort because its fares can be lower than those offered by its competitors.

Council Travel (www.counciltravel.com)

Having made a name for itself serving students and educators, Council Travel is now a broad-based travel discounter that negotiates volume discounts. It still has some deals solely for students, but there's enough here to make it worthwhile for most budget travel-ers. Searching the database for an early June trip from New York to London turned up a $282 round-trip fare, a pretty good price. But leaving in late June produced a best fare of $466, which may not be the best deal. Council puts its toll-free number on the site, so you can call if you have questions.

Go4Less.com (go4less.com)

Calling itself the "biggest discount vacation superstore on the Internet," Go4Less offers deals on vacation packages, cruises, airline tickets, hotels, and car rentals. But the deals are only to selected vacation spots, such as the Bahamas. A nice feature called **Search for**

Vacations enables you to input destination, months you can travel, and your budget; so, for example, you could search for a cruise to the Caribbean between January and March for under $1,200. Listings can be a bit thin—the Caribbean search for these winter months and a second search for summer months didn't yield any matching trips. However, a general search for vacation packages turned up some nice deals. Time will tell whether this site becomes a valuable service.

Hotel Reservations Network (hoteldiscounts.com)

HRN lists discount room rates at hotels in more than two dozen U.S. and international cities. This site is most useful for peak periods, especially if you're told the hotel you're trying to book is sold out. HRN prebooks blocks of rooms in advance, so sometimes it has rooms—at discount rates—at these "sold out" hotels. HRN sometimes comes up with some worthwhile discounts, even in cities where hotel rooms are expensive. But check around: During off-peak periods you may find a better deal through a travel agent or from a hotel's online specials. If you make a reservation through HRN, be sure to confirm it with the hotel, because HRN occasionally fails to make the booking.

LastMinuteTravel.com (www.lastminutetravel.com)

This is a new site, and it is too early to evaluate it, but its prospects look bright. Here's the idea: LastMinuteTravel serves as a clearinghouse for trips from all sorts of travel suppliers, including airlines, cruise lines, tour packagers, and others. Smaller companies, such as B&Bs, can participate as well, which is the true genius of this site: It lets the little guys get their last-minute deals in front of the public's eyes. Will it take off? Hard to say. When I wrote my first book about Internet travel in 1996, I highlighted a new site called Electronic Travel Auction, which appeared to be the next big thing. This site may have been a bit ahead of its time or may have lacked the financial backing to survive. Two years later Priceline.com—a similar site—launched with a massive ad campaign and quickly became one of the Net's most popular travel sites.

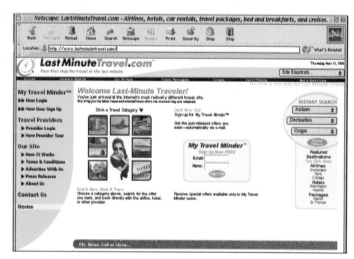

LastMinuteTravel (www.lastminutetravel.com) offers late-breaking deals on flights, cruises, B&Bs, travel packages, and more.

Lowestfare.com (www.lowestfare.com)

When corporate raider Carl Icahn ended his seven-year reign at TWA in 1993, he left with the option to buy $610 million worth of tickets at a 45 percent discount. No one knew how or if he'd sell these tickets, until the Net went mainstream. Today, Lowestfare.com sells TWA airline tickets at about a 20 percent discount. Though Lowestfare sells some other tickets, the vast majority of tickets sold are on TWA.

You Never Know Where the Best Deal Is

A 1999 study by *USA Today* compared Lowestfare.com with Expedia.com, Skytours, and a traditional, real-world agency, and found that in five of twelve sample domestic and international trips, Lowestfare did have the best deal, and in a sixth case it tied for the best. In other cases, however, it trailed well behind the others, for example, on a New York to Seattle flight, Lowestfare quoted a price of $378, while the other three agencies found tickets for $308.

This survey shows it's very hard to tell where you'll find the best deal for your itinerary. So the only sensible way to proceed is to check around, become informed about fares, and see if you find the best price online or through a travel agent. If an agent comes up with a better deal, reward that person for his or her hard work and buy the ticket through the agent. With all the commission cuts and other competition that agents face these days, they deserve to get your business when they find the lowest fare.

Smarter Living (www.smarterliving.com)

Best known for its e-mail dispatch of weekend deals on twenty airlines, Smarter Living also compiles lists of deals on its site. Search the **Deal Alert** section to view the latest specials on flights, vacation packages, cruises, and more; or sign up for the Deal Alert e-mail dispatch. *Note:* You can get two e-mail newsletters, one for airlines' weekend getaways and the second for other budget travel deals.

First Person: Linda Albert

Not everyone is convinced that buying online is the way to go. Linda Albert, who bought a ticket through Bestfares.com, realized she didn't really buy her ticket through Bestfares, which made it much harder to change. Here's her story, adapted from a letter to Arthur Frommer's Budget Travel site:

After buying a ticket through Bestfares.com, I tried to change the return date during the trip. I was willing to pay the $75 change fee to TWA, but TWA refused to change my ticket. They said it was illegal for them to do so. Only the travel agent through which I bought the ticket could change it.

I spent the next four hours on the phone. Bestfares.com told me they did not actually sell me the ticket, although I booked through them, and they took my charge card number. They gave me another agency to call.

The next agency told me they were not the ticketing agency either, that I would have to contact a rep at another number. This rep said, "Sorry, no seats available in your class on the day you want to make a change." Next time I'll pay a higher price to avoid such a hassle.

Online Travel Auctions

Though **Priceline.com** isn't the only auction site on the Net, it was the site that most rocked the online travel world on the eve of the millennium. With a glitzy, multi-million-dollar ad campaign featuring William Shatner of *Star Trek* fame, Priceline became one of the most recognized, most visited, and most discussed commerce sites on the Net. According to the *Wall Street Journal*, in mid-1999 Priceline was selling an average of 40,000 tickets a week, and sales were rising quickly.

First Person: Jon Goodstein

Jon Goodstein, a gardener in his 30s, recently used Priceline to book a round-trip ticket from his home near San Francisco to New York City. Here's Jon's story:

I wanted to visit my sister, her husband, and their two young children in New York, but I procrastinated until I realized I had only six days left to book a ticket. It was too late to get any of the advance purchase discounts, so I thought I'd try Priceline. The best fare for advance purchase tickets was $358, so I figured I'd add a bit to that and bid $398 because I really wanted a good shot at the ticket. It was mid-June and school had just gotten out, so I figured a lot of people would be traveling, and there might not be too many seats available.

Anyway, toward the end of the bidding procedure, Priceline offered to add another $40 to my bid if I applied for a credit card. So I did that and then went back and lowered my bid by $40, because the credit card application would add the $40 and give me the same bid. So I bid $358; the credit bonus upped the bid to $398, and I got the ticket. Not only that, it was a non-stop on Delta, and the flight times were convenient. As an added bonus, my outgoing flight was overbooked, so I volunteered to get bumped and got a voucher from Delta for $350 for a future flight. Then the flight on the way home was way oversold, so I got bumped again, this time for a $450 reward. So I ended up spending less than $400 and coming home with $800 in vouchers. Oh yeah, I forgot to mention that the flights I ended up taking were full in coach, so I got bumped up to business class both ways.

After launching as an airline ticket site in 1998, Priceline added hotel rooms and some nontravel products, such as new cars and home mortgages. The day the company went public in 1999, its net worth exceeded those of the three largest U.S. airlines—combined. Of course, these astonishing figures generated more hype, which obscured the key question: Is Priceline worth the trouble?

Here's how it works: Select a route and dates of travel, then name the price you're willing to pay for a domestic or international round-trip. You can't start ultralow and slowly inch up with new offers because Priceline only allows you to make one offer for any given itinerary. But if you change the dates of travel, you can make another offer. Priceline requires that you guarantee with a credit card, and if Priceline matches your price, it instantly charges your card. You don't have the opportunity to evaluate the times of travel or whether there's a stopover—you must take the ticket if Priceline meets your price. And it's not refundable, changeable, or transferable. If you can't use it, you're out of luck.

If you're flexible enough to work with these restrictions, Priceline can turn up some good deals. It's especially valuable if you can't plan far in advance and qualify for at least a seven-day advance purchase, or if you can't meet certain discount restrictions, such as staying over for a Saturday night. But research the going rate before making an offer. A good strategy is to bid about 20 to 30 percent lower than the best economy fare you can find

Priceline.com (priceline.com) encourages travelers to "name their price" for airline tickets and hotel rooms.

siteseeing

The Trouble with Priceline

Though Priceline.com's patented "name your price" premise sounds appealing, there are several factors you should consider before doing business with this site. Although Priceline can be good for travelers who have to take off on short notice (and who are thus unable to qualify for advance purchase discounts), for many other travelers it's no bargain. Here's why:

- If you overbid, Priceline pockets the difference. Some travelers, for example, might bid $400 for a February round-trip from New York to Paris. If Priceline can get this ticket for $250, it will keep the $150 difference. On the other hand, Priceline has occasionally sold tickets below cost because the company wants to increase its volume. So if you shop around to find the best price, then bid 20 percent to 30 percent less, you may bag a good deal.
- You can pick a date but not a time. Domestic flights may depart between 6:00 A.M. and 10:00 A.M. So you may get stuck on a flight that leaves at 9:30 P.M. and have to fly all night. International flights may depart anytime. You may also have to make one stopover. You can't see the itinerary before deciding whether to take a ticket. So if flight times are inconvenient, that's too bad.
- Tickets are nonrefundable, nonendorsable, and can't be exchanged. So if your plans change, you're out of luck.
- You won't earn frequent flier miles.
- Several leading airlines don't participate. Priceline has a limited number of carriers in its proprietary database. Priceline won't disclose which carriers these are but has conceded that several major airlines are taking a "wait-and-see" approach. In a 1999 Reuters story, British Airways Sales Director Dale Moss called Priceline's sales approach a "very interesting model," then added, "We've chosen not to participate."

through other channels if you are to have a decent chance of having your bid accepted.

Priceline maintains a proprietary database of flights on various airlines. Once you make a bid, Priceline searches this database to see if any airlines have a fare lower than your offer. Some, but not all, of the major U.S. airlines participate.

Other Auction Sites

Priceline isn't the only travel site to use the auction model. Other sites, such as **Travelbids.com (www.travelbids.com)**, use a form of auctions to lure travelers to their sites. Travelbids encourages travelers to research and reserve their trips but not to pay for them immediately. Instead, they are to give the information to Travelbids, which has a network of travel agents who bid for the business. The agent who can offer the lowest price gets to book the trip. The savings come from agents who are willing to rebate part of the commission to the traveler. The reasoning is that because the traveler did most of the research, he or she should get most of the commission. So Travelbids promises a minimum of 6 percent off. (The average commission is roughly 10 percent.)

Consider a cruise booking for two people at $1,200 each for a total trip value of $2,400. If a travel agent books this trip, that agent would get a $240 commission from the cruise line, based on a typical rate of 10 percent. That agent, because there was minimal work involved, kicks back a part of the commission, say $150, to the traveler. It all sounds good, but there are some issues to consider:

- The bidding starts at 6 percent off what you think is the best price. If that's not really the best price, you may get a bid (that you're obligated to accept) that really isn't the best deal.
- Your travel arrangements are taken over by an agency you don't know. Most are reputable, but what if you get stuck with one that isn't? What if you need assistance changing the date of your trip, and the agency isn't very helpful?
- There's a $5.00 fee for each part of the booking, so for a flight and hotel that's a $10 fee—if your total savings is $40, that is a fourth of what you save.
- In many cases you don't get your discount until after the agency receives its commission. So you have to keep an eye on this to make sure you eventually get the rebate. It may not be worthwhile for you to keep checking your credit statement for a relatively small savings.
- For the savings to be substantial, it would have to be an expensive trip, and you might not want go to an agency you don't know if you're spending several thousand dollars.

Several other sites offer travel auctions, and some are pretty cool. One is called **Travelfacts (www.bid4travel.com)**, which runs a fairly standard auction (as opposed to the reverse auctions discussed earlier), offering travelers the opportunity to bid on trips. Another is **Cathay-Pacific (www.cathay-usa.com)**, a Hong Kong-based airline, which occasionally offers auctions on hundreds of seats from the United States to Asia. When an airline auctions off so many seats, that means there's plenty of room for lots of people to "win." Recent auctions have seen many people fly to Asia at prices well below even the best discount rate. As the Web becomes an increasingly popular trading post for travel, look for auctions to proliferate. Five million eBay users can't be wrong.

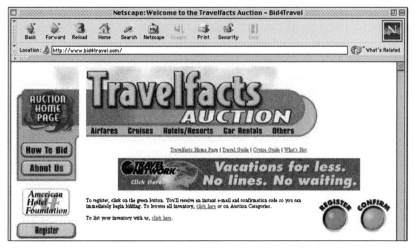

Travelfacts Auction (bid4travel.com) is one of several places to bid on travel packages.

Staying Informed *with* E-mail Newsletters

Airlines aren't the only travel suppliers that send out specials via e-mail. Lots of travel sites compile special deals on flights, cruises, hotels, and vacation packages, and many of these sites will happily send you weekly or occasional updates on their specials. Signing up is free and takes just a few seconds. But be sure to save the first mailing you receive, which should tell you how to unsubscribe if you get tired of receiving these dispatches. Most reputable newsletters also include a line across the bottom, letting you know how to unsubscribe.

Seven Leading Travel Bargain Dispatches

It can be daunting to try to keep visiting different Web sites to stay abreast of the thousands of deals out there. Rather than hunt them down, the following mailing lists deliver these deals to you. They don't cost a penny, and you don't risk any paper cuts.

This is just a sampling of the newsletters. By the time you read this, there will likely be more worthwhile dispatches. To find newsletters, see **Topica (topica.com)**, which lists about 200 travel-related mailing lists and is growing, or **Liszt (www. liszt.com)**, a Web site where you can search for newsletters by topic. A recent Liszt search for "travel" yielded sixty-six newsletters, including some destination specific ones, such as one called **europe4less**. Subscription instructions are on the site, but be forewarned that some newsletters are created to publicize Web sites. If a newsletter is hosted on a Web site, try to learn a bit about it before subscribing. (For more about mailing lists, see chap. 13.)

1travel.com Savings Alert (www.onetravel.com)

Click on "Savings Alert," and you can sign up for any or all of the four parts to 1travel's newsletter. The four sections cover airfares, resorts, cruises, and the all-around best deals, which 1travel.com calls "Hottest of the Hot." Also, 1travel.com lets you select the departure cities that interest you, customizing the newsletter for your possible departure points.

Air Travel Update

This mailing list (or listserv) is a nice roundup of air deals published on various Web sites. To subscribe, send an e-mail message to majordomo@listserv.prodigy.com and include the words *subscribe airtravel* in the body and subject line of the message. (For more on mailing lists, see chap. 13.)

Bestfares.com Hot Deals (www.bestfares.com)

Click on **"Hot Deals,"** enter your e-mail address, and you're set. This newsletter, penned by budget travel expert Tom Parsons, covers a wide range of bargains and is especially useful for those airfare deals that seem to disappear quickly.

Fare Wars Mailing List (www.travelersnet.com/farewars/index.htm)

Fare Wars is one of my favorite lists—it only sends me messages when a genuine fare war erupts. I've subscribed for years and have found it to be timely and well informed.

Information on Becoming an Air Courier (home.earthlink.net/~oracle/courier.htm)

Traveling as an air courier, as we'll discuss in the next section, is one of the cheapest ways to go. Simply give up your baggage allowance for use by an air courier company, and you'll travel for a fraction of the cost of discount tickets. This list is a fine place to learn about traveling as a courier. If you have problems with the Web address, send an e-mail message to courier@pastriesbyedie.com with the word *Subscribe* in the subject field.

Smarter Living (www.smarterliving.com)

Though Smarter Living's site isn't solely about travel, it has several excellent travel newsletters, including Internet Airfares, mentioned earlier in the chapter; Student Travel, which features an archive of back issues; and Deal Alert, which includes discounts on hotel rooms, car rentals, and vacation packages. No reason why you can't subscribe to them all—they're free!

TravelHub's Hub Club (www.travelhub.com)

TravelHub's Hub Club pulls together all sorts of deals from travel agents and compiles them in one e-mail message. Some of the deals are outstanding, such as the following, offered in May 1999:

BARCELONA, SPAIN FOR $449
Round-trip air via Iberia Airlines from New York
3 nights at 3-star hotels
breakfast daily, half-day sightseeing

The fare alert features discussed in chapter 2 are also a great way of staying on top of fares for a specific route. **Expedia.com**, for example, offers **Fare Tracker**, enabling you to keep tabs on the routes you fly most often. Each week Expedia sends an e-mail alert letting you know the fares on those routes and also pitches other offers. Other sites, such as **Travelocity.com**, will alert you each time the fare for the routes you select jumps or falls by $25 or more. **ITN.com** also has an excellent fare tracker.

Courier Flights: Fly *for* Almost Nothing

Flying as an air courier used to be one of budget travel's best-kept secrets. But in the last few years, the word has gotten out, and more travelers are flying this way, which means they aren't generally as cheap as they once were. Here's the deal: If you're willing to give up your baggage allowance, you can fly to international destinations for a song, for example, Los Angeles to Thailand for $300 round-trip. In addition to flying with just a carry-on, you have to fly when the courier company needs you, but some have almost daily departures. That doesn't mean you'll get that departure, but you can try. Also, you typically can stay no more than thirty days; sometimes the limit is less, typically fourteen days or sometimes just seven days.

One way to become a courier is to sign on with a courier company, which provides flight lists to members. Several of the companies are now online, for example, the **International Association of Air Travel Couriers (www.courier.org)**. This site will send you courier deals if you sign on as a member, which costs $45 a year. This fee is similar to those charged by offline courier companies, though it can be more efficient to get updates online. You'll also find testimonials

Learn about flying very cheaply to international destinations as an air courier at Air Courier Travel (www.courier.org).

from veteran air couriers and a special section for U.K. residents interested in becoming couriers.

Another courier site is **Worldwide Courier Association (www.wallstech.com)**, which answers "commonly asked questions." You can sign up to be a courier through WCA for $58, and for an additional $4.00 shipping fee, they'll send a flight guide. For links to other courier companies, look up "courier flights" on your favorite search engine.

Summing Up

The Net can be an excellent source for bargains, but just because a site says it has the lowest fares, doesn't mean that it does. As in the real world, it pays to shop around. Check various Web sites, from mainstream booking sites to online consolidators, and see what you can find. Then, if you have any doubts whether you really have found the lowest price, consult a travel agent who specializes in the type of travel you're planning. Finally, there are some deals, such as Net-only fares and last-minute deals, that are only available online. However, even these may not be the best deals out there, because as these specials have become more popular, they aren't quite as good as they used to be. It's the old law of supply and demand.

Other Chapters to Check

Chapter 2: "Booking Flights Online"—Flight bargains

Chapter 3: "A Room with a View"—Finding cheap lodgings

Chapter 5: "On the Road"—Booking rental cars

Chapter 9: "Cruising the Net"—Cruise deals

Chapter 11: "Taking Care of Business"—Tips on frequent flyer programs

Chapter 13: "Online Discussion Forums"—More on Internet mailing lists

---

FIND AN OUTFITTER *or* PLAN IT YOURSELF

The World's Largest Adventure Travel Catalog

Whether you're searching for a guided white-water rafting trip down Idaho's Salmon River or planning your own trek through the Himalayan foothills, the Net is a phenomenal resource. For both types of adventures, guided tours and self-planned trips, the Net can help you gather reams of information, connect with fellow travelers who can provide advice, and give you a taste of what to expect through travelogues, photos, even short video clips.

On the Net, you can read firsthand accounts written by adventurers who have just been to a particular place. Or you can visit newsgroups and Web forums, where you can ask fellow travelers about their recent journeys. Connecting online with other adventurers can be especially valuable for information about destinations that aren't covered in detail by guidebooks. As tour company managers say, the Net has given them a way to convey more information to window-shopping travelers.

Though a true adventure can never be completely planned, the Net can help you prepare for the unexpected and become more informed going in—which can help you escape intact getting out. On the following pages I offer some strategies for using Web pages, online forums, and e-mail lists to help you discover potential adventures you might never have considered and plan trips once you decide where to go.

Though it may sound far-fetched, the Net really is the world's largest adventure travel catalog. And it offers more features than any paper catalog. In addition to extensive descriptions and testimonials about each trip, you can see lots of pictures, hear sound clips, and perhaps most importantly, easily zap an e-mail message to an outfitter about any concerns you may have. Wondering if you need prior rafting experience to join a trip down the Zambezi—just ask. Another option is to scan press reviews. Major outfitters often feature newspaper or magazine stories written about them on their sites.

Any thoughtful adventure travel outfitter will have an e-mail address or toll-free number on its site. If a company doesn't, you should wonder about how thorough it is on its trips. Some might say it's unfair to judge an outfitter by its Web site. But every aspect of an outfitter's product is an indication of how safe and responsible it is. **Mountain Travel Sobek (www.mtsobek.com)** doesn't spend a fortune on its glossy print catalog because the company has money to burn. It does so because the catalog is more than a means to convey information—it's a statement about the company. Just like its Web site.

An Emotional Connection

Richard Bangs, formerly head of the adventure tour company **Mountain Travel Sobek (www.mtsobek.com)**, views the Net as an ideal tool for selling adventure tours. "To think that travelers made a major travel decision based on a single image and a few paragraphs of text is now astonishing. Today, people can learn so much more and better target their wants," he says. "The catalog is static. It is always somewhat out of date as soon as it's printed. The Net is convenient—you can ask a question in the middle of the night. Or a new trip to Korea can be posted immediately."

Until the Net came along, Bangs felt that adventure tour companies couldn't adequately convey what they had to offer. "We'd

Mountain Travel Sobek (www.mtsobek.com) offers an "emotional connection" for those considering an adventure tour.

always been frustrated with the lack of a suitable communications tool. To have a two-week trek through the Himalayas and try to convey that with one photo wasn't good enough," he says. "The question was how could we bring the experience closer. As soon as the Net started to show its hand, we knew this was the tool we wanted—not just because the Net can deliver more text and images. On the Net we can deliver sound and even video clips: the trumpet of an elephant, groan of a shifting glacier, or the gamelan of Indonesia. It's not just that you can provide infinitely more material—you can provide emotional material."

Finding Adventure Tours Online

With a whole world of adventure out there, it can be hard to know where to begin. If you know what you're seeking, you can go to any search engine and input key terms, for example "rafting AND idaho." Searching for this term at **Lycos (www.lycos.com)** yielded several white-water outfitters in the top ten listings, including **Outdoor Adventures (www.gorafting.com)**, which leads trips on Idaho's Salmon River.

On its Web site Outdoor Adventures includes all the catalog information you'd expect: river descriptions, guide experience, and prices and trip dates. And there's much more, such as updated projections for river levels and current flows. This information can give you a much better idea of what to expect and can help you make a decision about which trip to choose. For example, when moderate flows are expected, you might feel comfortable signing up for a challenging trip, but if high flows are anticipated, you might be more inclined to choose an easier river.

Another example: Searching for "scuba AND honduras" led to several interesting results on **HotBot (www.hotbot.com)**. The first page of results had a listing for **Captain Ron's Reef Resort (www.captainronsreefresort.com)**, which included an update on the Honduran island of Roatan's recovery from Hurricane Mitch. A message from Captain Ron, some local music, and links to related sites were among the other features here.

Searching for Adventure

If you're just fishing for a trip and don't have anything firmly in mind, you can drill down through a search directory, such as **Yahoo (yahoo.com)**.

For example, click on "Travel" and then "Tour Operators," where you'll find the following categories: Climbing, Dogsledding, Heli-Skiing, Llama Trekking, Sea Kayaking, and Safaris, among others. Click on any of these categories to find a multitude of links to outfitters' sites. By combing through the information on these sites, you can come up with some ideas for trips. Then follow up with e-mail or phone calls.

Another technique is to visit a directory of adventure travel outfitters. **Specialty Travel Index (www.spectrav.com)**, which started out as a print publication that listed various trips by region and type, has adapted well to the Web. From the home page, you can flip through listings in the **Interest/Activity Index, Geographical Index,** or **Tour Operator Listings.** Or you can simply search the site for key terms. Using an index such as STI can be a much more focused way to search; rather than wading though thousands of results on a search site, you can get a shorter and more relevant list for your query.

Let's say you were interested in a bicycle tour of Bali. Click on "Geographical Index," then click on "Asia," then "Bali." When you get to the Bali page, you'll see dozens of categories listed, from Artist Workshops to Yoga Retreats. The Bicycle Tours page includes several listings, each with a short description of the outfitter and links to contact information, which usually includes the outfitter's

tip

■ **You can also use sites devoted to a particular sport or activity; for example, visit GoSki (goski.com) to plan a ski adventure; or if you use AOL, check Ski Vacations (keyword: *ski vacations*). Each sport and activity has many Web sites and, in some cases, AOL areas devoted to it. These can be excellent starting points. (Because there are so many, we'll cover these sites in the Web directories at the back of the book.)**

Web site and e-mail addresses. Remember an outfitter may have a Web site even if STI doesn't list one—some listings are out of date. To check, just search for the outfitter's name on a search site, such as HotBot, and see what you find.

Once you narrow your choices, it can be a good idea follow up in newsgroups, Web site discussion forums, or in chat areas on AOL or CompuServe. Or if you subscribe to an e-mail list, such as Travel-L, you can post a message to the list, asking the hundreds of subscribers if they've ever gone on a Backroads trip, or any other trip you're considering. Most likely, a few people have, and probably a couple of them will get back to you and let you know how their trips went. We'll discuss these forums in detail in chapter 13; for now, suffice it to say that online discussions are a terrific place to get feedback from other travelers. (For a listing of some of the best adventure travel sites by category, see the Web directories at the back of the book.)

Great Outdoor Recreation Pages

When it comes to trail mix, GORP stands for "good ol' raisins and peanuts." On the Web, however, GORP means **Great Outdoor Recreation Pages (www.gorp.com)**, a vast database of information on planning your own outdoor adventure or finding an outfitter. GORP combines lively feature stories ("Fat Tires in Eastern Iowa") with extensive information on state and national parks and other outdoor destinations around the world.

GORP's **Attractions** category includes listings for parks, wilderness areas, national forests, and more. **Activities** has everything from camping and climbing to scuba and snorkeling. Or search by location, for the United States and around the world. Each of these main section pages has current features, such as "Tanzania: Scaling Mighty Kilimanjaro." If you dig down another level, you can find listings for all sorts of trips.

Not surprisingly, GORP hawks everything from destination guidebooks to outfitters' tours, but it's

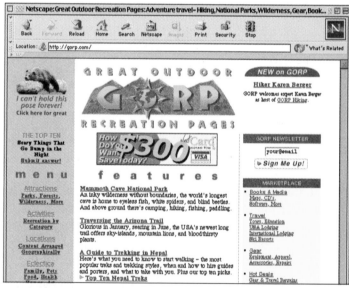

GORP (gorp.com) is an extensive guide to outdoor adventures.

pretty easy to distinguish between GORP's features and the stuff that's for sale. One of the coolest things GORP does is partner with destination guidebooks, offering an excerpt of the book. So if you click on a link for Hiking the Berkshires, you get routes and descriptions of four Berkshires hikes from the book *Fifty Hikes in Massachusetts*. This way, everyone wins: Readers get valuable advice without having to pay for it, and the book gets exposure that leads to increased sales.

Outside Online

Another superb site for active travel is **Outside Online (www.outsidemag.com)**. The site lets you plan your own trips, or if you're an armchair adventurer, you can follow other travelers' journeys from the safety and comfort of your own home. Outside's **Going Places** has a guide and insider tips for the hundreds of national parks in the United States. The site also features the latest dispatches from expeditions around the world, such as a recent ascent of Mount Everest.

Outside Online has too many worthwhile features to list here: Suffice it to say, you can find everything from ski conditions to an outfitter directory in the Going Places section. But don't overlook the other sections. **The Lodge**, for example, is a fine place to connect electronically with other travelers and occasionally chat with celebrities, such as Jon Krakauer, author of *Into Thin Air*.

Outside Online (outsidemag.com) includes a directory for active travelers and features from Outside magazine.

Adventure Tours with Nonprofit Groups

Many leading nonprofit groups, such as the Sierra Club and Audubon Society, lead adventure tours, often guided by experts in a field. By joining these tours, you not only enjoy a memorable vacation, you also help support these organizations. The following are some nonprofits that lead tours. You can find others by using a good search engine.

Audubon Nature Odysseys (www.audubon.org/market/no)

Have you ever dreamed of seeing penguins in their natural habitat? Well, Audubon Nature Odysseys can take you to Antarctica and all sorts of other locations around the globe to learn about birds. The Web site includes trip listings, leader profiles, a photo gallery, and information about Audubon's travel ethic.

Friends of the River (www.friendsoftheriver.org/html/rafting.html)

Friends of the River's (FOR) philosophy is that if you can get folks onto the river, the river will speak for itself. The conservation group offers trips primarily on California's American River, led by volunteer guides who have trained with FOR.

tip

■ To find resources for backpacking in Europe, see Eurotrip.com, with hostel reviews, packing advice, and destination descriptions.

For AOL Users:

ADVENTURE TRAVEL

AOL's **Adventure & Active** (keyword: *adventure travel*), with sections on biking, climbing, fishing, and scuba diving, is a good jumping-off point for adventure planning. A section called **Planning Guides** links to adventure Web sites; and another link goes to AOL's version of Outside Online (from *Outside* magazine). Adventure & Active links to related AOL pages, such as **Parks & Camping** and **Safaris & Ecotours.**

Outdoor Adventure Online (keyword: *outdoor adventure*) has sections such as **Guides and Tours**, and **Destinations and Resorts**. Or click on the link for "250 Ultimate Adventures," which is selected and organized into sixteen categories by OAO. This is a terrific resource; it not only lists trips but has instructional features, such as "Getting Certified on Your Vacation" in the scuba section. You can also participate in OAO's forum or scroll down the box in the lower right corner for listings by state.

The **Independent Traveler** (keyword: *traveler*) has a section called **Travelers' Journey**, with reports from other travelers who have recently visited such exciting destinations as Costa Rica. Other sections include resources for savvy traveling, an online bookstore, and late-breaking bargains to exotic destinations. And, of course, The Independent Traveler has plenty of online forums, where you can learn from others or share your thoughts.

Global Exchange Reality Tours (www.globalexchange.org/tours)

Global Exchange emphasizes building international understanding through personal connections. The trips include tours to Cuba, Africa, Southeast Asia, and Ireland, among other destinations. The online catalogs feature tours, listed by destination and by issue (health care, fair trade, women and development, etc.), as well as itineraries and prices. Although these tours can be educational, they can also be fun. A December 1999 tour of Cuba was entitled "Health and Healing with the Real Dr. Patch Adams."

tip

For a learning adventure in the wilderness, see the National Outdoor Leadership School site (www.nols.edu) or Outward Bound (www.outwardbound.com).

National Geographic Expeditions (www.nationalgeographic.com/ngexpeditions)

"Have you ever looked at a photograph in *National Geographic* magazine and wished you could be there?" So begins this site, which features an online catalog of expeditions and basic information about NGE trips. You can order a print catalog online.

Oceanic Society Expeditions (www.oceanic-society.org/ose.htm)

Thousands of people each year enjoy international natural history journeys, participatory research expeditions, and California whale-watching trips with the Oceanic Society. The site includes basic information on each of these categories. To learn more or to get a

the ultimate adventure

catalog, call the toll-free number on the site. (*Note:* It's hard to understand why an environmental group such as this doesn't have a paper-saving online catalog.)

Sierra Club Outings (www.sierraclub.org/outings)

Following in the footsteps of John Muir, the Sierra Club believes the best way to encourage people to preserve the environment is to get them into the wilderness. The Sierra Club site lists national and local outings, as well as lodges, such as the Clair Tappaan Lodge, where you can enjoy the great outdoors without breaking the bank.

World Wildlife Fund (www.worldwildlife.org/travel)

The World Wildlife Fund (WWF) offers a wide range of trips, spanning the globe from Mongolia to the Galapagos Islands. The Web site includes a catalog of upcoming trips, prices, policies, and a list of frequently asked questions (and answers!). If you have other questions, click on "Contact Us."

Lonely Planet's Thorn Tree

Speaking of dispatches from other adventure travelers, **Lonely Planet's Thorn Tree (www.lonelyplanet.com/thorn/thorn.htm)** is a computer bulletin board organized by region, which has special sections on activities, women travelers, and gays/lesbians. If you have a trip in mind and want to find someone to share your adventure with, link up with like minds in the **Travelling Companions** forum. Here's a sample post (this message included a name and e-mail address, which have been omitted to protect the writer's privacy):

Ghana . . . and other parts of Africa

(Timestamp: Sat. 29 May, 8:40 Tasmanian Standard Time)

I'm planning to visit Ghana this summer and/or fall—the
date of departure and duration of trip are flexible—to
learn African drumming. If you'd like to visit Africa send
me an e-mail. . . . I'm willing to visit other regions as well.
I'm interested in the music, culture, and natural beauty
of Africa, and I welcome anyone who wants to explore.

This is just one of several Lonely Planet forums—each has its own tone. Although the Travelling Companions board has a utilitarian slant, other forums typically are places where like-minded travelers share advice.

DIY: Do It Yourself

The Internet really shines as a travel resource when travelers head off the beaten path without the guidance of a tour company. Seattlites Susan Bott and Jim Klima (Jet City JimBo, as he's known on the Net) embarked on just this sort of around-the-world adventure, and Jim says the Net was essential for their pretrip planning and for getting updates during their trip. (*Note:* To read detailed accounts of JimBo and Sue's journey, see www.jetcity.com/~suebee.)

First Person: Jim Klima

The Net is the only way to get timely and biased as well as unbiased information. Travel agents are of little use to budget backpackers like me. For example, we checked Lonely Planet's Web site for postcards from readers.

The literature gets outdated rather quickly. Since I travel unreserved and prefer the unpredictable, my need for reliable information is paramount. There's no substitute for communicating with someone who's just been there. Even now, I get queries from people all over the world planning trips like the one I am on.

Before leaving, I prowled every travel-related discussion group I could find to locate people who had actually done an overland trip. Since few Americans travel this way, using the Net gave me access to Europeans and Australians who had firsthand experience. I received very good feedback, both negative and positive, about overlanding in general and specific (trucking) companies in particular. It also gave me a splendid opportunity to query these people about what equipment and precautions I should take.

Another great source of concern before we left was getting permission to enter the Central Asian countries, Uzbekistan, in particular. Everything there was in a state of flux since the collapse of the USSR, and corruption is quite rampant.

So once again reading travelogues posted by others who had been there really helped.

I joined [Usenet discussion] groups related to Russia and monitored them for relevant information. As I gathered useful electronic contacts, I e-mailed travel agents in Moscow, B&B proprietors in Uzbekistan, and even a pen-pal in Tashkent. Eventually, after using every search tool I could find on the Web, I stumbled across travel agencies in Seattle and Australia that could provide visa assistance.

One Net resource that was quite useful was the Travel-L listserv, which gave my posted queries international exposure. For example, I was worried about bandit hijackings of buses to Lamu, an island off the coast of Kenya. Online State Department information was not timely enough so I posted a query on Travel-L. A quick reply put me in touch with a man whose son goes there every year and was very knowledgeable about current conditions. Aside from being informative and up-to-date, this allowed

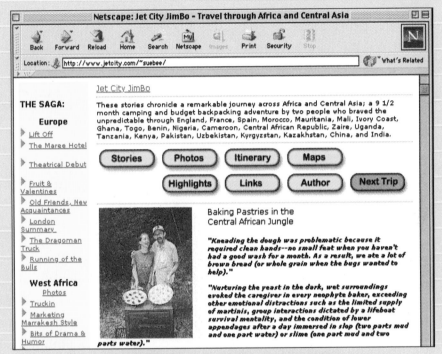

Netscape: Jet City JimBo - Travel through Africa and Central Asia

Back | Forward | Reload | Home | Search | Netscape | Images | Print | Security | Stop

Location: http://www.jetcity.com/~suebee/   What's Related

Jet City JimBo

THE SAGA:

Europe

▶ Lift Off
▶ The Maree Hotel

▶ Theatrical Debut

▶ Fruit &
Valentines
▶ Old Friends, New
Acquaintances
▶ London
Summary
▶ The Dragoman
Truck
▶ Running of the
Bulls

West Africa
Photos
▶ Truckin
▶ Marketing
Marrakesh Style
▶ Bits of Drama &
Humor

These stories chronicle a remarkable journey across Africa and Central Asia; a 9 1/2 month camping and budget backpacking adventure by two people who braved the unpredictable through England, France, Spain, Morocco, Mauritania, Mali, Ivory Coast, Ghana, Togo, Benin, Nigeria, Cameroon, Central African Republic, Zaire, Uganda, Tanzania, Kenya, Pakistan, Uzbekistan, Kyrgyzstan, Kazakhstan, China, and India.

Stories | Photos | Itinerary | Maps

Highlights | Links | Author | Next Trip

Baking Pastries in the Central African Jungle

"Kneading the dough was problematic because it required clean hands—no small feat when you haven't had a good wash for a month. As a result, we ate a lot of brown bread (or whole grain when the bugs wanted to help)."

"Nurturing the yeast in the dark, wet surroundings evoked the caregiver in every neophyte baker, exceeding other emotional distractions such as the limited supply of martinis, group interactions dictated by a lifeboat survival mentality, and the condition of lower appendages after a day immersed in slop (two parts mud and one part water) or slime (one part mud and two parts water)."

Intrepid travelers Jim and Sue Klima document their adventures with stories and photos (www.jetcity.com/~suebee).

me to cross-check and verify or chuck other information which I had accumulated—a necessity when you are doing independent travel.

We wanted to enter Kashgar, China, from a remote pass called Torgut in Kyrgyzstan, to avoid going the long way around via Kazakhstan, with its reputedly ugly border crossing. The LP Guide for Central Asia was not in publication yet, so information was scarce. But through TRAVEL-L, I was able to establish contact with people who had attempted this border within the last year or two.

Through the Net, Jim found reliable information from travelers who had just been to the places he planned to visit. For some regions, such as the former Soviet republics bordering western China, no printed guidebook could have helped Jim find what he was looking for. So he searched the Web for travelers' accounts and connected with others in online discussion areas and through Internet mailing lists. Through newsgroups, he learned what it would be like to travel overland and found a trucking company that led trips over the route he was interested in.

To get reliable news about border crossings, he posted a query to the Travel-L mailing list, where he could hear from more than one person, cross-checking and confirming his information. And after he returned, he served as a resource for other travelers. (For more about newsgroups and mailing lists, see chap. 13.)

Fielding's Danger Finder

Most adventurous travelers are willing to risk encountering some hazardous situations and meet these as they come. Yet there's another breed out there: unusually intrepid characters who go out and seek danger and hope they find a way out. If you're one of these people, or if you're just curious about the world's most dangerous places, have a look a **Fielding's Danger Finder (www.fieldingtravel.com/df/index.htm).**

In the Dangerous Places section, you'll find links to about three dozen countries, from Afghanistan to Iraq to the United States. Here's a sample from Afghanistan's Getting Around section: "Most talibs have never seen a Westerner up close and they have a bad habit of sticking their heads inside your car like deer at a drive-through zoo. My advice is to always smile and wave since most of the new talibs you run into are scared kids."

The adventure guide has a section called Save Yourself, which is mostly a listing for training schools. The Black Flag Cafe is an online forum where you can discuss your experiences or seek advice on where you're going. For some people, the material here may be inspiring; for others, intimidating. It's hoped that it will be a reminder to all that when you hit the dimly lit backroads of this planet, you're not in Disneyland anymore.

Michael Shapiro's Internet Travel Planner

the ultimate adventure

Adventure Travelogues

In my younger days when I traveled with a backpack and stayed at hostels, I sat up many nights with fellow travelers to hear stories about where they'd gone and what they'd found. Some of my most memorable adventures were spawned by tips from fellow travelers. Today, you can find these tips online, in the form of online travelogues. Perhaps not surprisingly, a good place to read travelogues is a site called **Hostels.com.**

Paul Otteson, author of *The World Awaits,* compiles Hostels.com's section on budget travel, which includes **Places and Tales (www.hostels.com/worldawaits/placestales. html)**, a roundup of fine travel writing, such as Brad Olsen's story on following his inspiration to the peak of an Egyptian pyramid.

One of the best things about online travelogues is that many list the e-mail address of the author, so you can drop a line to that person and get advice for your trip. Back in 1995 I put a trio of stories about Guatemala on the Web. Since then, I've had a few dozen travelers send me e-mail seeking advice about traveling there. It's been a pleasure to correspond with people interested in this beautiful land and to help give them a genuine picture of what's going on there, as opposed to the often skewed impression portrayed by "objective" media outlets.

The Russian Chronicles (www.f8.com/FP/Russia/index. html) represents another intersection between adventure travel and the Net. For this "experiment in interactive photojournalism," freelance writer Lisa Dickey and photojournalist Gary Matoso spent several months on a 5,000-mile journey, traveling through remote regions in Russia, documenting the outlook and opinion of contemporary Russians.

"E-mail was obviously our lifeline," says Lisa, "not only in the sense that it was the means of uploading our information to San Francisco, but also as a source of contact with our families and friends, feedback from readers of the Web site, and just generally getting news of what else was up in the world besides our monomaniacal drive to cross the trans-Siberian." In sum, not only did Lisa and Gary help inform the world about conditions in Russia as they discovered them, they also felt much less isolated because they were able to stay in touch with friends and family.

tips

■ Myriad sites focus on particular destinations and can be great sources of information. For an example, see Himalayan Explorers Club (www.hec.org), which helps independent travelers plan their adventures and even offers assistance to travelers in Nepal. Use search sites to find similar organizations for the region you plan to visit.

■ If you're on the road and don't want to spend a lot of time and money trying to dial into your home account, set up a freemail account through a Web-based e-mail service. Leading providers include Hotmail (www. hotmail.com) and Yahoo Mail (mail.yahoo.com). These services are supported by advertising that accompanies mail messages. (For more information on setting up a freemail account, see chap. 14, "Traveling with a Net.")

Where to Find Adventure Travelogues

There are two popular ways of finding online travelogues. The first is to use a search site, such as **LookSmart (looksmart.com)**, and search for key words. The second is to visit a collection of these stories. The following are some suggested sites where you can find a range of travelogues. Of course, not all travelogues here are stories of grand adventures, but each of these sites catalogs some inspiring trips.

- **Rec Travel Library (www.Travel-Library.com):** Round-the-world travelogues, tips for traveling and more.

- **Cyber Adventures (www.cyber-adventures.com):** Dozens of wired adventures and "strange-but-true" travel stories. Add your tale to the mix.

- **Yahoo's Travelogues (yahoo.com/Recreation/Travel/Travelogues):** An extensive list with lots of exceptional travel dispatches, categorized by region and country.

- **The Connected Traveler (www.connectedtraveler.com):** Veteran travel writer Russ Johnson posts some of his finest pieces and includes stories from a few other top travel pros. Many of the stories are embellished with sound, such as a piece on Fiji, which includes a sound clip from a local a capella chorus.

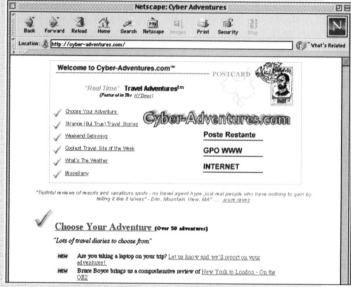

Cyber Adventures (cyber-adventures.com) is one of several adventure travelogue directories.

- **TravelMag's Travel Diaries (www.travelmag.co.uk/webwide/diaries.htm):** U.K. zine invites its readers to post their accounts.

- **Web Travel Review (webtravel.org/webtravel):** A selection of stories and images, most created by *Travels with Samantha* author Philip Greenspun.

- **TechNomads (www.microship.com/technomads):** Features Steve Roberts, who's best known for riding a computer-laden bike around the United States and is now readying the wired Microship for adventures in rivers and oceans.

- **Journeyfile (www.journeyfile.com):** Browse through others' travel tales or enter your own.

Around *the* World *in* Eighty Clicks

A trip around the world is the ultimate earthbound travel adventure. If you're contemplating an extended journey, visit the **Round-The-World Travel Guide (www.Travel-Library.com/rtw/html)**. Compiled by Marc Brosius of Florida, the RTW guide considers topics that range from whether to travel east or west to how long you can afford to be away. There are also discussions and tips on how and where to find work while traveling, how to stay in touch through e-mail and faxes, and how to find a reliable traveling companion. Marc posted the guide just before leaving on an around-the-world trip, another example of someone sharing his hard-won knowledge through the Web.

Like many of the best travel sites on the Web, the RTW Guide includes contributions from others. For example, fellow traveler Russell Gilbert warns prospective round-the-worlders that long-term traveling can be hard work at times. "Your new job will be to learn new currency, new local transportation, new languages, new places to sleep, new types of people, and new types of food. Every day, instead of driving to work, you will do these things. But the moments in between make it all worth it. So many people told us we were crazy for leaving our jobs. Don't listen to them! Go! You'll never regret it, even if you have a hard time finding a job when you get back. The trip was the best thing I've ever done in my life."

Another terrific site is called **Art of Travel (artoftravel. com)**, where you'll find a full-length manuscript with lots of great advice for traveling on a shoestring. Author John Gregory believes that how one travels is more important than where one travels, a philosophy shared by travel luminaries such as Arthur Frommer. Art of Travel covers mostly nuts-and-bolts topics, such as securing cheap flights and lodging, getting visas and passports, and essential equipment. It also ranges farther afield in sections on poetry, diplomacy, and non-verbal communication.

AirTreks.com (airtreks.com), formerly known as The Around-the-World Airfare Builder, lets travelers plan extended trips.

Summing Up

Clearly, a chapter on adventure can't be comprehensive: The options for adventure are far greater than can be listed in a few pages. By starting at the sites discussed in this chapter and following links to new sites, you can get advice from outfitters and fellow seekers. And through Net cafes, you can get online while traveling, in case you need some additional information while you're on the road or simply want to get in touch with the home front.

Other Chapters to Check

Chapter 1: "Destination Anywhere"—Guidebook-style advice

Chapter 7: "Budget Travel"—Tips on keeping expenses down

Chapter 13: "Online Discussion Forums"—Getting advice from fellow travelers

Chapter 14: "The Connected Traveler"—Learn how to stay online, with or without a laptop

CHOOSING *a* VOYAGE THAT'S RIGHT *for* YOU

Surveying the Field

The Internet has opened up a new porthole into the world of cruising. The entire process—from comparing cruise lines to shopping for the best deal—has been transformed. Just a few years ago, you might have visited a local travel agent, flipped through a few brochures, perhaps sought a recommendation from a friend or relative, and then plunked down thousands of your hard-earned dollars for a cruise that you might know very little about. Today, you can dive into cruise line Web sites, check reviews from fellow cruisers, and use other online resources to evaluate cruises on your own terms.

Reserving a cruise is a lot more involved than booking an airline seat. You pretty much know what you're getting when you book a flight; most seats are similar, and, unless you're in first class, the food will be mediocre at best. Cruises, on the other hand, seem almost limitless in variety. Ships range from the new megaliners (which are akin to floating suburbs, complete with multiplexes and shopping malls), to freighter cruises, where you ride along with the cargo and crew.

Each cruise line has its own personality: Some cater to those who want luxury at every turn, while others target travelers who like to party till dawn. Several Web sites, such as **TravelPage (www.travelpage.com/cruise)**, offer critical overviews of what you can expect from various cruise lines. You can also turn to cruise lines' own sites, which are akin to brochures, but with more information and interaction. Some sites, such as **Arthur Frommer's Budget Travel (www.frommers.com)**, offer cruise bargains that you can book online. And major booking sites, such as **Travelocity (www.travelocity.com)**, have recently begun selling cruises and sometimes offer specials on cruises that aren't filling up.

As in other travel categories, one of the most valuable aspects of planning trips online is that you can get opinions from other travelers. In some cases, you can even see those opinions tallied. One example is a site called **CruiseOpinion.com**, which assigns numerical scores based on lots of reviews. It's kind of like *Consumer Reports,* but by the people and for the people.

In addition to these sites are online magazines that cover the cruise industry and Web-based agencies, which sometimes offer pretty good deals and keep clients updated through e-mail newsletters. Though this wealth of information can sometimes seem daunting, the Net has become an invaluable resource for travelers. Using all this advice, particularly recommendations from other travelers (who don't have an ax to grind), can help you choose a cruise that's right for you.

Cruise Line Web Sites

Though some of the major cruise lines were slow to develop online sites and strategies, in recent years they've begun to perceive the value of the connecting online with prospective customers. Most of the major lines offer itineraries, prices, and information on ships, destinations, amenities, and onboard services. Some also have information on frequent cruiser programs, suggested travel agencies, and special theme or bargain cruises. And a few offer online booking. Despite recent improvements, however, most cruise sites have many leagues to go.

Royal Caribbean (www.rccl.com) is a perfect example. The glitzy home page looks good—once it finally downloads. Like many cruise sites, RCCL's is a bit heavy on style (and slow-loading images) and light on substance. I tried finding details on a weeklong Alaska cruise, but the only itinerary I could locate was a brief listing of the places where the ship docked each night. That's less than I'd expect from a print catalog. On the Web, you should get more, including details about each place the ship docks. In some other areas, RCCL does a good job. **Getting Your Feet Wet** helps clue in first-timers, and the information about onboard amenities and entertainment is nicely presented. You'll also find information on RCCL's Crown & Anchor loyalty program (for repeat guests) and a slideshow called Cybercruise.

Carnival's site **(www.carnival.com)** suffers from some of the same drawbacks as Royal Caribbean's site. The home page takes too long to load and is just a cover image with no information. Once you get to the real home page, there's a nice array of options, including descriptions of Carnival's "Fun Ships," destination information, and specials. Other sections include onboard activities, shore tours, online booking, and tips for first-timers. But the itinerary information can be thin here too. The Alaskan itinerary had links to more information, but the descriptions were still too brief, for example, shown here in its entirety is the information for Prince William Sound: "This grand collection of jagged glaciers encompassing 3.3 million acres includes saltwater beaches with protected coves, numerous jewel-like lakes, and lush forests."

tip

■ A Royal Caribbean executive recently said that as of spring 2000, the line's twelve ships will have Internet access terminals.

Holland America Line (www.hollandamerica.com) also has too many slow-loading images, including a useless cover page. However, HAL's site has some nice features: To get prospective clients excited about its cruises, it offers a virtual reality tour of one of its ships. This VR tour is optional, take it if you like, but if you aren't interested, it won't slow you down. There's also a feature called **Cruise Search,** which looks inviting, but when I clicked on the link for it, I got a message that said, "The database is currently being updated. Check back again soon." I checked back a few days later and got the same message.

Major Cruise Line Sites

Use these sites to find out about itineraries, prices, ships, destinations, amenities, and onboard services.

Carnival: www.carnival.com

Celebrity Cruises: www.celebrity-cruises.com

Crystal Cruises: www.crystalcruises.com

Cunard: www.cunardline.com

Disney Cruise Line: disney.go.com/DisneyCruise

Holland America Line: www.hollandamerica.com

Norwegian Cruise Line: www.ncl.com

Princess Cruises: www.princess.com

Royal Caribbean International: www.rccl.com

Seabourn Cruise Line: www.seabourn.com

Windjammer Barefoot Cruises: www.windjammer.com

Windstar Cruises: www.windstarcruises.com

Online Reviews

The most valuable advice online doesn't come from cruise companies—it's freely given by fellow travelers who offer independent assessments and opinions. A couple of sites, each featuring thousands of reviews, can help you decide what type of cruise you want, and perhaps more importantly, what you don't want. A nonstop party on a Carnival cruise might sound like a dream come true for some people—and a nightmare for others. What's most valuable about these databases is that they offer insightful and well-informed opinions from travel agents and people who have recently returned from their cruises. They can tell you what worked, and what didn't, on topics from getting to the port to whether it's worth paying more for an outside cabin.

CruiseOpinion.com

With more than 2,400 personal reviews, **CruiseOpinion.com (www.cruiseopinion. com)** is an excellent source for evaluating cruises. Reviews are sorted by cruise line and ship, with numerical rankings for about forty categories, from midnight buffets to shore excursions. The written reviews are often the most valuable part of CruiseOpinion.com, offering informal yet illuminating advice. Most reviewers include their age, occupation, and number of cruises they've taken, and some add their e-mail address so you can send follow-up questions.

Reviews are sorted by cruise line. There are nine categories: eight for each of the eight major lines and a ninth for the rest. Clicking on the link for Princess Cruises leads to a page of reviews for various Princess ships. It's a good idea to check reviews for different ships, even if they're all run by the same line, because they do vary. Most reviewers numerically rank dozens of categories, from the quality of the midnight buffets to whether a cruise would be good for honeymooners. But most valuable are reviewer's written descriptions, which offer insight into the cruise experience. Here's a critique of the *Dawn Princess*:

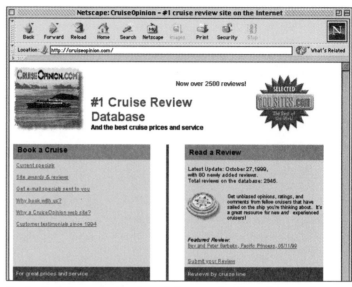

We had a verandah room and the balcony was really worth it. Not only for the views but for the extra room it affords you in the cabin. If you book real early (we were one year ahead), it doesn't cost that much more than an outside cabin. The large entertainment lounges were the only disappointment. They were comfortable, but the entertainment was weak and repetitive.

CruiseOpinion.com (cruiseopinion.com) offers thousands of frank reviews from other cruisers.

This is just a snippet from a much longer review. You may be amazed by the depth of the critiques and the lengths to which your fellow travelers are willing to go to share their experiences. CruiseOpinion.com is also an agency, featuring a free newsletter with some late-breaking deals.

TravelPage.com: Cruise Travel

Another useful site for choosing a cruise is called **TravelPage.com (www. travelpage.com/cruise).** This site has assessments of hundreds of cruises and a forum where you can find postings from others or ask a question of your own. Scroll down on the home page to the dozens of cruise lines and select one, then choose one of the ships for an assessment. At the top of each critique, you'll find the facts on each ship, including year built, number of cabins, and size of the ship. Lower down is a detailed review, including cabins, dining, public areas, and information.

The CruiseQuery feature is very helpful. Input where and when you want to go, what you can spend, and how many days you want to travel and CruiseQuery will suggest cruises that meet your criteria. And these are all linked to TravelPage's evaluations of each cruise, so you can comparison shop. If you find one you like, you can book through the agency behind this site, which promises a 10 percent discount on the cruise line's list price. Still, it's worth shopping around, because this discount might not be the best available.

Though TravelPage doesn't have the liveliness of CruiseOpinion.com, it does have some frank assessments of various lines. Here's a sample of TravelPage's review of Celebrity Cruises: "Why our beef with this line, especially since they provide a perfectly capable product? In our experience only Seabourn Cruises has so baldly employed the snob appeal in its attempt to win passengers. What Celebrity attempts to pass itself off as being, it cannot be, because the fares they collect do not permit them to operate the type of product they claim to be. And nothing in this business sets our teeth so badly on edge as pretense . . . and, whew, this fleet is full of it!"

TravelPage is also in the business of selling cruises, which could color the reviews, so be forewarned. It's hard to tell; they appear objective, and they can be critical, but most large agencies—online and off—favor some lines over others. Not surprisingly, they often have share arrangements with those they favor. Share agreements stipulate that if an agency sells a certain number of cruises on a particular line, they get extra commissions or bonuses, so they have incentives to recommend that line. That doesn't mean you can't trust reviews here; it just means you shouldn't rely solely on this site.

Fielding's Cruise Finder

If you're looking for advice from a well-known name in the guidebook business, consult **Fielding's Cruise Finder (www.fieldingtravel.com/cf/index.htm)**. The site reviews the major cruise lines and evaluates them in more than a dozen categories, including tips on the ships, cuisine, and who should (and should not) go. You'll find general categories on the home page, with tips for choosing a cruise, getting ready to go, and alternative cruises, among others. And you can search by region or name, or scroll through Fielding's rankings. **The Best of . . .** section lists top cruises for food, romance, value, families, adventure, and wheelchair access.

Unlike cruise agencies, Fielding's isn't trying to sell you anything (except their cruise guidebook), which lends more credibility to the reviews. As you might expect, reviews here can differ from those on other sites. Here's an example: While TravelPage rips Celebrity (see previous segment), Fielding's gives it two thumbs up: "In today's world, with value for the vacation dollar so important, it's comforting to sail with a cruise line that delivers high-quality food and service on a stylish ship at moderate prices."

One word of caution on Fielding's reviews: Some appear a bit dated. If a review is a year or two old, it may be inaccurate because cruise lines can make great leaps or sink in a hurry.

Cruise Lines International Association

As the leading trade association, **Cruise Lines International Association (CLIA); (www.cruising.org/index2.htm)** doesn't offer criticism, but it is an extensive database that can help you select a cruise. CLIA considers its endorsement to be akin to a Good Housekeeping seal, and for the most part, the major lines that are members are reputable.

Use the **Cruise Expert Locator** to find a cruise specialist in your area or an online agency that specializes in the type of cruise you're seeking. In **Choose Your Cruise,** more than one hundred major ships are profiled, while the **Vacation Travel Guide** lists dozens of cruise destinations worldwide. **Cruise News and Specials** has news releases about bargains, but again be forewarned that some of these "bargains" might not be such good deals.

Travelocity's Cruise Critic

If you're looking for an independent expert's opinion, **Cruise Critic**, hosted on Travelocity, **(www2.travel ocity.com/vacations/ html/cruiseCritic)** is a good place to look. Penned by author Anne Campbell, who a few years ago wrote *Fielding's Guide to Worldwide Cruises,* this site offer frank opinions about various lines. A section called Cruise Reviews covers all the major

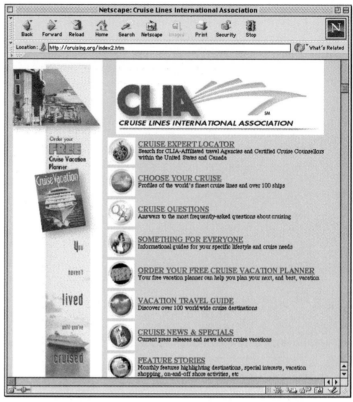

Cruise Lines International (cruising.org/index2.htm), a trade association, can help you select a cruise.

lines and ships, while other sections include general advice, tips for first-timers, and editor's picks. *Note:* If Cruise Critic's URL is too long to type, just go to **www.travelocity.com** and follow the links from the cruise section.

For AOL Users:

CRUISE CRITIC

Cruise Critic (keyword: *cruise critic*) includes news and bargains, advice to help you choose, tips for first-time cruisers, and picks from cruise critic Anne Campbell. The AOL Cruise Critic is similar to the one offered on Travelocity (see earlier section), but on AOL it's even simpler to navigate.

AOL's **Cruise Center** (keyword: *cruise*) teams with Travelon to offer a cruise selector. The site also includes links to late-breaking bargains and a forum of member opinions.

Seeking Advice *from* Fellow Travelers

Newsgroups and conference areas have been used extensively by cruise-goers and by people considering taking a cruise for the first time. The following account shows how younger people, who are seeking alternatives to formal cruises, are using the newsgroups to find the right cruise (for more information on how to use newsgroups, see chap. 13):

Ethan Solomita, a twenty-something software engineer for Silicon Graphics, wanted to spend his vacation on a cruise ship, but he didn't want to play shuffleboard and dress up for dinner every night. The following is an excerpt from a message entitled "Choosing a cruise when you're weird," which Ethan posted to the **rec.travel.cruises** newsgroup.

> I am not comfortable if I'm dressed up. I can do a suit and tie for a couple of dinners if I must, but I'd feel really uncomfortable in a suit for a whole evening. I don't want a touristy cruise. I have images of the boat docking at yet another Caribbean island, with yet another set of locals selling goods to the tourists. I don't enjoy shopping. I can't just sit on a beach for hours. Hiking, snorkeling, and ancient ruins all sound great. Driving in a bus to a "Mayan ruin" surrounded by tourists and people selling T-shirts is less than I'd hope for.

During the next few days, several people wrote back to Ethan, assuring him that no one is too young to cruise, that many cruises don't expect people to dress formally for dinner every night, and that he should look for long port visits, giving him time to explore.

"You might try cruising out of San Juan, and get there a couple of days early. That way, you could independently (we sense that's your style) take in Old San Juan, some nightlife, then take your cruise," wrote a veteran cruiser from Nashville, who suggested that Windjammer's sailing ship cruises might be what Ethan is looking for. Because Ethan said he's not into the big party scene, another cruiser recommended he avoid Carnival cruises and not travel during spring break.

Clicking over to **Windjammer Barefoot Cruises (www.windjammer.com)**, Ethan found information about Windjammer's fleet, departure dates, special singles' cruises, and an informative FAQ (frequently asked questions). Ethan could see images of the Windjammer sailing ships and ask follow-up questions through an e-mail address or toll-free number on the site.

Finding Cruise Deals

As mentioned in the chapter on budget travel, not too many cruise lines offer the type of last-minute deals available on flights, hotels, and cars. But that's likely to change soon as the world's big cruise companies continue to add megaliners to their armadas and will be eager to find ways to fill unsold cabins. And when the economy noses down, fewer people will be inclined to travel, which should lead the major cruise lines to look for new ways to fill those empty cabins.

One firm that's already using the Net to offer last-minute deals is Windjammer (mentioned earlier). Known for its tall-masted sailing ships, Windjammer recently introduced a program called **CyberSailors.** Sign up online for e-mail alerts, and ten days before departures, you'll receive an update on any available cabins, which can be booked at half-price. Of course, these are valid only for new bookings—you can't cancel an existing reservation and then book one of these deals.

Other sites, such as **1travel.com (onetravel. com)**, collect cruise deals, displaying these specials on their sites and sending them to subscribers of 1travel.com's e-mail newsletter. You can also find cruise deals at major sites, such as **Expedia.com**, by visiting the cruise sections of these sites and checking specials there. However, just because a price is listed online as a special bargain, that doesn't mean it's the best price available. It can pay to shop around—online and at traditional agencies.

> **tip**
>
> ■ Freighter cruises offer a different type of sea-based vacation—for more information, see Freighter World Cruises (www.freighterworld.com).

Online Cruise Magazines and Booking Sites

Each of the sites that follow can help you learn about cruises, from how sanitary the ships are to news about upcoming bargains. Some offer e-mail alerts to keep you posted about upcoming specials, but remember, agencies sometimes make these deals sound better than they really are. It usually pays to shop around.

CDC Vessel Sanitation Program (www.cdc.gov/nceh/programs/sanit/vsp/scores/scores.htm)

See how the Centers for Disease Control ranks ships on cleanliness and sanitation. Just about all of them pass (with overall scores above 85) but some are cleaner than others.

Cruise Fun (www.cruisefun.com)

Cruise Fun is one of those online agencies that can put you in touch with a cruise specialist in your home town. Just enter your zip code and Cruise Fun will recommend agencies near you. You can also use this site to search for cruises based on criteria (destination, price, number of days, etc.). The list of results has some prices, but Cruise Fun, which is also a travel agency, recommends you call for the current price, which is usually below the list price. Cruise Fun has some reviews from travelers, but not nearly as many as CruiseOpinion.com.

Cruise News (www.cruise-news.com)

Cruise News offers information on seasonal and themed cruises and about upcoming launches of new ships. You'll also find links to agents who specialize in selling cruise vacations.

Cruise News Daily (www.reply.net/clients/ cruise/news.html)

This site gives you a matter-of-fact daily update on cruise news, such as delays on a cruise line unveiling a new ship or special deals on off-peak cruises. You can sign up for a weekly e-mail dispatch or check the Web site for news items.

Cruise News: Exploring the World by Ship (www.romanticgetaways.com)

A couple of veteran travel writers compile this collection of features, advice, and infor-

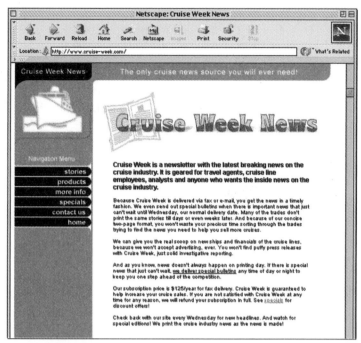

Cruise Week News (www.cruise-week.com) is one of several sites that provide updates by e-mail.

mation on what's new in cruising. You'll find ideas for shore-based excursions, tips for reducing the single supplement, and suggestions for coping with seasickness. Sign up, if you wish, for the biweekly e-mail newsletter.

Cruise Week News (www.cruise-week.com)

Cruise Week News posts a concise roundup of the week's cruise news each Wednesday. You can also have this dispatch delivered via e-mail.

Dialysis at Sea Cruises (www.dialysis-at-sea.com)

"Dialysis doesn't take a vacation—but you can . . . " says this Web site. Learn about cruises in the Caribbean and other destinations, all on ships outfitted to care for dialysis patients. Also see **ADA Vacations Plus (www.vacations-plus.com).**

Get Cruising (www.getcruising.com/cruising)

The site lets you sort its database, using such categories as average per diem cost, passenger space ratio, and number of cabins. You can also input your preferences and scan a list of suggested cruises, though this feature is a little clunky.

Internet Cruise Travel Network (www.cruisetravel.com)

The Internet Cruise Travel Network is an online cruise agency. You can check prices and look for special deals here. It has far too many unnecessary images, which makes surfing slow. A toll-free number is provided for latest fare quotes.

Summing Up

The options for cruising are almost as vast as the seven seas. Through online reviews, the opinions of fellow travelers, e-mail newsletters, and cruise line Web sites, it's become much easier to get informed and find good deals. And all this information should help you find what you want at a fair price. After your vacation, you can return the favor by reviewing your cruise, helping to keep fellow cruise-lovers informed about the latest developments.

Other Chapters to Check

Chapter 7: "Budget Travel"—Cruise deals

Chapter 13: "Online Discussion Forums"—Online bulletin boards that discuss cruises

---

USE THE NET *to* FIND THE IDEAL TRIP

Vacation Packages *and* Tour Directories

Many people work most of the year just to have a couple of weeks to do what they please. So they don't want to fritter away their hard-earned vacation time on trips that don't meet expectations. By using the Net, travelers can get a much better idea of the types of trips out there, and learn more by using these sites effectively. The Net is ideal for finding information about specific types of vacations, such as Elderhostel trips for seniors. It's also superb for off-the-beaten-track destinations, such as a honeymoon on the island of Ibiza. And for those who aren't quite sure how they want to spend their next vacation, the Net's a wonderful way to get ideas.

Travelers searching for vacations online can be divided into two main camps: Those who know what they want and are seeking more information, and those who are fishing for ideas. If you know what you want, for example, a Club Med vacation in the Caribbean, you can go straight to the **Club Med** site **(www.clubmed.com)** and check out the options.

If you're looking for ideas, it's helpful to start with a search directory, such as **Yahoo (yahoo.com)**, clicking on "Travel," and then "Tour Operators," where you'll find tours in dozens of categories, including **Boat Charters, Bus Tours,** and **Birdwatching**—and that's just some of the B's. Click on any category that appeals and visit tour operator Web sites to see if any of the trips strike your fancy. If you find a trip that looks good, you can follow up with questions via e-mail or phone calls.

Vacation Directories

Of course, search sites aren't the only places where you can find vacation ideas. Several Web sites provide directories of trips by location and by category. One of the most wide-ranging is called **Travelon (www.travelon.com)**, which includes such categories as **Golf, Romance, Ski, Family,** and **Learning and Culture**. Many of these categories have subcategories; under **Sports**, for example, you'll find Kayaking, Mountain Biking, Diving, and others.

Travelon has a nifty search feature. Here's how it works: Select "Golf," for example, and then choose a destination (let's try U.S.) and price (such as $1,000–$2,000). When I made this query, Travelon found nineteen trips at hotels and resorts from Florida to Hawaii. Each was listed with a brief description, contact information, and a link to more information if desired. Using an index like Travelon can be a more efficient way to search; rather than sorting through thousands of results on a search site, you typically get a shorter and more relevant list of links. But this is a selective list: You'll only get listings for companies that have paid to be on Travelon.

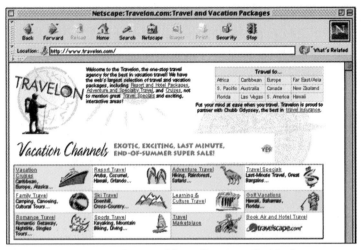

Travelon (www.travelon.com) is a directory that helps locate vacations by category.

Specialty Travel Index (www.spectrav.com discussed in chap. 8, "The Ultimate Adventure") is another search directory that lists trips by type and by location. From the home page, you can search for key terms or flip through listings in the **Interest/Activity Index, Geographical Index,** or **Tour Operator Listings.** Say you're looking for a literary tour in the United Kingdom. Go to the Interest/Activity Index, click on "Literary Tours," then click on "UK." Up come your choices, including **Select Travel Service,** which has a brief description of its tours, a link to its Web site, and e-mail address for further information.

Or you could check **Online Vacation Mall (onlinevacationmall.com),** a site that collects and sells vacation packages and tours. Featuring trips to popular destinations, such as Las Vegas and Florida, this site lets you explore options and book online. It can also update you with an e-mail alert for specials. And for last-minute deals on vacation packages, don't forget sites mentioned in chapter 7, such as **LastMinuteTravel.com** and **1travel.com**.

For AOL Users:

VACATION CENTER

AOL's **Vacation Center** (keyword: *vacation center*) includes sections on cruising, adventure, theme parks, casinos, and many more. *Bargains* lists trips by departure city and by type (resort packages, specialty vacations, etc.). You'll find a section listing deals from travel supplies such as Renaissance Cruises.

More Sources for Vacation Packages

Arthur Frommer's Budget Travel (www.frommers.com) produces a daily newsletter made up mostly of the latest package deals to destinations from Fiji to Florence and just about every place in between. Frommer, who's been scouring the globe for almost half a century searching for great deals, delivers his findings seven days a week in an e-mail newsletter. You can sign up for the newsletter at the site or search the archives **(www.frommers.com /search/news_search_ adv.html)**. If you simply want to peruse the newsletters from the past thirty days, go to **www.frommers.com/ newsletters/archives)**.

It's also a good idea to check the big booking sites, such as **Expedia.com** and **Travelocity (www.travel ocity.com)**, which list vacation packages and often have special deals.

Travelocity also has well-organized and extensive list of specials. From the home page, click **"Vacations and Cruises,"** where you'll find **Hot Deals,**

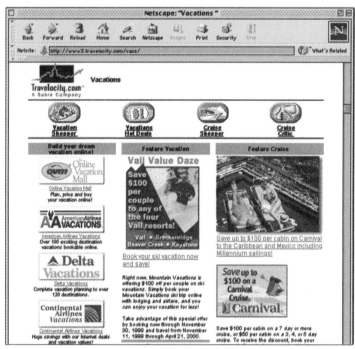

Travelocity, like other major booking sites, has a section on vacation planning (www3.travelocity.com/vacs).

such as the recent offer of five nights at Bangkok's Royal River Hotel for $669, including round-trip airfare from any of the western United States. You can also use the **Vacation Index** to find trips by region.

Expedia.com takes a different approach, featuring links to package vacation providers, such as **Backroads (backroads.com)**, and to sites that offer vacations by type, such as **Golf Travel Online (gto.com)**. This is a nice feature because it zips you directly to some of the leading sites by category, whatever your interest. Of course, these aren't the only worthwhile sites for each category—you can find many more through search sites, where you can search for key terms or drill down by category.

Family Vacations

There are probably as many different family vacations as there are families. Although some destinations, such as Walt Disney World, are almost universally popular among families with young children, there's much more out there. You can find cruises that cater to kids, restaurants and hotels that are especially friendly to kids, and attractions in cities around the world that will delight children of any age—and maybe even their parents.

siteseeing

Disney Theme Parks

If you were to poll a thousand kids, there's little doubt that their top travel choice would be a Disney theme park. From Disney's main page (disney.go.com), you can leap into Walt Disney World or Disneyland. We'll discuss Disney World's site (disney.go.com/disneyworld) here, which will also give you a pretty good idea of how to navigate Disneyland's site.

Walt Disney World's home on the Web is a vast virtual wonderland designed to help you take care of the real-world tasks necessary to make your Disney fantasy come true. In the left-hand column of the home page, you'll find tools for planning and booking your vacation, as well as links to advice about the theme parks, resorts, entertainment, and dining options. The rest of the home page features what's new at Disney World, such as the most recent addition to Disney's Animal Kingdom. And don't miss the calendar link near the bottom of the home page, which gives you a month-by-month update of what's going on.

tip

■ Pamela Lanier's familytravelguides.com includes family travel tips, destination advice, suggestions for enjoying the great outdoors, and special deals for family travel.

Here is a thumbnail sketch of what you'll find in each section of Disney World's site. All the following sections are reachable from Disney World's main page:

■ **Vacation Planning:** Start by getting oriented with maps of Walt Disney World, and then peruse the hotel and restaurant options. Use the Theme Park Attraction Search to locate attractions suited to any age group at Epcot, the Magic Kingdom, or any of the other theme parks.

■ **Tickets Online:** Learn about all the choices for theme park passes, as well as packages that include park admissions and lodging. You can then order online. Click on "Resort Reservations" to make hotel reservations and order park admission passes.

■ **Theme Parks:** All the latest details on Epcot, Magic Kingdom Park, Disney— MGM Studios, and Disney's Animal Kingdom are here. Information includes operating hours, ticket information, parade descriptions, maps, and special services for disabled visitors. There are even Web cams that let you see live images from Disney World.

■ **Entertainment, Shopping, and Dining:** Consider this a starting point for each of the major entertainment areas, such as Disney's BoardWalk. From here you can explore dining, shopping, and entertainment options to get a better sense of where you want to go. There are also links to kids' programs, baby-sitting services, and Camp Disney, so that you'll know your children will be taken care of while you enjoy a night on the town.

■ **Water Parks, Recreation, & Sports:** Descriptions of water parks, golf courses (and minigolf for the kids), tennis courts, and fishing holes; health clubs and spas; and Disney's Wide World of Sports Complex are just part of what's listed here.

Family.com: Travel

The **Family.com** travel page **(family.go.com/Categories/Travel)** is almost as enticing, and as overwhelming, as a kid's first glimpse of Disney World. Hosted on the **Go** network **(go.com)**, which is owned by Disney, Family.com is a remarkably extensive set of resources that can help you find and plan your family's next trip.

But don't get too excited, this site has some drawbacks. I took the **Family Travel Planner** for a test drive, first searching for a trip in the western United States. This yielded some good options but also included a link to New York State Park resorts. Hmmm. I tried another search: this time for theme parks under the Vacation Type heading. What came up was a full-page ad for a Ford minivan, which was really confusing. The page said it would quickly roll over to my search results, but it didn't, so I had to click a link to get there. When I went back and tried again, it did roll over quickly, but this ad was still an irritating distraction. Maybe that's the price we'll soon be paying for all this free information, though I hope not.

On the positive side, Family.com's Travel page has some great feature stories from magazines like *FamilyFun,* such as a recent piece on fifty-three "must-see" attractions. Even better is a section called **Family Friendly City Guides,** which has suggestions for kids' activities in fourteen U.S. cities. The list of cities was a bit odd—Jacksonville was covered while San Francisco wasn't—but the listings were outstanding. For example, clicking on Philadelphia yielded dozens of listings, such as one for the Crayola factory tour, including a review and suggestions for the tour and a link to Crayola's site.

Rounding out the site is a forum called **Road-Tested Vacations,** where you can read other travelers' posts about their trips or post a message of your own. Say you were interested in taking a family cruise on the Big Red Boat. Click on "Road-Tested Vacations," then "Cruises," and you'll see several comments on Big Red Boat. A sampling of the online reviews produced one family that loved their cruise and two reviewers who thought it was merely above average. Beyond the rankings were some comments that can help you decide whether a particular trip is for you.

A Gateway to Family Travel Sites

Although Disney and Family.com provide some outstanding resources for planning a family trip, lots of other worthwhile sites can help plan family trips. If you want to see what's out there, you can simply type "family travel" into your favorite search engine or visit a collection of family travel sites, such as the one culled by **About.com**. Each topic in About.com has links chosen by a human guide, not a bot. The collection for **Family Travel (travelwithkids.about.com)**, selected by guide Teresa Plowright, is quite helpful.

tip

■ Road trips can make great family vacations. (For tips on using the Net to plan road trips, see chap. 5.)

There are general categories, such as **Children's Museums,** as well as sections for destinations, such as **Hawaii with Kids.** Each section has plenty of links to Web sites where you can explore possible family vacations. You'll also find some short feature articles, such as "Summer Vacation Ideas," that can help you decide where to go. And if you have questions, you can send e-mail to Teresa (just click on her byline for a page that lists her address), and she may respond with advice.

Expedia's Family Travel (expedia.com/daily/family) includes offers on vacation packages for families, tips from author Eileen Ogintz on taking the kids, an airport survival guide, and forums where you can discuss family trips with other travelers.

One Family Lives Its Dream

Many folks dream of selling their house, quitting their jobs, packing up the kids, and hitting the road for a year or two. David Cohen, his wife, and their three children, did just that, embarking on a year-long, round-the-world odyssey. But thanks to the Net, they didn't have to sever all ties to their life back home. The Cohens packed a laptop computer, which enabled them to communicate with their friends and family throughout the United States. David's nine-year-old daughter Kara used the laptop to send trip reports to her classmates at Park School in Mill Valley, California, and to chat with her friends and classmates.

First Person: David Cohen

(*Note:* David wrote the following dispatch during his family's round-the-world trip. His book, *One Year Off,* was published in 1999 by Simon & Schuster.)

E-mail is very useful to us, and we log in wherever we can. My mother is handling a lot of our business while we are gone. I gave her an old Powerbook, and we communicate with her most conveniently through AOL. We get 5 to 10 messages a day.

I also wrote an article for the *San Francisco Chronicle* about selling the house, quitting the job, and hitting the road for a year with the three kids. I put our e-mail address at the bottom and was surprised to get nearly 50 responses. Most were from people who had done, planned to do, or wished they could someday do, the same thing. A lot of encouragement. Several people invited us to drop in when we were in India or South Africa, for example.

The e-mail relationship between Kara and her class is very positive. The kids in the class are learning a lot about the world, and Kara loves getting the e-mail and keeping in contact. It is also a good writing discipline for her, and has taught her how to use the computer and the Net pretty painlessly. It is not magical to her at all. She has been around computers since she can remember, and thinks it is all as normal as the TV or the telephone or traveling around the world.

Later in the trip, Kara was on AOL at the same time as Kara's friend and classmate Christine Ogawa. Kara and Christine used AOL's Buddy feature, a type of instant messaging, to see that they were online at the same time and began a chat session, whereby they could "talk" to one another by typing messages back and forth.

A trip around the world may not be your cup of tea, but even if your family journey is just for a month or so, letting the kids stay in touch with friends back home is great idea. E-mail lets them share the excitement of the trip with their peers during a time when they are cooped up with two stuffy grown-ups, and it can help keep homesickness at bay.

For AOL Users:

FAMILY TRAVEL NETWORK

Family Travel Network (keyword: *family travel network*) is chock full of ideas, including trips listed by interest (kids' museums, dinosaur treks, etc.) and bargains for family travel. The Destinations section includes planning advice, features about top vacation spots, and information on the best places for families to stay.

Learning Vacations

For those who want to do more than lie on a beach during their vacations, **Learning Vacations (www.learningvacations.com)** is a site that offers you trips ranging from sailing schools to safaris. Or you could join a field research team through **Earthwatch Institute (www.earthwatch.org)** where, for example, you can sign up for a trip to Nanning City, China, in an effort to help preserve the habitat of the white-headed langur, a highly endangered primate.

Others may be interested in a birding tour in Costa Rica's forests. Or an excursion to Nepal to see the Dumje Festival, a four-day celebration with chanting, dancing, and exotic costumes. To explore these and dozens of other travel alternatives, see **EarthWise Journeys (www.teleport.com/~earthwyz)**. Several groups, such as **Elderhostel, Inc. (www.elderhostel.com)**, offer learning vacations for seniors (see "Seniors" later in this chapter.)

Honeymoons in Paradise

Lord knows, couples are busy enough when they're planning a wedding. So it's not surprising that many impending newlyweds are employing the Web to find ideas for their honeymoons or simply corresponding via e-mail with agents who are planning their week or two of postnuptial bliss. For those wanting to get a jump on what to consider when planning a honeymoon, the Net can help.

Honeymoons.com and Modern Bride

Honeymoons.com (honeymoons.com) is a terrific resource. **Destinations** covers mostly Mexican and Caribbean getaways, with hints for honeymoons for each place. An example for Cozumel: "Best Bargain Bet: Playa Azul, $52–$59. Small, sweet, and simple. No frills, on the beach." The site has other ideas to help couples get the most from their vacations, such as this one, also from the Cozumel page: "Bring your own snorkel mask so you won't have to wait in line getting fitted for rentals."

A section called **Tips** discusses what couples should consider during the planning process ("Do you want to save or splurge—do you want to be lively or lazy?"). These may sound like obvious questions, but lots of couples overlook the basics. Tips also has hints, such as "Everybody loves a lover. Tell everyone along the way: your travel agent, airline personnel, hotel front desks, etc., that you're on your honeymoon. You'll be surprised at the number of smiles and perks this can bring you!" It's no surprise that Honeymoons.com is such a fine resource; it's written by Susan Wagner, who spent a decade producing the honeymoon section of *Modern Bride* magazine.

Speaking of *Modern Bride,* the online version of the magazine has a honeymoon section **(www.modernbride.com/honeymoonplanning/index.cfm)** that has lots of valuable advice. **Best Places to Go** lists top destinations by category, such as Most Romantic, Best Value, Best Beaches, and Best Destination Weddings (for couples who want to get married at their honeymoon destination). It also has sections for popular honeymoon destinations, such as Hawaii and France. **Hot Spots & Cool Ideas** covers dozens of destinations (scroll to the bottom of the page for links).

For AOL Users:

THE KNOT
The Knot (keyword: *knot*) is a general wedding site that has a link to Honeymoon Escapes, which lists top honeymoon destinations and sorts trips into categories, including adventure, beach, exotic, Hawaiian, European, etc.

Other Honeymoon Sites

Many of the strategies discussed in chapter 1, "Destination Anywhere," can help when you're looking for a honeymoon. However, there are sites such as **Honeymoon Travel (www.honeymoontravel.com),** that feature solely trips for newlyweds. Honeymoon Travel is an agency that's specific in focus, covering primarily Caribbean destinations and highlighting all-inclusive resorts, such as **Sandals (www.sandals.com)**. Honeymoon

Travel negotiates rates for its clients and provides a request form online that you can send via e-mail to get price quotes. The company also has promotions and incentives, such as a recent offer for $300 worth of free dinnerware for any couple booking a stay of six nights or longer at any Sandals resort.

A great source for honeymoon bargains is **1travel.com (onetravel.com)**, which frequently updates its list of deals for honeymooners. From the home page, scroll down to the **Specialty** section and click on "Honeymoons." Typically, you'll find more than one hundred listings, including special airfare deals and bargains and package vacations. These deals are offered through travel agencies that are part of 1travel.com's network. Here's a recent deal offered through New Jersey–based Resort Outlet: free air transportation for two from the United States to any Sandals resorts for any couple staying six nights or more.

An Internet Honeymoon

Leslie Camino-Markowitz, a public relations specialist from Santa Rosa, California, planned her honeymoon on the Net and ended up realizing more benefits than she ever imagined. Here is Leslie's story:

First Person: Leslie Camino-Markowitz

I'm a real rookie. I just got in there and started exploring, searching for travel in Spain. I got a list of travel agents through **Webcrawler (webcrawler.com)**, and one had a description for the island of Ibiza (near Spain's east coast). I sent e-mail to the agency called **Festive Travel (www.festivetravel.com/ibiza.htm)** that had the Web page on Ibiza. I received a response the next day. They asked for more information and said, "Tell us what your tastes are."

We told them we wanted something that's adventurous, romantic, and a good deal. They responded the next day with some ideas and found a great place for us in Ibiza. They know the area and can find what you want. They made it very simple. We were blown away because it was the first time we've done anything through the Net. I just get in there and play. I'm not a techie person.

We were in the middle of getting married and forgot the paperwork about what hotel we were staying at. We couldn't find the agency in any phonebooks. Just then, I remembered there was an Internet cafe in Barcelona. So we rented a computer and sent e-mail saying we forgot our paperwork and need to know our hotel for the island of Ibiza. We asked them to fax the information to our hotel, but we never received a fax.

When we got to Ibiza there were two gentlemen with a big sign saying "Camino-Markowitz." It was the two travel agents who made the arrangements from Ibiza, two Americans who are working from the island. They met us and took us to the hotel. Not only that, they got us a room with a beautiful view because they wanted to make sure our honeymoon was perfect.

Leslie and Michael may have eventually found the hotel without a Net connection, but their story highlights the Net's usefulness both before and during a trip. Would they have ever learned of remote Ibiza without surfing the Net? Maybe. But then again, maybe not. And, remote as it was, their e-mail plea for help reached the travel agents in Ibiza and solved their problem.

Seniors: Special Trips and Discounts

Though some people view the Net as the domain of the young and shiftless, seniors have gone online in droves. And they're finding that it can be an essential planning tool for everything from last-minute weekend getaways to learning vacations for elders. Best of all, seniors are using the Net to become more informed about discounts available on airlines, cruises, hotels rooms, and more. Most airlines, for example, have special deals for seniors, and publicize these offers online. Other travel suppliers, such as tour companies, often offer last-minute deals at deep discounts, deals that retired seniors can snap up, if they can be flexible.

An Online Senior Center

Wouldn't it be nice if there was one place on the Web where you could find a whole compendium of resources for senior travelers? Well, there is, and it's part of a larger site you've already heard about. The **Yahoo Seniors' Guide** has an excellent **Travel** section **(seniors.yahoo.com/seniors/travel/index.html)**, which highlights special trips and deals for seniors.

Yahoo Seniors' Guide has done a terrific job of combining Top Picks, such as **European Walking Tours (www.walkingtours.com)**, with other tour operators and travel agents who specialize in trips for seniors. You'll also find links to airlines' and hotels' discount programs and offers for seniors. At Yahoo's online travel forum for seniors, you can discuss a wide range of topics, such as "Seasonal Accommodation in Florida." Yahoo's senior center also links to Yahoo's main directory, which has more sites to check out, such as **Seniors Home Exchange (www.seniorshomeexchange.com)**, which helps seniors arrange home swaps to save on hotel costs.

tip

■ **The American Association of Retired Persons maintains a travel page (www.aarp.org/travel) that includes travel stories, an interactive forum, and information on AARP's Purchase Privilege Programs, which provide discounts on hotel rooms, airline tickets, cruises, and more.**

Airline Deals for Seniors

To find discounts for seniors, visit an airline's Web page, such as **United Airlines (www.ual.com)**, and look for information on senior fares. United's convoluted site isn't easy to navigate, so it's best to go directly to the airline's **Silver Wings Plus** program by typing in its URL **(www.silverwingsplus.com)**. Currently, this program, for those 55 and older, has a fee of $150 for two years, or $225 for lifetime membership, but the airline says the free coupons, vouchers, bonus frequent flier miles, and other savings can more than make up for the fee.

Silver Wings Plus has some interesting offers, such as a program called **USA Collection** (I know, it sounds like they're after unpaid bills), which calculates fares based on number of miles flown, and can be an especially good deal for midrange flights. For example, if you fly between 1,001 and 3,000 miles round-trip, you'll pay $178 Monday through Thursday and $198 Friday or Saturday. The program doesn't appear to offer Sunday flights.

Now, if you were flying from Minneapolis to Billings, which is about 1,500 miles round-trip, you could fly for as little as $178. Because these airports don't have much traffic between one another, it would probably be much more expensive to fly on a conventional ticket. United also works with all sorts of other travel suppliers, including Holland America Line and Sheraton hotels, which has offered as much as 35 percent off rooms in Hawaii.

United isn't the only airline offering discounts for seniors. **American Airlines (aa.com)** has a program for seniors called **Senior TrAAveler Fares.** From the home page, go to the pull-down menu for Specials and select "Senior Fares" to learn about current deals. The discounts, offered to anyone sixty-two and older, include 10 percent off tickets to most destinations, coupon books, and other bargains.

> **tip**
>
> ■ SeniorNet (www.seniornet.org) is a general site for seniors that has a lively discussion group, where you can discuss travel issues.

Many other airlines have similar deals. For a list of airlines and their Web addresses, see the Web directories at the back of this book, or **Airlines of the Web (www.flyaow. com)**.

Elderhostel for Lifelong Learning

One of the most popular travel options for seniors is **Elderhostel, Inc. (www.elder hostel.org)**, which offers courses for seniors in inviting locations around the world. At the Elderhostel site, travelers can peruse a catalog of courses that appeal to older travelers, such as a weeklong course in California on San Francisco's literary heritage or an astronomy course in New Hampshire. Other programs travel to more than seventy international destinations, including Greece, to study the art and architecture of this ancient civilization.

To help people get more familiar with Elderhostel's programs, the site has sections, such as **Elderhostel Exper-ience** and **First-Time Visitor,** that let you know what to expect. **Program Options** lists various types of Elderhostels, including Active Outdoor, Intergenerational, as well as courses for the hearing-impaired.

Elderhostel has put its catalogs online **(www. elderhostel.org/cata log)**, so you can search the U.S. and Canada catalog or the international catalog. Find trips that match keywords (such as *myth*), or just browse through the catalog by choosing types of programs. For example, click on "Adventures Afloat," then "Natchez to New Orleans," and you'll get a long page with a detailed course description, dates and prices, and information about the accommodations. You can sign up online to have the printed catalog sent to you or subscribe to e-mail alerts that let you know when a new online catalog is posted to the Web site.

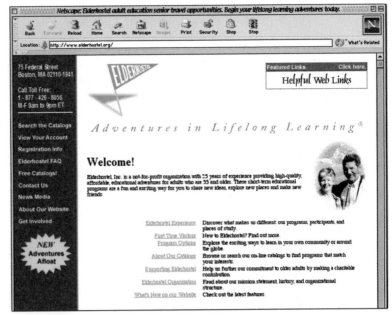

Elderhostel, Inc. (www.elderhostel.org) offers adventures for lifelong learning.

Other Programs for Seniors

ElderTreks (www.eldertreks.com) says it's "the world's first adventure travel company dedicated exclusively to people 50 and over." Whether that's true or not doesn't much matter—what counts is that the company appears to offer some terrific tours wrapped in a philosophy of continued learning and active adventure. Here's a snippet from the site: "Our trips explore the culture and nature of a destination while traveling sensitively in small groups limited to 15 people." The site goes on to say you should be in reasonable shape but don't have to go through boot camp to prepare for one of these trips.

ElderTreks' home page greets visitors with a signpost pointing to various destinations, such as Europe, the Americas, and South Pacific. Click on one to gain more information on programs to that region. A click on "Southeast Asia" led to information on trips to Laos, Thailand, and Borneo, among other destinations. Each was listed with a brief description, tour dates, and prices. A click on "Photo Library" yielded a page of compelling images for each destination. If you're on the fence, a peek at the photos may convince you to go. And if you ever want more information, you can send e-mail or call the company's toll-free number; both are listed at the bottom of most pages.

Because seniors tend to have the time and disposable income to travel, many Web sites cater to seniors. (For more sites, see the Web directories at the back of the book.)

Sites *for* Disabled Travelers

Earlier we discussed how the Net, at its root, is about people helping one another. For travelers with special needs or physical challenges, this type of communication is even more essential. Fortunately, several excellent sites serve the disabled and some have trip reports from travelers evaluating the accessibility of travel destinations around the world.

Access-Able Travel Source

Created by Carol Randall, who has multiple sclerosis, and her husband Bill, **Access-Able Travel Source (www.access-able.com)** is an essential site for disabled travelers. Here's the message from Access-Able's welcome page:

> We have always liked to travel, and, like many of you, don't get to do it enough. Carol has MS and uses a wheelchair or scooter. This has given us some first-hand experience with unpleasant surprises and access problems. That's why we started Access-Able Travel Source. We are not travel agents, just travelers. We think we have come up with a way to help fellow travelers help themselves.

Here's what you can expect from each section:

- **Tips:** Answers to FAQs (frequently asked questions) on topics ranging from traveling with oxygen to finding a hotel room.
- **Travel Agents:** A list of those who specialize in planning trips for people with special needs.
- **Cruise Lines:** A listing of ships accessible to those with physical challenges.
- **Forums and Bulletin Board:** An online discussion area where you can read others' posts or speak out yourself.
- **Relay and TTY Telephone Numbers:** A listing of travel companies' (Hertz, Hilton, etc.) phone numbers for the hearing impaired.
- **More Links:** Below the major headings are links to travel accounts submitted by readers, featured tours, a monthly newsletter, and links to other Web sites.

Other Resources for Disabled Travelers

Emerging Horizons (emerginghorizons.com) is an accessible travel magazine and newsletter, with lively features, such as "The Kiwi Way." Most useful is the **Travel Resources** section, where you can find links for accessible tours, lodgings, transportation, and recreation around the world. The lodging section, for example, includes links to other Web sites that list accessible accommodations, such as **Ireland Accessible Lodging List (www.iol.ie/infograf/dtour/intro.html)**. Columns such as **Travel Tips** and **The Curious Traveler** have insightful tidbits for planning vacations or finding accessible destinations.

GlobalAccess (www. geocities.com/Paris/1502) is another site where disabled travelers can find resources to ease their journeys. Richard Stricker, who maintains the site, has collected dozens of links to other Web sites, such as **Dialysis Finder (www. dialysisfinder.com)**, that can help you find a dialysis unit anywhere in the United States. You'll also find excellent resources for traveling in Europe, such as **Everybody's Hotel Directory (www. everybody.co.uk)**, which lists thousands of accessible lodging options in the United Kingdom.

A section called **Tips, Trips and Resources** offers advice on trip planning, including suggestions for choosing a travel agent and taking an attendant. In a section called **Readers Write,** disabled travelers share their concerns, tips, and advice, such as reports on what hotels are accessible. "The greatest strength of Global Access lies in its ability to provide disabled travelers with a place to network and share ideas and experiences," Stricker says.

Access-Able (www.access-able.com) is a rich source of information for disabled travelers.

Connecting Online with Other Disabled Travelers

Finally, if you have specific questions about travel for the disabled, the best sources can be newsgroups, forums, and e-mail lists, such as the Yahoo Seniors forum discussed earlier.

An excellent e-mail list for disabled travelers is called **Travable**. To subscribe, send e-mail to listserv@maelstrom.stjohns.edu and in the body of the message, put "subscribe travable" (without the quotations). Once on the e-mail list, you get a copy of each message delivered into your e-mail box, which helps you get to know the other members, fostering a virtual community.

For special needs travel, try Usenet newsgroups (discussion forums), such as **misc.handicap**. You can also post to general newsgroups, such as **rec.travel.cruises** and mention that you have special needs. A helpful tool for finding forums by topic or subject is a Web site called **Deja.com**. (For more on online forums, see chap. 13.)

For Women Only

It's no secret that most women take a different approach to travel than men do. And the Web offers lots of sites created by women travelers that reflect the desires and interests of women on the go. The Web can be the perfect place to find a women-only tour, get tips about traveling solo, connect with like-minded female travelers, or simply follow the adventures of intrepid women who are blazing trails across the globe.

A good way to start your search is with a directory, such as **Femina (femina.cyber grrl.com),** that includes a travel category with sites for women travelers. You can also consult a mainstream directory like Yahoo and search for "women travel," which yielded more than 200 sites when I tried it, or drill down from Travel to the section for women travelers. Here's a sample of what's out there:

Hitchhiking Vietnam: Letters from the Trail (www.pbs.org/hitchhikingvietnam)

Although *Hitchhiking Vietnam* author Karin Muller has been criticized for misrepresenting her journey, she has assembled a compelling site documenting her "solo hitchhiking" odyssey through Vietnam. This site is produced by PBS, which aired a documentary covering Karin's trip.

Journeywoman (www.journeywoman.com)

Journeywoman is an outspoken online magazine that offers a free subscription to an informative e-mail newsletter. The Web site includes **Girl Stuff Guides** to cities around the world, while **Ms. Biz** has advice for female execs. **Fab Travel Treats** includes tours, lodging, eco-adventures, and much more, all catering to women. Each new issue of Journeywoman has lively features, such as "Solo Dining: Make it Fun" and "Two Women and a Baby in Africa." At the bottom of the home page is a terrific directory. Its topics range from "The Older Adventuress" to "Her Spa Stop."

Maiden Voyages (maiden-voyages.com) has a directory of tours for women.

Maiden Voyages (maiden-voyages.com)

This magazine for women travelers has an excellent directory of tours, lodgings, and Web sites. Categories include Cruises, Packing, Kayaking, Spiritual, and many others.

Rough Guides: Women Travel (www.roughguides.com/women)

If you enjoy travel tales written by some of the world's leading women writers, you'll be enthralled by this site. Dozens of exquisitely rendered tales appear here, such as excerpts from Sara Wheeler's "Travels in a Thin Country," which describes her time in Chile.

Wild Women Adventures (www.wildwomenadv.com)

Wild Women Adventures is just one of many tour companies that cater to adventurous women travelers. But not every adventure has to include shooting down a river in Borneo. Wild Women offers trips for women who like to have a good time and who enjoy their comforts. Sample trips include Les Femmes Sauvages en France and Fiesta de los Locos in Mexico. For other tour companies for women, look up the keywords *"women travel tours"* in Yahoo or another search directory.

WomenNetworking.com's Weekend Passport (www.women-networking.com/weekendpassport/Welcome.html)

With a **Virtual Survival Kit, 10 Commandments of Travel,** and some basic destination guides, this nice little site can help you plan trips to wherever your journeys may take you.

Especially *for* Gays & Lesbians

Finding destinations, lodgings, and nightspots that welcome gays or lesbians can make or break a vacation. Though prejudice and bigotry rear their ugly heads all over the world, employing online resources can lead to better choices about places that welcome gays and lesbians. And the Web is a fine place to find tours specifically for gays or lesbians, such as **Olivia Cruises & Resorts (www.oliviatravel.com)**, which specializes in tours for women.

Getting Your Feet Wet

PlanetOut Travel (www.planetout.com/pno/travel) calls itself "the definitive source for lesbian and gay travel information." The site includes a guide to destinations around the world; wide-ranging features, such as "Mazatlan: Mexican Charm on the Beach"; and a travelogue section called **Pink Highways: Tales of Queer Madness on the Road**.

Story Categories has several sections, including **Fun in the Sun, Outdoor Adventures,** and **Lesbian Travel,** great places to get personal accounts of trips, such as "Amsterdam for Lesbians." PlanetOut Travel also has a search page—I searched for "London" and got about a dozen listings, including guidebook information, features, and other listings.

Of course, there are loads of other guides for gay and lesbian travelers. You can find many simply by searching for key terms, such as "gay paris" or drill down at Yahoo. Here's an example: Go to Yahoo and click on "Travel" (under the Recreation & Sports heading), then click on "Destination Guides," then on "Lesbians, Gay and Bisexuals." Et voilà, you'll find dozens of links to gay guides, from **Acapulco Gay Directory (casa condesa.com/gay. acapulco.directory. htm)** to the **Rio Gay Guide (ipanema.com/ rio/gay)**.

PlanetOut Travel (planetout.com/pno/travel) is an extensive guide for gay and lesbian travelers.

For AOL Users:

PLANETOUT TRAVEL

PlanetOut Travel (keyword: *PNO Travel*) is also available on AOL and includes many of the same features found on the PlanetOut Web site, plus lots of message boards and chat rooms to connect with other gay and lesbian travelers.

Advice from Fellow Travelers

As many gay, lesbian, and bisexual travelers already know, some of the most useful advice comes from fellow travelers. The Net has made it possible to network with the gay community at large, as travelers from around the world offer one another advice on Web forums, newsgroups, and AOL boards. Here's an example: Yahoo has a series of travel bulletin boards—go to **messages.yahoo.com/index.html**, click on "Travel," then "Lifestyles," then on "Lesbian, Gay and Bisexual," where the following message appeared:

Traveling to Miami or Key West

Hi, I am looking to possibly take a vacation in Late Feb/Early March to either Miami or Key West, traveling from CT. I am looking for one of two things. Either info on some reasonably priced places to stay that cater to a gay clientele or are at least gay friendly, or someone who might be interested in being a travel partner and splitting the costs. I am not looking for sex with this person, but in either event, you must be sane and mature, not into drugs, etc., a non-smoker, between 25 and 40. Anyone who has any information on lodgings or interest in sharing the hotel room can leave a message here with a way to contact you. Thanks, any and all replies appreciated.

The author left his first name and e-mail address, so people could contact him directly or post a note in the forum. Soon afterward, the following response was posted:

Hey Mark—Newton Street Station is a nice place, a little off the beaten path but very reasonable. John is the owner and he lives next door. Bruce and I stayed for a week last August in room #6 for $60 per night. The room was small but clean, good air-conditioning (which is important in the Keys), had a 1/2 bath connected to room, but the shower you used was the outdoor one by the pool. The other guests at that time were all in your age bracket and well behaved. Because of the short distance to the nightlife on Duval Street, bike rentals are included in the price of the room—we had no problem riding around town—in fact, it was fun. Oh yeah, they have a decent free continental breakfast poolside each morning with Miami and Key West newspapers and fresh squeezed orange juice, coffee, and pastries.

This response shows how much detail fellow travelers are willing to offer. And this information has more authenticity than a hotel's Web site, because the writer isn't trying to sell a room; he's just recommending a place he enjoyed. There are lots of other online forums where you can connect with travelers; we'll discuss these in chapter 13.

Studying, Working, & Living Abroad

Whether you're a college student who'd like to spend a year abroad or someone who's interested in working on another part of the planet, the Net is a valuable resource for planning your trip. In chapter 8 we discussed resources for planning around-the-world trips—here we'll focus on travelers who plan to stay in one destination for some time.

Studyabroad.com

If you're serious about spending part of your academic career overseas, don't overlook **Studyabroad.com**. Whether your pleasure is a semester at sea or studying Spanish in Guatemala, Studyabroad.com is a good starting point, with listings for thousands of study-abroad programs in more than one hundred countries throughout the world. Studyabroad.com also includes the following:

- ▪ **The Studyabroad.com Handbook:** This nuts-and-bolts guide has topic headings such as Reverse Culture Shock, Immunizations, and Costs and Documents.

- **Search for a Study Abroad Program:** This is a directory of study-abroad programs, including intensive language programs, summer programs, and others.
- **Study Abroad Discussion Boards:** Scroll through others' messages or post one of your own.

For dozens of other resources for studying abroad, see **Yahoo's Study Abroad Listings (dir.yahoo.com/Education/Programs/Study_Abroad)** or simply enter the term "study abroad" in your favorite search engine.

More Resources for Extended Stays Abroad

Transitions Abroad (www.TransitionsAbroad.com) began as a print magazine, and like much of the best online content, combined its established content with new material for the Web. Transitions' well-designed site has sections called **Work, Study, Travel,** and **Living**, each with short descriptions of programs, internships, and resources for working or studying abroad. Most of these have e-mail or Web links where you can learn more. You can also preview *Trans-itions Abroad*'s bi-monthly issues, and if you see one that has stories you're interested in, you can buy that issue through an online order form.

The **Council on International Educational Exchange (www.ciee.org)** is another useful site for those interested in studying, working, or volunteering abroad. The home page includes a clickable map: Start with the place where you live and see what overseas programs are available. You'll also find advice on essential items, such as student I.D. cards. Faculty programs are also listed. Once you know where you're going, you can click over to **Council Travel (www. counciltravel.com)**, where you might find good deals on airline tickets, rail passes, and more.

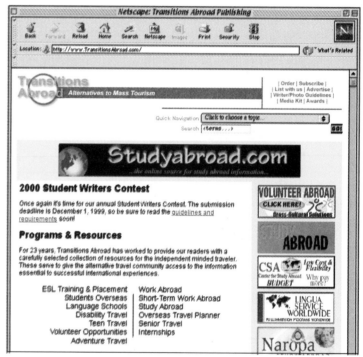

Transitions Abroad (www.TransitionsAbroad.com) helps those who want more than a week on a beach when they travel.

Summing Up

Whew, what more can you say. The 7,000 or so words in this chapter are testimony to the range and diversity of vacation planning sites. Whether you're a senior searching for educational trips to England or a gay man trying to figure out where to stay in Sydney, there's most likely a site or a person out there willing to help. We've entered a new age in which travel agents aren't the primary source of travel information. Communities of travelers are using the Web to inform one another, leading to richer journeys for those willing to avail themselves of this advice.

Other Chapters to Check

Chapter 1: "Destination Anywhere"—Strategies on learning about places to visit

Chapter 7: "Budget Travel"—Affordable vacation ideas

Chapter 8: "The Ultimate Adventure"—Active vacations

Chapter 9: "Cruising the Web"—Cruises appealing to various interests

Chapter 13: "Online Discussion Forums"—Ways to connect directly with other travelers

PLAN TRIPS & MANAGE FREQUENT FLIER ACCOUNTS ONLINE

Business travelers demand efficiency. They don't have weeks or months to think about where they want to travel—they know where they have to go and want the trip to be as painless as possible. Enter the Net. Through the Internet, business travelers can book flights, find appropriate lodgings and facilities, stay in touch with the home office (or the office at home), and get quickly oriented in unfamiliar cities. They can even use the Net to find ground transportation from the airport to the hotel. In the following pages, we'll discuss how the Net has become a lifeline for business travelers.

Business Travel Resources

Many of the sites mentioned throughout this book, such as **Mapquest.com**, are useful to business travelers as well as travelers in general. In addition, there are sites such as **Biztravel.com**, geared specifically to business travelers. You can use these sites to book flights, hotels, and cars; to read the latest business travel news; to track frequent flier accounts; and to store profiles of air travel preferences, such as whether you prefer an aisle seat or require a special meal. Some of these same services are available at general booking sites, such as **Expedia.com**; however, business travel sites wrap these tools in a package of resources tailored to mobile professionals.

Biztravel.com

Featuring express booking and lots of useful magazine-style features, **Biztravel. com** has become a favored destination for business travelers. For my money, what distinguishes Biztravel are all the services it offers to make business travel easier. For example, it can use your preferences to automatically request airline upgrades. BizTravel's magazine, which includes columns such as **The Techno Traveler** and **The Tactical Traveler,** along with the deals on flights and hotels. A section called **Biztravel Reports** has features on topics such as jet lag and travel insurance.

The most prominent column is the **Brancatelli File,** penned by veteran business traveler Joe Brancatelli. Sometimes he's quite informative—at other times his prose turns a bit purple. Here's a snippet from a 1999 column on the crash of American Flight 1420:

On a day when a plane goes down and fellow travelers die, all of us who live our lives on the road feel empty. We know that our lives, such as they are, have changed forever—and not for the better. We know that nothing will ever be the same. Were you in a hotel room yesterday morning? Did you flip on the tube to catch the news and see the horrifying pictures of American Flight 1420 broken and ablaze in Little Rock? Did you make your way, zombie-like, through the day's meetings and presentations? Did you mindlessly guide your rental car back to the airport and trudge blank-eyed through the terminal? Did you then, in a supreme act of denial, step on another airplane?

In addition to its magazine, Biztravel offers regular specials for business travelers, such as cash awards or bonus frequent flier miles. Check these specials at Biztravel's site or sign up for a free weekly newsletter, sent via e-mail. The weekly e-mail alert usually includes about five specials, as well as a blurb about Brancatelli's latest column.

Biztravel used to have a very cool frequent flier mileage tracking tool, but most airlines no longer share mileage data with Biztravel, so although this tool still exists, for most programs all you can do is track bookings purchased through Biztravel. Air-lines want people to visit their own sites, so they can

Biztravel (www.biztravel.com) offers express booking and magazine-style features for business travelers.

build traffic and hawk their deals, rather than having people check mileage accounts at outside sites like Biztravel. However, several sites, including Expedia, have stepped in and filled the void by partnering with MaxMiles to offer subscriptions to a frequent travel program manager. (To learn more, see "Keeping Track of Your Mileage" later in the chapter.)

Trip.com: Business Travel and Beyond

Trip.com started out as a business site, but it relaunched in 1999 with broader appeal, while continuing to focus on mobile professionals. Included in the relaunch is a feature called **intelliTrip (intellitrip.com)**, a booking engine that searches a wide range of different databases to find the cheapest flight. At this time, intelliTrip seems a bit slow, but by the time you read this, they should have the bugs worked out, and it might be a great way to find cheap fares. Anyway, though Trip.com is no longer solely for business travelers, it continues to offer many worthwhile features for them, such as the following:

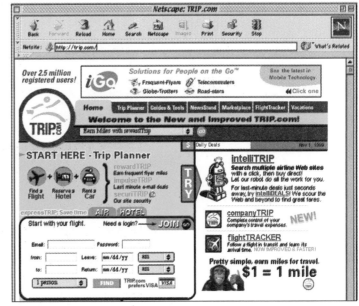

Trip.com (trip.com) caters to mobile professionals but has lots of cool features for leisure travelers.

- **Advanced Booking:** If you join Trip.com (membership is free), you can use booking features that show you how many seats are left on a plane. Those with more seats often have cheaper fares—at the very least, they're more comfortable.

- **Guides & Tools:** This feature includes a world clock, guides to about forty U.S. airports (including an airport map, view of the terminal, and a regional map), a domestic and international per diem guide, and a guide to international holidays.

- **Newsstand:** You'll find lots of feature stories for business travelers here, including the following columns: **Road Warrior** (with coping strategies for frequent travelers), **Plugged In** (a guide to using high-tech gadgets), and **Mileage Maniac** (penned by frequent flier guru Randy Petersen). You'll also find late-breaking deals and travel news headlines, such as the latest on fare wars.

- **Flight Tracker:** This is one of the coolest features created in recent years: You can get up-to-the-minute information on when a flight is due in, and even see an animated image of where the plane is. In other words, if you're tracking a flight that's due in to New York at 5:30 P.M., enter the airline and flight number (if you have it; if not, you can still use this feature though it involves some additional steps). Flight Tracker will show you where the plane is, tell you what time it's due in, even show you its present altitude and speed. Sure, you could simply call the airline, but you might have to wait on hold for a few minutes, and it isn't nearly as much fun as seeing all this information on your computer monitor. With the graphical dials showing speed and altitude, you almost feel like you're in the cockpit.

Eleven Leading Business Travel Sites

The sites mentioned earlier have become favorites of business travelers. The following are other valuable sites that will keep you informed about the latest trends, help you cope with frequent travel, and even teach you what gestures to avoid while you're on the road.

About.com: Business Travel (businesstravel.about.com)

This massive collection of business travel links is nicely organized and it includes categories such as **Passport/Visa, FT Resources,** and **Customs & Etiquette.** With links to hundreds of sites, About.com's Business Travel section almost certainly has what you're looking for.

CNNfn's Travel Center (www.cnnfn.com/services/travel center) includes business travel news and city guides.

Business Traveler Online (www.btonline.com)

Business Traveler Online combines lively features, such as a story on first-class train travel, with destination information. This is a worthwhile site for business travelers, especially those heading to Europe.

CNNfn Travel Center (www.cnnfn.com/services/travelcenter)

CNNfn is a collection of CNN stories related to fare hikes and sales, as well as travel tools, including booking services, city guides, and a currency converter.

Doing Business Abroad (www.getcustoms.com/omnibus/dba.html)

Though this site is buried deep in the Get Customs site, Doing Business Abroad is a fantastic resource for knowing how to act in various countries. If you want to avoid insulting potential business associates, or simply want to understand what's expected from Hong Kong to Italy, visit this page.

Executive Woman's Travel Network (www.delta-air.com/womenexecs)

Though this site targets women, much of its advice applies to all business travelers. You'll find tips on laptops, luggage, and frequent flying, as well as sections like Family Matters and Health and Fitness on the Road. If you choose to join (membership is free, but you have to join Delta's Sky Miles program and fill out a survey), you'll become eligible for special offers from major companies, such as Hyatt, American Express, and National Car Rental.

Expedia.com: Business Travel (expedia.com/daily/business)

Expedia does a terrific job rounding up excellent resources for business travelers. **MileageMiner** is a nice tool for managing frequent flier tallies (but it's not free; more on this later in the chapter), while the airport guide can help you get oriented before take-off. Click on **Insider Advice** for features from experts, such as NBC's Peter Greenberg. For daily business travel news, see **Business Travel Update,** with stories such as the recent "New Service Means No More Lost Bags." (Hmmm, what does this service do, rename them "temporarily missing bags"?)

tip

■ American Express (www.americanexpress. com) has services for business and leisure travelers. The company also has a site for corporate travel planners; see www6.americanexpress. com/corporateservices. (For a detailed look at AmEx's site, see chap. 12.)

Gestures of the World (www.webofculture.com/edu/gestures.html)

Did you know that when you're in Sudan you should avoid showing the bottom of your shoe to another person? Or that in Belgium it's considered rude to slap someone on the back? Gestures of the World imparts these tidbits for dozens of countries around the globe. Part of the Web of Culture site, Gestures is well organized and worth checking before that big meeting in Malaysia (because if you put your hands on your hips there, you'll be expressing anger). Even if you're not planning a trip abroad, this site makes good reading.

New York Times: Business Traveler (www.nytimes.com/library/travel/business)

This site is an archive of updates, usually with four or five short items per column. Of course, the *Times* isn't the only newspaper with columns and features for business travelers. To find other newspapers, try searching at **Newspapers.com**, then follow the publication's link to its business or travel section. Also see *USA Today*'s index of business travel stories **(www.usatoday.com/life/travel/business/ltb000.htm)**. The *Wall Street Journal* has a site **(interactive.wsj.com)**, but its content is available only by paid subscription.

Roadnews.com (www.roadnews.com)

Chock full of informative articles, Roadnews is a must-visit site for road warriors. Topics include using services such as **iPass (www.ipass.com)** to log on from abroad. A section called **Tricks of the Trade** discusses Net cafes and other places where business travelers can log on without a laptop; **Road Reports** has accounts from business travelers, such as "Vietnam Moves Slowly onto the Information Superhighway." Sign up for the e-mail list and get weekly digests on the latest mobile computing news. If you still have questions, send a note to Roadnews editor Bob Lawson, who lists his e-mail address. This site is so informative that it's hard to do it justice in one paragraph. In sum, if you plan to log on while traveling and need some advice, check here.

Rosenbluth International (www.rosenbluth.com)

This is another source for the corporate travel planner, including travel management, services, and a section called **Travel Doctor**, which answers readers' questions. Also see **Carlson Wagonlit Travel (www.carlsonwagonlit.com)**.

U.S. State Department: Business Travel (www.state.gov/www/about_state/business/business_travel.html)

With reams of valuable advice, this site includes guidelines for personal security, advice for protecting business information, and links to travel warnings and consular information sheets. You'll also find a section on doing business overseas, which includes foreign travel per diem rates and country background notes.

As you may imagine, this is just a sampling of sites serving business travelers. For more see the Web directories at the back of the book. Also see chapter 12, "A Traveler's Toolbox," which has lots of information about general tools, such as ATM locators and a currency converter.

For AOL Users:

Business Travel Center

AOL's **Business Travel Center** (keyword: *business travel*) includes the same booking features found in AOL's general travel section. Added to this are some mapping features (including airport maps and point-to-point directions), city guides, and MaxMiles's tool for managing frequent flier accounts.

A Brief Guide *to* Airport Services

Getting acquainted with airports before you go can be reassuring and helpful. You can check whether an airport has a business lounge, find ATMs or Internet kiosks, or learn about ground transportation. Many of these topics are covered toward the end of chapter 2, but the following paragraphs offer a brief summary of the information there.

Trip.com (mentioned earlier) has a serviceable directory of airport maps. To get there click the **Airport Guides** link on the home page. You'll see a listing of dozens of domestic airports. Click "Airport Map" to get an overall view of the airport or select "Regional Map" to see where the airport is located relative to the city it serves. Terminal View lists services and shops, including ATMs, airport lounges, and Internet kiosks. Trip.com also lists strategies for moving efficiently through airports **(trip.com/strategies/airport)**.

Because Trip.com covers only domestic airports, you'll have to look elsewhere for international airport maps. **QuickAID (www.quickaid.com)** has an extensive list of international airports, offering links to airport home pages outside its site. So when you click on the link for the Oslo, Norway, airport, you'll get information from Oslo. Thus, the quality of the information depends on the airport site you link to. QuickAID also puts Internet terminals in major airports around the world. A typical charge is $2.50 for ten minutes. For a guide to QuickAID's Internet stations, see **www.quickaid.com/qis.**

Another terrific resource is **Airlines of the Web (www.flyaow.com)**, which has links to hundreds of airline sites. To find airline lounges, for example, select the airline whose program you belong to and follow the links at that airline's site. (For more on airlines, see chap. 2.)

On *the* Road, but Not Out *of* Touch

Not long ago saying, "Oh, I was on the road," was an excuse for not responding quickly to colleagues or clients. But no longer. Business leaders expect their co-workers to be electronically accessible and to respond quickly to questions or problems. Here is an overview of the technologies available to keep today's mobile executive in touch:

▉ **Mobile computing:**
Toshiba Portege **(www. csd.toshiba.com)**, Sony Vaio **(www.ita.sel. sony.com)**, Sharp Actius **(www.sharp-usa.com)**, and other lightweight laptops squeeze the power of a desktop PC into ever smaller packages. These slimmed-down notebooks, or handheld "personal digital assistants," like the popular Palm Pilot **(palm.com)**, sync with office networks to manage e-mail and appointments and download information from corporate databases. iPass **(www.ipass.com)** and other Internet-roaming networks make it possible to get connected with a local phone call throughout much of the world.

Learn about the latest gizmos and gadgets at Palm Computing (palm.com) and other sites.

Keeping Pace with the
Latest Gizmos and Gadgets

Mobile communication technologies are changing rapidly, with smaller and more ingenious gizmos coming into the marketplace at an astonishing pace. Fortunately, the Web itself can help you stay on top of the latest developments. Here are some useful sites to follow:

- **Outlook on Communications and Computing (outlook.com)** is a subscription-based newsletter published by mobile computing guru Andrew Seybold. Executive summaries and some articles are published free online.

- CNET's **Gadgets Topic Center** features product reviews, news, message boards, and comparative shopping resources in a variety of categories, including handheld computers and cellular telephones. Go to **computers.com** and click on "Gadgets" under the heading More Resources. The ZDNet Web site has a similar section called **Equip (www.zdnet.com/equip)**, which include a free e-mail newsletter.

- For more free online resources, check out Yahoo's mobile computing directory (dir.yahoo.com/Computers_and_Internet/ Mobile_Computing).

- **Pocket-size data storage:** The Franklin Rex **(www.franklin.com)**, a tiny electronic device the size of a credit card, stores address lists, appointments, and other essential data that you load from your desktop. Similar storage systems may be squeezed into pagers, portable phones, even wristwatches.

- **Web-based e-mail and data storage:** Free password-protected online services allow users to send and receive e-mail and consult address books or appointment calendars from any place with Web access, including Internet cafes and hotel business centers. Yahoo **(yahoo.com)** offers all three functions; Day-Timer Digital **(digital.daytimer.com)** and Web Address Book **(webaddressbook.com)** specialize in managing appointments and contact lists.

- **Wireless connectivity:** Pocket-size alphanumeric pagers like the SkyWord Plus **(www.skytel.com)** can receive e-mail messages in the hundreds of characters. Laptops equipped with radio modems (such as the Ricochet, **www.ricochet.net**) and handheld digital assistants with built-in wireless modems (such as the Palm VII, **palm.com**) offer portable access to e-mail, the Web, and other Internet applications. Smart mobile telephones—some with compact keyboards (Nokia 9000 series, **www.nokia.com**) and others with pen-based interfaces similar to the Palm Pilot (Qualcomm pdQ, **www.qualcomm.com**)—can send and receive e-mail without need of a computer.

- **Mobile telephony:** Satellite telephone services under development, including Iridium **(www.iridium.com)** and Teledesic **(www.teledesic.com)**, make it possible for travelers to place and receive calls from almost any point on the globe. Even without satellites, standard portable phones enabled for international roaming can be used in urban areas around the world.

- **Global positioning:** Handheld or automotive receivers made by Magellan **(www.magellandis.com)** and other manufacturers use satellite transmissions to calculate your exact location and altitude anywhere on Earth. These GPS devices can interact with geographical databases to generate customized maps and precise point-to-point driving directions.

Managing Frequent Flier Programs

Though some people might view business travel as glamorous, veteran road warriors know it's an ordeal. However, there are some nice perks, and perhaps the most cherished benefit is that if you travel often, you can quickly accumulate frequent flier miles. It's no secret that these programs have become infinitely more complex in recent years, yet once again, the Net comes through to help you learn how to best accumulate, manage, and cash in those hard-won mileage points.

Everything You Wanted to Know about Frequent Flyer Programs . . .

A site called **WebFlyer (webflyer.com)**, created by frequent flier expert Randy Petersen (see box following) is the definitive site for frequent fliers. Mileage programs have become confoundingly complex in recent years, but WebFlyer has risen to the challenge and helps travelers make the most of these programs.

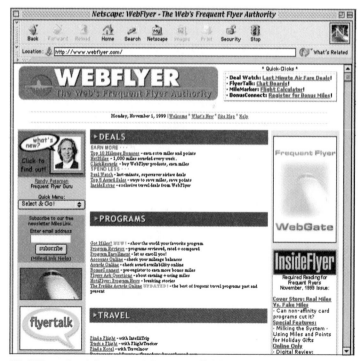

- **Program Reviews:**
  Analysis and rankings for dozens of airline and hotel frequent traveler programs. Programs are evaluated based on earning ability, award choices, partnerships, elite levels, and general value to consumers. Petersen also reviews the Web sites of these programs.
- **Top 10 Mileage Bonuses:**
  This frequently updated area has the latest ways to earn extra miles, such as a

WebFlyer (webflyer.com) is the definitive frequent flier site.

recent American Airlines offer of 40,000 bonus miles on flights between the United States and several South American destinations.

- **NotiFlyer:** Late-breaking news on programs make up this section. There are also lots of tips here for earning more miles.
- **Ask Randy:** This is where you get to pose a question to the frequent flier guru and check his answers to others' questions. You can join the lively forums at WebFlyer, where frequent fliers help one another, or post a question to one of the message boards. It's quite likely you'll get a quick response, as those who participate in this group are generally helpful. But first scroll through the board to see if your question has recently been posted: It's poor "netiquette" to parachute into a forum and ask a question that's just been discussed.

siteseeing

Behind the Scenes at WebFlyer

Randy Petersen had no grand goals when he started boning up on various frequent flier programs in the 1980s. He simply wanted to be informed about those he used. But as these programs became more complicated, "My family, friends, and co-workers depended on me for the latest information on their awards. Then, I started getting calls from travel agents I'd never met—that's when I knew there was a business niche waiting for me."

Petersen started by publishing a newsletter called *InsideFlyer*, which blossomed into a full-fledged magazine. In the mid-1990s, when the Web was in its infancy, Petersen saw the opportunity to reach a new audience and created WebFlyer (webflyer.com). Today, travelers earn about half their miles on the ground by using mileage credit cards, signing up with MCI, buying flowers, or even gambling in Vegas. WebFlyer spotlights these opportunities and offers advice on the most savvy ways to use the miles once travelers have earned enough for a free flight. (See "Bonus Miles for Internet Users" later in this chapter for ways to earn miles by surfing the Net.)

So how many miles has Petersen accumulated? About eight million, he says, enough, if he used them, for 320 round-trip flights in the United States. But, remarkably, Petersen says he doesn't use his miles, preferring to pay his own way. "I fly like everyone else (coach) so I can see how the system works" and talk to fellow passengers, he says. "I haven't left my roots—I'm still the guy in 22F with the other road warriors."

Keeping Track of Your Mileage

For a couple of years, one of the best business travel sites, **Biztravel.com** (discussed earlier), was also the best place on the Net to manage frequent flier accounts. With a few clicks of the mouse, you could get data on all your mileage programs rather than having to go to each airline or hotel site to check your account. But in the late-1990s, United blocked Biztravel's access to United's mileage data in an attempt to get people to visit United's site. It worked; many other airlines followed suit, and now, for most airline programs, Biztravel can only track miles for flights booked through Biztravel. (However, to Biztravel's credit, the site helps travelers book flights that maximize their mileage accounts.)

Enter **Expedia.com.** The massive general booking site from Microsoft recently partnered with **MaxMiles** to offer a service that lets you check all your frequent flier accounts at once (or at least accounts with all companies that participate, which includes just about all of the major ones). If you have accounts with American, United, and Hilton, you could check all these accounts in one place. To get to **MileageMiner,** visit **Expedia Business Travel (expedia.com/daily/ business)**.

tip

■ **Frequentflier.com** is another terrific site for advice on choosing a program, maximizing miles, and late-breaking frequent flier news. This site also has an informative newsletter that can alert you to new ways to accumulate miles. Sign up for the newsletter at the Web site: frequentflier.com.

MaxMiles's **Account Summary** shows how many mileage points you have in each of your accounts and if/when they expire. Lower down on the MaxMile page, the **Activity Summary** shows the most recent credits or debits in your accounts, while **Special Offers** includes deals in the programs that you belong to, such as bonus miles for flying to certain destinations.

Expedia has been offering a free introductory year of MileageMiner. After that the annual fee is $9.95, unless you book three tickets a year at Expedia, which makes membership free. MaxMiles is available on several other Web sites through similar subscription programs, including **Excite (excite.com), ITN (itn.com)**, and **American Express (americanexpress.com)**, where it's free to those enrolled in AmEx's Member Reward program. MaxMiles is also available on AOL.

Is MaxMiles worth paying for? That all depends on how much you value your time. If you don't mind checking various Web sites to monitor different accounts, probably not. But if you want a clean, easy-to-access, and up-to-date summary of your accounts, MaxMiles may be worth the fee.

Bonus Miles for Internet Users

These days you don't have to fly frequently to accumulate lots of flier miles. You can earn miles by sending flowers, talking on the phone, or simply using the right credit card. In fact, about half of all frequent flier miles are acquired without taking to the skies. What follows are some popular ways to earn miles through the Net. Given the nature of all Net "offers," these may have changed or disappeared by the time you read this. Yet even if a specific offer is no longer in effect, this list provides an idea of what's available.

■ **Book your flights online:** Many airlines award bonus points for buying tickets

siteseeing

Northwest Airlines Frequent Flyer Center (www.nwa.com/freqfly)

Northwest's Frequent Flyer Center is a fine example of the way an airline should organize this program information. The airline makes it easy to find what you're seeking, with clear links to major topics from the home page. Here's what you'll find:

■ **WorldPerks Member's Guide:** Learn how to earn free travel, track your miles, redeem awards, and reach elite status. To sign up, click on "WorldPerks Enrollment."

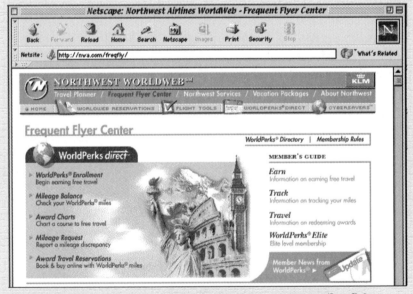

Northwest Airlines' Frequent Flyer Center (www.nwa.com/freqfly) includes mileage balances, award charts, program information, and booking capability.

- **Mileage Balance:** Simply enter your name and account number to access your balance. This procedure differs from most other programs in that Northwest doesn't require you to establish a password.
- **Award Chart:** Scroll down to the bottom of the page where you'll see two pull-down menus, one for origin and another for destination. After selecting these, click "Show Award Chart" and find out how many miles you'll need for a trip and when blackout dates are in effect. You'll see several different award levels for the same destination. From the United States to Europe, you can fly round-trip for only 40,000 miles October through May—during the summer months, you'll need 50,000 for the same trip. You can also find how many miles you'll need for upgrades.
- **Mileage Credit Request:** Did you take a flight and not get credit for it? If it doesn't show up on your account within a couple of weeks (and this happens quite often), you probably didn't get credit. Use the online form to request the miles you've earned.
- **Award Travel Reservations:** This is where you can book award trips online. If you're not comfortable finalizing your arrangements online but want to start the process on the Net, you can make reservations that are held for twenty-four hours and follow up by booking through a toll-free phone number.

through their Internet sites. **US Airways (www.usairways.com)** recently offered 1,000 miles for booking online, while United offered 20,000 bonus miles for those who booked ten round-trip flights.

■ **Invest:** Open a brokerage account with **E-Trade (etrade.com)**, where you can earn up to 50,000 miles a year. Call 800–ETRADE–1.

■ **Shop online:** A site called **ClickRewards (clickrewards.com)** offers miles whenever you buy from their partners, including **Barnes & Noble (bn.com)**. These miles are good for most major U.S. airline programs—you choose the program in which you want your miles placed.

Signing Up, Getting Informed, and Booking Awards Online

Several airlines, including **Northwest (www.nwa.com)**, have begun to let travelers book frequent flier award trips online. And just about all major airline Web sites have program descriptions, online enrollment forms, and award charts that list how many miles you need for various routes. You can also check your mileage balance online, usually after you set up a password.

Some airlines don't have simple Web addresses for their frequent flier pages. You have to enter through the home page, such as United's at **ual.com**, and then click on frequent flier links. Others let you go straight to frequent flier pages with simple URLs. Northwest's **WorldPerks Frequent Flyer Center (www.nwa.com/freqfly)** is one site that makes it easy.

Northwest's Frequent Flyer Center includes program news and updates and special offers, such as a 1,000-mile discount for booking online. That means you could get to Europe from North America for 39,000 miles during nonsummer months—not a bad deal.

Each airline site has its own way of conveying frequent flier program information. Northwest's Frequent Flyer Center is particularly good. At other airline sites, it can be a bit harder to find what you're looking for. But don't despair, the information is there, even if it's not organized as well as it could be.

Summing Up

Online business travel tools, such as the Palm VII, are at the leading edge of technological development and thus evolve quickly. To keep abreast of the latest developments, check the sites listed in this chapter, such as **Roadnews.com**, which track recent trends. Also have a look at Chapter 14, which discusses strategies for traveling with a laptop.

Other Chapters to Check

ESSENTIAL ONLINE RESOURCES & ADVICE *for* STAYING HEALTHY ABROAD

What's the weather forecast for Madrid? Do you need a visa to get into Jordan? What's the Danish word for bathroom? How many rubles can I get for my dollar (or do I even want to change my dollars into rubles)? These and dozens of other small but significant questions will inevitably come up as you prepare for an international journey. Fortunately, the Net hosts a phenomenal range of resources that can answer most questions that arise. This chapter lists some of the most essential online tools for travelers. (If you don't see what you need here, try using the search techniques described in chap. 1.)

Finding ATMs around the Globe

It wasn't long ago that an international journey began with the purchase of travelers' checks. Although travelers' checks are not quite obsolete, it makes more sense to buy a small amount and use your ATM card to get foreign currency at your destination. Banks typically get a good exchange rate and pass this rate onto customers, though this benefit can be offset somewhat by fees for using foreign ATMs. A good rule of thumb is to get a couple of days worth of cash at a time, enough to make it worth the fee, but not so much that you'll get wiped out if you lose your money or get robbed.

Visa, MasterCard, and American Express have made it easy to locate ATMs online. If you're concerned you might not find one where you're going, don't worry, unless you'll be in very remote regions. Almost all international airports now have ATMs, though you can't always count on them functioning.

If you're looking for ATMs near your destination, visit the ATM search page for **Visa (www.visa.com/pd/atm)**, **MasterCard (www.mastercard.com/atm)**, or **AmEx** (see next section). The following are techniques for using the MasterCard page—the Visa and AmEx pages are somewhat similar:

- **Worldwide ATM Locator:** Use this to search for MasterCard/Cirrus ATMs outside the United States by entering a city and country on the main page.
- **United States ATM Locator:** At this site, you can find ATMs that accept MasterCard/Cirrus cards by entering the city you're planning to visit. If you want to be more specific, which is advisable if you're visiting a big city, enter an address or

zip code, if you know it. (*Note:* The address can be any valid address. The locator will use this address to give you listings for nearby ATMs.) When you get to the results page, click "Map It" to see the ATM's location.

- **Find ATMs by Region:** This section at the bottom of MasteriCard's ATM page lets you choose a continent, such as Asia, then get more specific (South Korea, Seoul), until you get a list of ATMs.

Finally, MasterCard has a wide range of online resources for its cardholders, and many of these are helpful for travelers. For example, **Smart Tips for ATM Usage (www.mastercard.com/atm/tipsfrm.html)** has a section called **Tips When Traveling Abroad.**

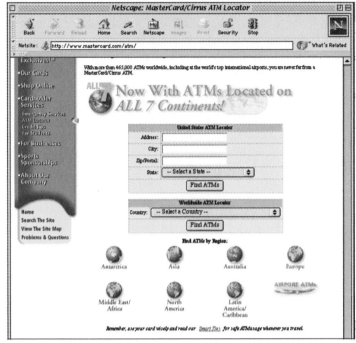

The MasterCard/Cirrus ATM Locator (www.mastercard.com/atm) helps pinpoint automatic teller machines around the globe.

Cold Cash

Just for the heck of it, I took **Mastercard's ATM Finder (www.mastercard.com/atm)** for a spin, in search of a cash machine in Antarctica. Here's what I found:

The following ATM locations match your search request in:

ANTARCTICA

WELLS FARGO BANK
MCMURDO STATION
Additional Info: MCMURDO STATION
Accepts MasterCard and Cirrus. Available 24 hours.

Frankly, there aren't a lot of places to burn money in Antarctica, unless you're trying to stay warm. Still, it's somehow reassuring to know that even at McMurdo Station, you can get cash twenty-four hours a day.

American Express Travel

"Don't leave home without it" was the old slogan for the American Express card. Well, these days, with Internet access becoming almost ubiquitous, you can log on wherever you go and find the nearest American Express office.

American Express (travel.americanexpress.com /travel/personal) devotes most of its travel page to weekly specials and last-minute deals, some for AmEx cardholders, others available to anyone. A section called **Last Minute Travel Bargains** includes specials on flights, hotels, cars, cruises, and package vacations. Though AmEx gives most of its virtual real estate to these bargains, the most useful tools are just a click away. In the upper-left hand corner of the page is a link to **Travel Resources**—click it to get a page full of useful information. Business travelers will likely be most interested in the **Travel Insight** section, which includes tips for driving overseas, gratuities, and personal safety.

SkyGuide includes the latest frequent flier promotions, a roster of business services and amenities at major U.S. airports, advice on ground transport from major U.S. airports, even the configurations of the most popular aircraft. **Travel Tools** has features like a world time clock and a temperature conversion chart, while **Travel Necessities** covers travelers' checks, foreign currency, and visa information. You can find out what currencies you can buy through American Express and currencies in which AmEx's travelers' checks are available.

Finally, under **Maps & Locators,** you can pinpoint AmEx offices around the world and locate ATMs that let you use your American Express card.

To find an office, click on **Travel Service Office Locator,** where you'll get an index by region. If you're searching for the AmEx office in Buenos Aires, for example, scroll down to Caribbean and Latin America, select "Argentina," then click on *B* for Buenos Aires. You'll find the office address, phone, hours, and holidays on which the office is closed.

All in all, American Express has done a nice job in providing useful tools, though the site organization could be improved. Rather than mixing business travel resources with bargains for leisure travelers, American Express could better serve mobile professionals by creating a business travel center and making it easy to locate from the home page. The site could also have shorter Web addresses, which would make it easier to go straight to the resources you're seeking.

tips

■ When traveling abroad, it can be a good idea to use a credit card for purchases. The exchange rate is good, and doing so keeps you from carrying a lot of cash. On the downside, some cards charge fees for international purchases: Check with your bank or card issuer to see whether your card imposes these fees. If your card company does charge a fee, voice your displeasure and consider switching to a card that doesn't.

■ The URL for AmEx's ATM page is long, so most people follow the links described here. But if you want to go directly to the ATM page, see maps. americanexpress. com/expresscash/ mqinterconnect? link=home.

Currency Converters: How Much Is It Worth?

The following sites can help you quickly and easily figure out how much your dollars, pounds, or any other currency is worth abroad:

■ **Universal Currency Converter (www.xe.net/currency):** Start with the amount of money you expect to change, say $100, choose your currency (dollars), then choose the currency of the country where you plan to change money (e.g., Japanyen). Click "Perform Currency Conversion," and you'll see how many yen your dollars are worth.

■ **Oanda Currency Converter (www.oanda.com):** Available in seven languages, this converter has features similar to those of the Universal converter. You can track currency fluctuations from day to day on a personalized page. The home page also includes currency forecasts, news, and historical tables.

Knowing approximately how much your money is worth before traveling is helpful because you'll be better able to gauge how much you should get. In general, avoid changing money at hotels and banks, which almost always have disadvantageous rates.

Weather Forecasts Worldwide

Years ago, on the eve of an international journey, I would scan the newspaper and check the temperatures for my destination. Today, on the Web, you can get much more than yesterday's high or tomorrow's forecast. You can see satellite images, get extended forecasts, and even view forecasts for specific activities, such as sailing or golf. Here are three popular weather sites and some of their features.

AccuWeather.com

The most straightforward of the major weather sites, AccuWeather.com has links to U.S. and international forecasts on the upper-left-hand corner of its home page. For international forecasts, select a country or continent from the pull-down menu to get a weather map listing highs and lows for the major cities. Use the links below the temperature data to get forecasts for subsequent days. For U.S. destinations, you can enter the city name or zip code of your destination to get a five-day (or even a six- to ten-day) forecast.

Intellicast (intellicast.com)

There are two ways to use Intellicast: Either enter your destination in the search box, or click on the world map and select a continent and then a destination; for example, Asia and then Bali. You'll find a detailed four-day forecast, with temperatures in Fahrenheit and Celsius. Intellicast's home page also has custom forecasts for golfers, sailors—even kite-flyers. A problem with Intellicast, however, is that when you search for a destination, instead of getting a forecast, which is what most people want, you get a set of links, including several to satellite imagery, and you have to sort through these to find the link to the forecast, and then click on that.

Weather.com

Weather.com is another weather site that doesn't quite get what people want: quick and easy access to forecasts. Instead, Weather.com, spawned by The Weather Channel, seems more excited about breaking weather news around the world. Still, you can get forecasts by clicking on the links on the left side of the screen called

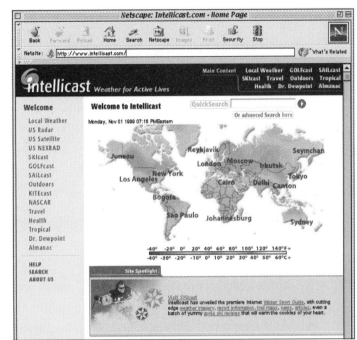

Intellicast (intellicast.com) offers forecasts for hundreds of cities in the U.S. and around the world.

U.S. City Forecasts or **International City Forecasts.** After clicking one of these links, enter your destination by using the pull-down menu, to select "Australia/New Zealand," for example. You'll then see a long list of cities. Click on the one you're interested in to get a forecast.

All these sites have many other bells and whistles. Most people just like to get forecasts, but if you're a weather enthusiast (and it seems many people are—these weather sites are heavily trafficked), visit any of these sites and poke around.

For AOL Users:

Resource Center

AOL Travel's **Resource Center** (keyword: *resource center*) includes trip-planning advice and sections on passports, money, health and safety, and packing, among other topics. The center also includes timely features, such as a recent piece on drinking water abroad. If you don't see the subject you're interested in, try the center's search box.

Foreign Languages *for* Travelers

Though some boorish travelers expect the entire world to speak English, it's amazing how learning a little of the local lingo can open doors wherever you travel. Phrasebooks and tapes can be helpful, but the Web offers a unique resource for practicing and studying before you go or as you travel.

Foreign Languages for Travelers (www.travlang.com/languages), also known as Travlang, has language primers for more than seventy languages. Click on the language you speak (English) and on the language to want to learn (Polish). Then select the category you want, for example, **Basic Words, Shopping/Dining, Directions,** etc. Clicking on "Basic Words" leads to about forty terms translated from English to Polish. You can print Basic Words or any of the other primers and study them on the plane en route to your destination.

Travlang's greatest feature is its collection of audio files associated with the words and phrases; if you click on a term, you can hear it spoken. Listening to the words can help tune your ear, so when someone responds to that singular phrase you've mastered, you may be able to come up with a way to respond.

Travlang also has more than one hundred translation dictionaries **(dictionaries. travlang.com)**. With each you can enter a term in a search box and see the word or phrase it translates into. For example, enter the word *museum* in the English-Spanish dictionary, and Travlang produces the result, *museo*. Of course, a little online study is no substitute for a good language class, but it can certainly help you learn a few basics before you go.

Packing Light

Lugging around a couple of heavy suitcases for a week or two away is almost always unnecessary. A friend once said, "Leave behind half of what you plan to take." Sage advice, though the trouble is figuring which half. The sites that follow will help you sort the necessities from the dead weight:

- **The Travelite FAQ (www.travelite.org):** Tips on packing light, choosing luggage, and selecting appropriate travel wear are offered here.
- **eBags (www.ebags.com):** Purchase travel gear online from leading manufacturers, including Samsonite, Jansport, and Eagle Creek.
- **Tips for Travelers (www.webfoot.com/travel/tips/tips.top.html):** This is a long Web address but worth entering for tips on what to take, what to pack it in, and even how to pack a bicycle.
- **Walkabout Travel Gear (www.walkabouttravelgear.com):** One-stop shopping for active travel gear and advice for the adventurous are offered at this site. See **www.walkabouttravelgear.com/packit.htm** for space-saving travel gear.

Passports *and* Visas Online

If you're planning your first trip outside your home country, you'll have to get a passport. This is one area where it's worth planning ahead: The U.S. government advises that it takes up to twenty-five business days to process a passport. However, if you have to take off in a hurry, there are ways to expedite processing, for a fee, of course. In a pinch, you can even get a passport in just a couple of days through a private passport agency. Read on to see how.

Passport Advice from the State Department

The U.S. government has yet to enable citizens to apply online for passports, and given the documentation required and the speed with which the government adopts new technologies, this is one service that probably won't migrate to the Net anytime soon.

However, the **State Department (travel.state.gov)** has a very thorough Web site, which includes a section called **Passport Services (travel.state.gov/passport_services.html)**, with information on how and where to apply, fees, and applications you can print and send with your check. Software called Adobe Acrobat, which can be downloaded, is necessary to print application forms. (To download the Adobe Acrobat Reader for free, see **www.adobe.com/prodindex/acrobat/readstep.html.)**

Frequently Asked Questions covers a range of topics, such as passport renewal, getting passports quickly, and what to do if your passport is lost or stolen. The **How To...** section also has information on applying, adding pages to a full passport, and obtaining passport records. To find a place to apply, click on **"Where to Apply"** and enter your city name. If nothing comes up, try the nearest large city and see what you find.

If you need a passport in a hurry, choose Expedite service; mark the envelope "Expedite" and add the extra fee ($35 at press time). The State Department strongly suggests sending expedited orders via overnight mail and providing a paid overnight mail envelope for return delivery. If you follow these steps, you can usually get a passport in about a week.

When You Absolutely, Positively Have to Have It Overnight

If you have to travel overseas on very short notice and have less than a week to get a new passport or renew an existing one, there are several private agencies that can help. For about $100 (plus the government's $95 fee for an expedited passport), these companies will arrange to get your passport to you in about three business days.

Here's how it works: Go to a post office or other government agency and sign the forms in the presence of an authorized agent. Then, pay the standard passport fee plus the supplement for expediting the passport and overnight the materials to a private passport service (see listings that follow). They can usually process the passport in about twenty-four hours and then overnight the passport to you, meaning you'll have it about three days after you've submitted your application. These agencies also expedite visas, which can be a great help when you're short on time.

Here are four agencies that can expedite passports. For others visit a search site such as Yahoo and search for "passport services."

American Passport (americanpassport.com)

Using a three-tiered structure based on how fast you need your passport, American charges $100 (plus the $95 government fee) for twenty-four-hour Urgent Service. For Express Service, which will get your passport to you in about a week, American's fee is $55 (plus the $95 for Uncle Sam). They'll also process regular applications for a $40 service fee, but if you're not pressed for time, you may as well do it yourself and save the fee.

Passport Offices for Other Countries

Canadian Passport Office (www.dfait-maeci.gc.ca/passport/passport.htm): Learn how to obtain a passport whether you're in Canada, the United States, or outside of North America. You can also find out about application locations, fees, and how long the process should take.

U.K. Passport Agency (www.open.gov.uk/ukpass/ukpass.htm): Find out how to apply, what to do if your passport is lost or stolen, and how to inquire about passports that are being processed.

Passports Australia (www.dfat.gov.au/passports/index.html): Find out where to apply and what you need (photos, identification, etc.).

Express Visa (www.expressvisa.com)

Express Visa says it has been processing visas and passport for more than twenty years. In addition to processing passports rapidly, Express can help quickly replace a passport that's lost or stolen abroad. The company also maintains a twenty-four-hour/seven-days-a-week emergency line for anyone in a pinch.

Instant Passport (instantpassport.com)

This private agency can get you a passport in a jif and also provides visas in a hurry. Fees for tourist visas start at $20. This site is primarily informative. To order services call the toll-free number listed on the home page.

Passport Express (www.passportexpress.com)

Passport Express first helps you figure out if you need your

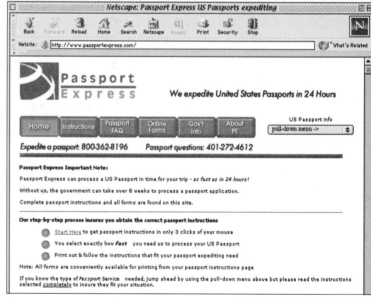

Passport Express (www.passportexpress.com) is one of several sites that can process a passport in twenty-four hours.

passport expedited, and if so, what level of service you require. Like the other agencies, the faster the turnaround, the more expensive the fee. The company says that if it receives an application in the morning, it will ship a passport that afternoon, meaning you can get it in just a couple of days (including delivery time) or possibly faster if you live near a Passport Express office.

Visas: Online Help

If you need a visa quickly, or simply want to learn about visa requirements, see **Traveldocs (www.traveldocs.com)**, an extensive site devoted to informing travelers about visa requirements and procuring these visas—rapidly if necessary. Start with the clickable world map and drill down to the country you're planning to visit, or scroll to the bottom of the home page, where you can click on the first letter of any country. Select "Georgia" (the former Soviet state), for example, and you'll get a page listing entry and visa requirements, travel conditions and advisories, and information about the country and its people.

Another site that can get you a visa in a hurry is **G3 Visas and Passports (g3visas.com)**, which uses two pull-down menus to make it easy to find what you need. Simply select the length of stay and the country you're visiting to get information about what you'll need. Inputting a two-week stay to Cambodia showed that a $20 tourist visa is required along with three passport-size photos for the three copies of the application. G3 lists its toll-free number for those who have questions or want to use G3 to expedite a visa.

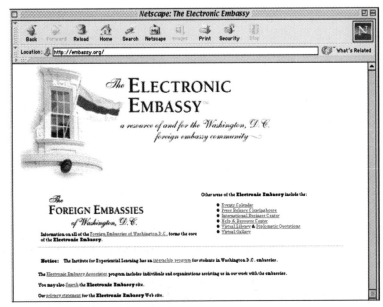

Finding Embassies

Not surprisingly, two other excellent sources of advice for travelers are embassies and consulates, and many countries have created online embassies to answer basic questions. A good place to start is the **Electronic Embassy (embassy.org)**,

The Electronic Embassy (embassy.org) links to foreign embassy sites.

which focuses on embassies in Washington, D.C., but has links to embassy pages for countries around the world. If you are planning a trip to Brazil, for example, scroll down to Brazil and click on its link. You'll find an e-mail address and a link to Brazil's online embassy, as well as contact information for

Brazil's embassy in Washington, D.C. **Embassyweb. com** is another site for finding embassies, but I find the Electronic Embassy to be more straightforward and easier to navigate.

U.S. Customs: Traveler Alerts

Most people find going through customs as pleasant as being audited by the IRS. Yet the **U.S. Customs Service** site **(www.customs.gov)** can answer questions for U.S. citizens traveling abroad, as well as for those from other countries who plan to visit the United States.

Traveler Alerts **(www.customs.gov/travel/ travel.htm)** has sections including **Visiting the U.S.** and **Medications/Drugs.** The **FAQ** (frequently asked questions) answers queries, such as "Why Did U.S. Customs Take My Food?" It also addresses what travelers can take to other countries. Most extensive is the **Know Before You Go** section, covering what you can bring home, penalties for failure to declare, how to transport pets, and duty-free shopping. Here's an excerpt regarding sending stuff home:

> Personal belongings taken abroad, such as worn clothing, etc., may be sent home by mail before you return and receive free entry, provided they have not been altered or repaired while abroad. These packages should be marked "American Goods Returned."

tip

■ Another great site for finding country information is the Tourism Offices Worldwide Directory (www.towd.com). Choose a country and get links to tourism offices online and addresses and phone numbers for real-world offices.

Travel Advisories *and* Warnings

There are several Web sites for updates and travel advisories, from government sources, such as the State Department and CIA, to online guidebooks, such as Lonely Planet. You can also get travel news from online outlets, including **CNN's Travel Guide (cnn.com/TRAVEL)**, **USA Today (www.usatoday.com/life/travel/ltfront.htm)**, and many other newspaper travel sections. It's wise to check a variety of sources to get a well-rounded picture of what's happening at your destination.

State Department Travel Warnings

The **U.S. State Department (travel.state.gov)** provides a wealth of resources for travelers going overseas, information that can help you learn more about the potential hazards of a place and what to do to get out of a jam while traveling. Naturally, the department is cautious, some might say overly cautious, but its warnings can help you become more informed about the country you plan to visit.

To find the latest update, visit **Travel Warnings and Consular Information Sheets (travel.state.gov/travel_warnings.html)** and scroll down the alphabetical list of countries. Though the department's travel warnings can sometimes be more than a year old, they're often valuable sources of information. Some can be quite current. When I checked for Zimbabwe, for example, the information had been updated just a week before. The date is listed, so you can tell how fresh the information is. Here's a snippet from the Zimbabwe sheet.

SAFETY/SECURITY: Land mines along the Mozambique border, which is outside the main tourist areas, make travel to that border area potentially hazardous. U.S. citizens should avoid political rallies and street demonstrations and maintain security awareness at all times.

CRIME INFORMATION: Muggings, rape, purse snatching, car thefts, and credit card fraud are on the increase and as Americans and other foreigners are perceived as being wealthy, these groups are frequently being targeted. . . . Car doors should be locked and windows rolled up at all times.

The warning goes on to say travelers should leave valuables in hotel safes, not carry much cash, and make a copy of their passport photo page. As you can see, much of the advice is common sense. Yet these warnings are still worthwhile: They list medical facilities, information on road travel advisories, aviation safety updates, restrictions on photography, and embassy locations.

The State Department also puts its popular pamphlets online—see **Travel Publications (travel.state.gov/trav el_pubs.html)**. These include *U.S. Consuls Help American Abroad, Crisis Abroad,* and *A Safe Trip Abroad.* Other pamphlets include advice for seniors, for those residing abroad, and for sending money overseas. About a dozen pamphlets cover specific regions, such as *Tips for Travelers to Mexico,* and *Tips for Business Travelers to Nigeria.* Finally, an essential online pamphlet called *Foreign Entry Requirements* **(travel. state.gov/foreignentryreqs.html)** lists entry restrictions by country. This information is usually dependable, though it's always a good idea to check with the State Department by phone or with a country's consulate or embassy before you go to an unstable country.

tips

■ The State Department offers several e-mail lists, including one on travel warnings. If you sign up, which is free, you'll get regular updates delivered via e-mail. To subscribe to any of these lists, visit www.state.gov/www/ listservs.html and enter your e-mail address.

■ The Canadian government's Travel Information and Advisory Reports site (www.dfait-maeci.gc.ca/travel report/menu_e.htm) provides international updates in English and French and has an e-mail alert to which you can subscribe.

The CIA World Factbook

Ever since its inception, the Central Intelligence Agency has been spending Americans' hard-earned tax dollars to amass information on countries around the globe. So it's high time we the people get a little return for our money. **The CIA World Factbook (www.odci.gov/cia/publications/factbook)** has basic information on just about every country on the planet, and the agency shares this unclassified material on this Web site.

Start by clicking "Country Listing," then scroll down to the country you want to learn about (or click the first letter of the country to go there more quickly). The information here covers any number of topics, including People, Government, Economy, and Transportation. Here's a sample from the section on Belize's economy:

The small, essentially private enterprise economy is based primarily on agriculture, agro-based industry, and merchandising, with tourism and construction assuming greater importance. Sugar, the chief crop, accounts for more than one-third of exports, while the banana industry is the country's largest employer.

Okay, so this information sounds like it came from an old *World Book* encyclopedia, but the Factbook is a decent place to get a quantitative overview of what to expect. The site also contains reference maps that aren't too detailed but are good for a quick orientation.

Updates from Online Guidebooks

Even if a guidebook is updated annually, the information is several months old by the time it hits the shelves. Until the advent of the Net, there wasn't much that publishers could do about this, but today, they can post updates that complement the guidebook. (You can find online updates of this book at www.internet travelplanner.com.)

In the late 1990s, Lonely Planet, which has a book on just about every country under the sun, launched a new feature they called **Upgrades (www.lonely planet.com/upgrades)**, which updates dozens of its most popular guidebooks.

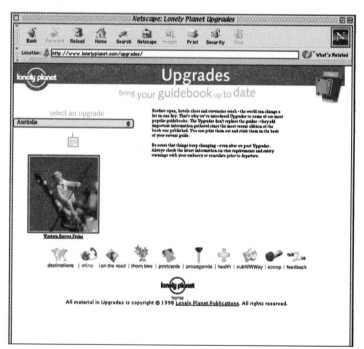

Lonely Planet's Upgrades (www.lonelyplanet.com/ upgrades) offer online updates by country from LP's writers and editors.

Upgrades are compiled by LP's writers and editors and include recent information on safety, political situations, currency, and health conditions. These updates are designed to work in tandem with the print guide, but even if you don't have the book, they can be useful.

"Most books are on two-year cycles," says Virginie Boone, Lonely Planet's online producer. "We were collecting all this information and it was just sitting there. So we decided to offer it online—it fills the gaps." With Upgrades, LP has added a selling point that book-sellers can use to promote the brand, and travelers benefit by getting updated information from knowledgeable sources. Here's a sample from the Nepal Upgrade:

Nepal remains politically volatile, with governments seeming to come and go with alarming frequency. This month's elections will bring in the fifth government in the last three years. A "People's War" is being waged against the government by the anti-monarchical Nepal Communist Party-Maoist. In the three years since the insurgency started more than 600 people have been killed.

Lonely Planet has several other sections with updates:

- **Scoop (www.lonelyplanet.com/scoop):** Scoop lists the latest news from each destination—use the pull-down menus to select a country.
- **The Thorn Tree (www.lonelyplanet.com/thorn):** This online forum allows you to read dispatches from other travelers and post a message of your own. These bulletin boards are organized by region (Central America, Europe, etc.) and by category (Travelling Companions, Women Travellers, etc.).
- **Postcards (www.lonelyplanet.com/letters):** Lonely Planet readers send updates of what they're finding around the world. Most of these dispatches are sent via e-mail from the destination. Though they're not as authoritative as an update from an LP author, most are very informative, and some are compelling.

Other online guidebooks can be helpful with updates as well. Among the best are **Arthur Frommer's Budget Travel (frommers.com)** and **Rough Guides (travel.roughguides.com)**.

Staying Healthy Wherever You Go

First things first: The Net is absolutely not a substitute for medical advice from a knowledgeable physician. However, it is a terrific resource for becoming more informed about health hazards and medical conditions abroad. Travel health sites also provide advice about immunizations and precautions, as well as tips for putting together a compact first-aid kit for your trip.

Advice from the Centers for Disease Control

If you're planning to visit a country and you're not sure about its health conditions, start at the U.S. government's **CDC Travel Information (www.cdc.gov/travel/travel.html)**, which has advice on immunizations, travel preparations, and general health conditions. Begin by clicking on the **"Graphical Travel Map,"** then select the region you're visiting. Here's what I found by clicking on "India":

Food and waterborne diseases are the number one cause of illness in travelers. . . . Malaria is a preventable infection that can be fatal if left untreated. Prevent infection by taking prescription anti-malaria drugs and protecting yourself against mosquito bites. Malaria risk in this region exists in some urban and many rural areas, depending on elevation. For specific locations, see Malaria Inform-ation for Travel-ers to the Indian Sub-continent. Most travel-ers to the Indian Subcontinent at risk for malaria should take mefloquine to prevent malaria.

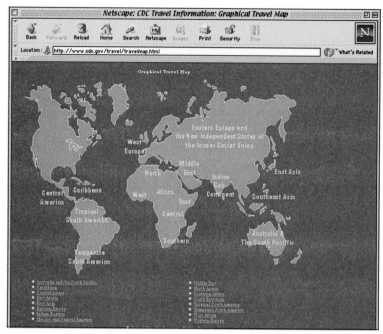

The CDC's graphical map (www.cdc.gov/travel/travelmap. html) lets travelers click on their destination to learn about health conditions throughout the world.

The advisory for India, which is similar to other advisories, includes recommended vaccinations, tips for staying healthy, and essential items, such as insect repellent.

The CDC home page lists other precautions and recent outbreaks of disease around the world. All in all, the CDC site is an extensive resource and well worth visiting when preparing for a trip abroad.

The Travel Doc Is In

Expedia.com, Microsoft's big booking site, has a section called **Insider Advice (expe dia.com/daily/experts)**, with regular columns by several leading travel experts. One of these experts is Dr. Alan Spira, who tackles a travel health issue every couple of weeks in **Travel Doc** (go to the main Insider page and click on "Travel Doc").

Recent topics have ranged from altitude sickness to fighting infections. The Travel Doc archive **(expedia.com/daily/experts/default.asp#doc)** lists stories dating back more than a year. I recently used the archive to dig up a story Spira wrote a couple of years ago on putting together a first-aid kit for travel abroad **(expedia.com/daily/experts/October1997/Oct31- 97firstaid.asp)**. Here's an excerpt:

Read a first-aid manual before you travel, or take a first-aid class. Adventure travelers who'll be out of immediate reach of medical assistance should take an emergency medical technician or wilderness medicine course, which covers

tip

 The World Health Organization (www.who.int) is another good source of international health data.

a traveler's toolbox

medical basics, treatment of injuries and illnesses, and cardiopulmonary resuscitation (CPR). Along with basic knowledge and common sense, you should bring a first-aid kit and know how to use it. Finally, be ready to improvise, and to adapt to circumstances by using your first-aid kit and your ingenuity.

This excerpt is the introduction—a list of essentials follows in Spira's story. This column is just one of many sources that can help you become better informed, without spending a lot of money on medical books.

Prepping with Travel Health Online

Travel Health Online (www.tripprep.com), which is frequently updated, combines news of international health conditions with other foreign travel advice, such as crime information. However, most of the site is devoted to health concerns, and Travel Health is a very clear and straightforward resource for getting basic overviews of conditions at your destination. Here's a sample from the page on Haiti:

Medical care in Port-au-Prince is limited, and the level of community sanitation is low. Medical facilities outside the capital are generally below U.S. standards. Life-threatening emergencies may require evacuation by air ambulance at the patient's expense. Doctors and hospitals often expect immediate cash payment for health services.

Healthy Flying

Have you ever come down with a cold or flu just after a flight? Recirculated cabin air can cause these illnesses, says Diana Fairechild, a former international flight attendant. Fairechild flew more than 10 million miles before retiring due to illnesses she says were caused by the cabin environment. To share what she's learned about avoiding illness while flying, Fairechild wrote the book *Jet Smarter: The Air*

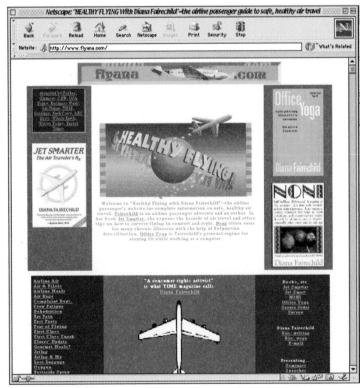

Healthy Flying (www.flyana.com) has tips for preventing airborne diseases.

Traveler's Rx and created a Web page called **Healthy Flying (www.flyana.com)** to help travelers reduce the risk of getting sick en route.

"As soon as the Net became available in Hawaii, I got online and searched my field of expertise, but there wasn't anything," she says. So she created Healthy Flying, with topics ranging from avoiding jet lag to overcoming fear of flying.

Fairechild tells travelers what they can do to stay healthier: Request that the pilot circulate more fresh air. She also responds to readers; for example, the mother who asks why she should put on her own oxygen mask before taking care of her children. Other topics include ear pain, dehydration, and air rage. Most valuable are basic tips for avoiding illness, such as drinking lots of water, getting up and moving about every hour or two, and taking supplements to boost your immune system.

Other Travel Medicine Sites

Another excellent resource for travelers is a site called **Staying Healthy in Asia, Africa, and Latin America (www.moon.com/staying_healthy)**, which features content from Moon's book of the same name. This is a remarkably detailed work, covering immunizations, malaria, blood transfusions, signs of dangerous illness, and many other topics. This guide is so good, that Tony Wheeler, publisher of the rival Lonely Planet guidebook series, had this to say about it, "Probably the best all-around [travel medicine] guide to carry, as it's compact but very detailed and well organized."

The U.S. State Department has a site called **Medical Information for Americans Abroad (travel.state.gov/medical.html)**, which lists dozens of medical organizations and resources, including those covering insurance, medical evacuation, and clinic listings overseas.

A site called **Armchair World** has a section called **Your Health Abroad (www.armchair.com/info/health.html)**, which has advice on everything from health insurance to insect bites. One section covers swimming precautions, while another offers blood transfusion guidelines for international travelers.

When you're on the road, you never know when you might need a clinic, so it's worth checking a directory hosted by the **International Society of Travel Medicine**. The ISTM directory at **www.istm.org/clinidir.html** lists clinics in the first world and developing countries that are members of this organization. Most listings include an address, phone, and e-mail address.

If you travel frequently, especially to remote areas, chances are that sooner or later you'll become ill. If you do, try to access Lonely Planet's **Pills, Ills and Bellyaches (www.lonelyplanet.com/health/health.htm)**, where you'll find remedies for those nasty road bugs. Sections include predeparture planning, keeping healthy, women's health, diseases and ailments, and links to other travel health sites. With information supplied by Australia's Traveller's Medical & Vaccination Centres, this site goes as far as specifying drug dosages for some ailments, but of course LP recommends seeking the advice

tip

■ To learn more about jet lag and how to prevent it, see nojetlag.com.

■ If you have a chronic medical condition, you may want to get a Medic-Alert bracelet before traveling—for more information, see MedicAlert (www.medicalert.org).

of a qualified physician whenever possible. For minor ailments, such as cuts, bites, or less severe altitude sickness, this is a good site to visit. If you'll be miles from Net access, which is quite likely in the developing world, print out a few key pages and make them part of your custom guidebook or fold them into your first-aid kit.

For more travel health sites, consult Yahoo's listing **(dir.yahoo.com/health/ travel)** or simply enter the term "travel AND health" into your favorite search engine.

Summing Up

Although it can be fun to be spontaneous while traveling abroad, there are some requirements that can't be left to chance. You'll need to have your documents in order, convert currency, get the proper immunizations, and learn about any instability in the country or region you plan to visit. In all these cases, the Net can help you take care of the essentials. By being mindful of these basics, you can make your journey safer, easier, and more fulfilling.

Other Chapters to Check

Chapter 1: "Destination Anywhere"—Destination information
Chapter 13: "Online Discussion Forums"—Get advice directly from other travelers
Chapter 14: "The Connected Traveler"—Tips on logging on while traveling

---

WEB-BASED BULLETIN BOARDS, NEWSGROUPS & E-MAIL LISTS

The Value *of* Online Forums

Though some people believe the Web *is* the Internet, there's much more to the Net than simply millions of Web pages. Most prominent among the Net's other components are discussion groups, which occur online in various forms: in online services such as AOL, in Usenet newsgroups, on e-mail lists, and, not surprisingly, on Web sites.

The phenomenal growth of the Web during the past few years has obscured one of the most useful features of the Net: two-way communication between individuals. Many people see the Net as a one-way medium: They visit their favorite Web sites, get the information they want, and move on. Yet one of the most remarkable features of the Net is that it enables people with similar interests to converse—at virtually no cost—no matter where they live.

The value of these groups cannot be overstated. Most Web sites, no matter how good—and some are outstanding—have a certain perspective and operate within legal boundaries. For example, a site that reviews B&Bs may be hesitant to post a really scathing review. Furthermore, some hotel and restaurant sites sell space, so the listings are really glorified ads. But in online discussions, most people just say what they feel and give honest opinions. You may not always love someone else's favorite beach or bar, because people have different tastes and preferences. But you can get advice straight from the source, and this is often the best advice around.

Until the Web became so prominent, these person-to-person connections were at the root of the Net. Prior to the mid-1990s, much of the communication was in Usenet newsgroups. Usenet, a network of more than 30,000 mostly unmoderated discussion groups, still provides freewheeling forums where people can rant or provide information on any topic. Although Usenet remains popular and is accessible directly through Netscape and Internet Explorer browsers, many people access it today through the **Deja.com** Web site, which makes it relatively easy to find discussions on topics you're interested in.

However, newsgroups have their faults. In recent years, many have become cluttered with spam (unwelcome messages by someone who's selling or promoting something). Another problem is that in some forums lots of people are asking for help while not many are volunteering answers. And perhaps the biggest drawback is that sometimes when you post to these discussion groups, people grab your e-mail address and send you junk e-mail with subjects like, "Work 2 hours a day from home and earn $150,000 a year!!!" This is really unfortunate, and I must admit it often makes me hesitant about posting to these groups.

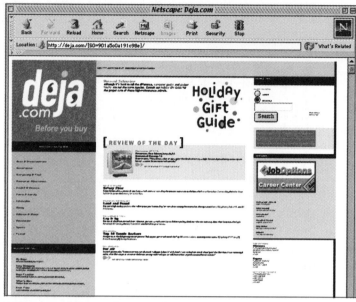

Deja.com (deja.com) makes it easy to access newsgroups and find travel discussions.

This is not to say that every newsgroup is filled with spam—spammers typically hit the most popular and more heavily trafficked groups. Other groups, such as **soc.culture. bulgaria**, are more intimate and cover more specialized topics. These "smaller" forums are less prone to getting bogged down in mindless drivel, and they often are places where you can get answers to arcane questions, such as, "Is it really dangerous to visit Angkor Wat?" A good rule of thumb is that the narrower the group's focus, the more likely you are to find someone who can respond to challenging questions. But, as in many areas of the Net, rules don't always apply. Some forums are so narrow and have so few people who scan the posts that they're not of much use at all.

In addition to Usenet newsgroups, the Web has spawned many other ways to help you connect with fellow travelers. Among the most popular are Web-based forums—the discussion areas hosted on leading travel sites—such as **Rough Guides Travel (travel.roughguides.com)**. Major search sites like **Yahoo (yahoo.com)** and online services like AOL also host travel forums as well as live travel chats, where people type messages back and forth in real time. AOL has become a rich source of information, as AOL users by the millions participate in online discussions. On the flip side, however, AOL discussions are often riddled with inane comments and juvenile sexual innuendoes.

Not to be overlooked are mailing lists, which deliver messages via e-mail. When you subscribe to a list, you sign up to get a copy of each message posted. In this way, list members get to know one another, even if they never actually meet in person. Sometimes these virtual connections lead to real-world get-togethers (as we'll see later in the chapter).

Web Site Bulletin Boards

Popular travel Web sites, especially online guidebooks such as **Arthur Frommer's Budget Travel (frommers.com)**, have become virtual gathering places for travelers seeking advice. Many people find that these forums are simple to access and provide the information they're seeking. Anyone can browse these discussions, which are typically arranged by topic (travel companions) or region (Washington/Oregon). To join a discussion, you often must register, but registration is free and only takes a minute or two. Then, you can post your own queries and see who responds.

The following is a look at some popular online guidebooks that host forums, with some tips on how to use each these discussion areas. Keep in mind that this is just a small sampling—lots of travel sites have active discussions. As these become more established, more people participate, which adds to their usefulness.

Arthur Frommer's Budget Travel (frommers.com)

Frommer's message boards include some regional discussions (Europe, Caribbean, etc.) and several topical forums (Cruising, Bargains, etc.). To join in click "Travel Message Boards." Unlike some other sites, you don't have to register to participate. Perhaps most noteworthy are the **Ask the Expert** forums. In these discussions, an expert, usually the author of a Frommer guidebook, moderates the discussion and answers questions. Every couple of weeks they cover a new region. These experts typically answer questions for just a couple of weeks, then their responses are archived on the site so you can check them to help you plan a trip. For example, here's an archived response from Alaska expert Charles Wohlforth:

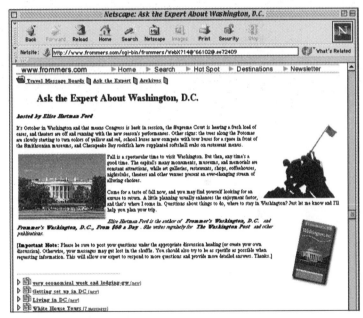

Frommer's Ask the Expert message boards let travelers pose questions to guidebook authors. See the home page (frommers.com) and click on "Travel Message Boards."

For buying Native crafts, there are a number of good choices. Alaska Native Arts and Crafts, on Fourth Ave., is a cooperative of Native artists. The Alaska Native Heritage Center, a $15-million facility built by Native groups and just finished last month, has a large gift store, which I haven't seen yet, but it should be excellent. The best I've seen is a local secret, the small gift shop at the Alaska Native Medical Center, on Tudor Road east of Bragaw. Everything there is on consignment from the Native people who use the hospital.

For AOL Users:

TRAVEL BOARDS

Many of AOL's travel areas have dedicated space to bulletin boards or forums, where you can review messages posted by others or add a query of your own. Enter the keyword *travel boards* for a list of forums. The results are extensive and include message boards for destinations, issues, and activities. Each of these boards is broken down into subtopics; for example, the **Destinations** board includes forums on the Caribbean, Europe, and the United States. The ambitiously titled **World Traveler Board** includes folders on lots of international destinations and one covering around-the-world trips.

Because AOL has close to 20 million members, there are plenty of people who participate in these discussions, meaning there's a pretty good chance your question will be answered. Here's a brief example of the type of advice found on the around-the-world board: "Just a note to strongly suggest that you hide a couple of $100 U.S. bills along with a copy of your passport. This has saved my butt twice now in remote areas of the world."

AOL is a hub for chat of all kinds, including travel discussions. If you're an AOL member, type in the keyword "travel boards" to join the conversation.

Real Discussions (www.realdiscussions.com)

At the Real Discussions home page, you'll find a Yahoo-style directory. Click on "Travel" to see the range of discussions going on. When I checked I saw topics such as "Don't Leave Home Without It" and "Around the World in 80 Days." Real Discussions's forums are often quite active and the level of discussion is generally intelligent, a refreshing change from blather frequently found in AOL chat rooms.

Rough Guides Travel Talk (travel.roughguides.com)

Rough Guides hosts discussions on nine different regions, including Africa, Asia, Central America, and the Middle East. In addition to these regional discussions, Rough Guides hosts a forum called Find a Travel Partner. To read the posts in any of these discussion, click on "Travel Talk" at the bottom of the page and then select the group that interests you. To read a post, simply click on its subject line ("Driving Across Africa," for example). To join the discussion, you need to register.

Lonely Planet Thorn Tree (www.lonelyplanet.com)

"Thorn Tree" refers to a tree outside of Nairobi on which travelers posted notes. To get to LP's online version, go to the home page and click on the Thorn Tree icon. LP has fourteen destination forums and six that cover assorted topics, including Travelling Companions, Women Travelers, and Kids. (For more on Thorn Tree, see chap. 8.)

WebFlyer (www.webflyer.com)

Let's face it, frequent flier programs have become one of the most complicated incentives ever invented. If you'd like advice from travelers who know how to get the most out of these programs, or if you know enough to help others, go to WebFlyer's home page and scroll down to the Interactive section. Here, you'll find a link to FlyerTalk, and you'll find dozens of discussions—some are devoted to a specific airline or hotel program, while others are more general, such as **In the News,** where people discuss the latest deals, or **The Buzz,** which is the most active group. I've participated in The Buzz and have found the regulars to be remarkably knowledgeable and helpful. However they expect you to browse the discussions before posting a question so you don't ask something that's recently been addressed.

Deja.com: Gateway *to* Usenet Newsgroups

There are several ways to access newsgroups, but the easiest is through a Web site called **Deja.com**. The miraculous thing about Deja is that it organizes millions and millions of newsgroup postings and makes them accessible through keyword searches. Formerly known as DejaNews, the site underwent a dramatic redesign in mid-1999 and added **Deja Ratings.** These ratings let consumers evaluate everything from digital cameras to roman-

From Deja.com's home page (deja.com), click on "Travel" and then on "Discussions" for a list of travel-related newsgroups.

tic getaways, but they clutter the site and distract from its former focus: online discussions.

As with search sites, there are two ways to find newsgroups (online discussion forums) and postings on Deja: by searching for keywords or by drilling down through categories and getting more and more specific until you find what you're seeking. In the Siteseeing entry on the next page, we'll discuss these two methods and Deja's other features, such as how to pose your own questions to newsgroups.

Although Deja.com might sound a bit complicated, it's really quite simple once you get the hang of it. I've found it's a good way for those who are getting started with newsgroups to begin participating, but keep in mind it's not the only way to access newsgroups. Both leading browsers—Netscape Communicator and Internet Explorer—offer access to newsgroups. Because the instructions for using these groups vary by browser, it's best to follow the procedures laid out by the particular browser you're using. If you have questions, call or send an e-mail to the support staff of your Internet service provider.

Advice *for* Using Newsgroups

Ami Claxton, who used **rec.travel.europe** to research her trip to Italy (see chap. 4), has this to say about the value of newsgroups:

> The Usenet community is a *fabulous* source of travel information. The best part of Usenet is that it is up to the minute. Very often, people who wrote had just returned from Rome within the past month, so that the information is timely and relevant.
>
> It's also much cheaper than buying a guidebook and/or making many international phone calls (to people who don't necessarily speak English). Another bonus is that these are just regular people (most times) who are trying to help you enjoy your experience—they have no financial stake in where you stay or visit. If you go to travel agents, you're just never sure if they are directing you to a certain place because it really meets your specifications or because they have a nice little deal worked out for commissions!

Ami doesn't just turn to the newsgroups when she has a question; she also scans them often, and if she spies a topic she's knowledgeable about, she responds to the person who posted the query.

It may sound like newsgroups are good for just about everything under the sun, but those who frequent these groups appreciate it if you do your homework first. If you can easily find the answer on the Web, try that route first. For example, if you're wondering what the exchange rate of dollars to francs is, use an online currency converter. If you want to know how hot it gets in Bali in December, consult an online guidebook. And scroll through recent

tip

■ Asterisks around a word indicate emphasis. They are often used in e-mail communications when using italics or other forms of emphasis can prove problematic.

siteseeing

Deja.com

Travel is one of the most popular categories of the Usenet newsgroups, featuring groups such as rec.travel.europe and rec.travel.cruising. And these groups are excellent forums for learning about Europe or cruise travel—the challenge is finding them. If you didn't know about them, how would you know they exist? One of the best ways to find groups for any interest is through Deja.com.

I like to start by searching for a keyword or key term, such as *travel*. To do this, simply enter the word or words in the search box in the upper right corner and click on "Search". My search produced three top matches, including the two groups mentioned earlier. For more forums, click on "Get more groups related to travel"; in this case I got about forty groups. Of course, like any Net search, some matches were quite relevant, while others had nothing to do with what I was looking for. But among the forty or so that came up, close to half were legitimate travel discussion groups, not a bad ratio.

One of the top groups to come up is rec.travel.asia, next to it is the letter *S*, which you can click on to subscribe to the group, and the letter *P*, for posting to the group. But before you decide whether to subscribe (free, of course) or post, it makes sense to browse through the postings to see if this is the type of information you're interested in. Click on the rec.travel.asia link and view recent postings, some regarding subjects such as "Homestay in Japan" and "Traveling India with an Infant."

If you click on one of these subject headings, you'll see links for the entire thread. A thread is all the messages exchanged on a particular topic, so if someone posts a message that leads five others to join the discussion, there would be six messages in this thread. If you see a thread that interests you and want to stay apprised of future posts, click on "Track this thread for me," and Deja.com will archive these messages on a page called My Deja. Deja Tracker can also send you e-mail notification when there are new messages. To use this tracking service, or to subscribe to newsgroups or post messages, you need to become a member of Deja.com. Again this is free; however it does require you to enter some information about yourself.

postings in the forum to be sure you don't pose a question that's recently been asked—and answered—in the group. Newsgroups are best for finding obscure information and personal opinions and for making contacts with people.

Lurk Before You Leap

Remember, you can learn from newsgroups by "lurking" in them. Lurking is the practice of reading messages without posting a question yourself. It's typically good netiquette (Net etiquette) to lurk for awhile to get a sense of a newsgroup before posting to it. It's also wise to read the Frequently Asked Questions (FAQ) summary, which often answers the most common questions posted to a group. Someone else may have already asked the question you had in mind, and the answer will appear alongside the question. You can start at the beginning of a thread and follow it to its culmination.

When you're done lurking and are ready to jump into a newsgroup, how do you know where to begin your online conversation? Among the most popular places for travel newsgroups are those in the **rec.travel** category, such as **rec.travel.air**, **rec.travel.europe**, and **rec.travel.usa-canada**. Also useful are the **soc.culture** newsgroups, if you're planning a trip to Brazil and want to learn more about Brazilian culture, for example.

How do Usenet Newsgroups Get Their Names?

At first glance, it may appear that Usenet newsgroup names are arbitrary, but they are organized under a naming system. The first part of the name (such as "rec," "alt," or "soc") is called the hierarchy. As you move from left to right, the subjects get more specific. For example, rec.travel.europe, starts with the recreation category, then shows it covers travel, then tells you the topic is travel in Europe. There many top-level hierarchies—here are a few:

■ **alt:** alternative, indie, or underground topics

■ **biz:** commercial postings—the one place where unsolicited sales pitches are acceptable

■ **comp:** computer-related discussions

■ **misc:** miscellaneous topics

■ **news:** no, not current events; this group covers Usenet itself

■ **rec:** for recreational activities, such as travel

■ **soc:** mostly social and cultural topics, also very useful for travelers

Most major newsgroups have FAQs. For those new to the group, this is a good first stop. FAQs are set up by newsgroup moderators so people don't have to waste time answering the same questions each time a new member joins, for example, "What does this group do?" "Can I post pictures in this group?" If your question is not answered in the FAQ and it seems that the group is the appropriate place to post your question, then go ahead, don't be shy. Post it.

When you post, be sure to craft a short but descriptive subject line. As frequent traveler Troels Arvin, creator of a popular Web site called Budget Accommodation in Copenhagen, says,

> The flow in the travel newsgroups is quite high. When I look through the headers of newsgroups, I don't want to spend too much time doing it. So I only take a closer look at messages which immediately look interesting from their specific subject headers. For example, if you want to receive answers to a question about accommodation in Copenhagen, don't post a question a subject line that reads: "A question about traveling" or "Help." Instead, use "Question about Copenhagen," or even better: "Copenhagen accommodations?"

You may ask potential responders to send e-mail directly to you (rather than just posting the response in the newsgroup), but be forewarned that some people resent this unless you have a good reason. Because the whole premise of using newsgroups is to share information, some feel it's selfish to mine the group for what you need without contributing to the discussion. So, unless there is some pressing privacy-related reason to do so, try not to ask for a personal e-mail response. If you're afraid you'll miss the response because you don't check the group regularly, then ask the person to both post a response and "cc" a copy to your e-mail box as well. Most people will gladly oblige if you ask politely.

A Sampling of Travel-related Newsgroups

Here are some of the most popular Usenet discussion groups for travelers. (*Note:* If there's no description that means the subject of the group is clear from its title.)

rec.travel sites

rec.travel.europe
rec.travel.usa-canada
rec.travel.asia
rec.travel.latin-america
rec.travel.caribbean
rec.travel.africa
rec.travel.australia+nz
rec.travel.air: airline and airport info
rec.travel.cruises: cruise reports and reviews
rec.travel.marketplace: buy/sell tix, travel bargains
rec.travel.misc: miscellaneous travel topics

Other rec newsgroups

rec.backcountry: hiking and backpacking

rec.outdoors.camping: camping in campgrounds

rec.outdoors.rv-travel: travel in campers or RVs

rec.outdoors.national-parks: national parks (all nations, not just U.S.)

rec.scuba.locations: dive sites and destinations

rec.outdoors.fishing: where to fish

rec.bicycles.off-road: for mountain biking

rec.climbing: for rock climbing

rec.boats.paddle: rafting, canoeing, and kayaking

rec.skiing.alpine: downhill skiing

rec.skiing.nordic: cross-country skiing

rec.skiing.snowboard: hitting the slopes without skis

soc.culture newsgroups

With more than 150 soc.culture newsgroups (from soc.culture.afghanistan to soc.culture.zimbabwe), there's almost certainly a soc.culture newsgroup that applies to your destination. The soc.culture groups are among the most useful Usenet groups for getting a sense of place and an idea of the way people think. For travelers who seek to be more sensitive and respectful of the local culture, these groups are excellent sources of advice, whether you have a question or want to learn by lurking. Here are some popular soc.culture newsgroups:

soc.culture.african

soc.culture.brazil

soc.culture.british

soc.culture.canada

soc.culture.china

soc.culture.europe

soc.culture.french

soc.culture.indian

soc.culture.italian

soc.culture.japan

soc.culture.usa

soc.culture.vietnamese

Other useful newsgroups

bit.listserv.travel-l: general travel topics

alt.rec.camping: where and when to camp

alt.travel.road-trip: choice routes, sights, and places to stay

misc.kids.vacation: ideas for family vacations

Newsgroup Contacts Serve as a Virtual Guidebook

A few years ago, before the phenomenal growth of the World Wide Web, author Allen Noren found Usenet newsgroups most useful in researching a three-month motorcycle trip around the Baltic Sea. "I research all my trips before departing, but this one had a twist," Allen said. "I planned and researched it almost exclusively over the Internet. I made it a challenge to myself to see just how much I could accomplish online."

First Person: Allen Noren

The recently liberated Baltic states of Estonia, Latvia, and Lithuania had just broken free from forty years of repressive Soviet control. Not a single guidebook existed. Accounts of independent travelers having navigated through them were as rare as a youth hostel in Siberia. I called their U.S. embassies, and the common refrain was, "You'se vant tour informasons? Ha Ha! Ve don' have even telephone in Estonia, an' you'se vant tour informasons!"

Within days of getting online, I was able to find current political and cultural information on Usenet soc.culture newsgroups (such as **soc.culture.russia** and **soc.culture.baltics**). Russians warned me of bandits on the road to St. Petersburg and how to avoid corrupt police. An Estonian gave me the name of a man who could help me obtain a travel permit for the island of Saaremaa, an area that had been closed even to Estonians since World War II.

A Latvian student gave me directions to a beach where I could find amber, and the address of his uncle who sold black market gasoline. A Lithuanian astronomer invited me to his observatory. Within two weeks I had been invited for dinners and weekends. I was even offered a job, and I hadn't even left home.

In the **rec.travel.europe** newsgroup I met a Dutch businessman who had recently driven part of the same route I would be taking, and when I wanted more information from him, he invited me to a private chat room on IRC [Internet Relay Chat], where we communicated for half an hour uninterrupted.

I created IRC discussion groups on Finland and each of the three Baltic States, and before long I was deluged with good information. On more than one occasion I used IRC as a place to meet people I'd exchanged e-mail with and wanted to have lengthier discussions with.

Did I find answers to all my questions on the Internet? No, and that's not the point. For me, traveling is about a constantly unfolding set of questions that only grow more complex the farther one goes. What the Net did was enable me to create an informed context, one that allowed me to become a better traveler.

Note: Allen Noren's book *Storm: A Motorcycle Journey around the Baltic Sea* is published by Travelers' Tales.

Conversing on E-mail Lists

If you're interested in staying informed about the latest travel topics, from last-minute air deals to conditions along the Tibetan border, e-mail lists (or listservs) are among the most up to date. On a listserv every message posted is delivered into your e-mail box. If a topic strikes your interest, you can easily join the discussion by simply replying to the message. And if you want to address an issue or ask a question, that's as simple as sending an e-mail to the group.

What's so cool about e-mail lists? Well, you don't have to search the Web to find information: Once you sign up for a list, it's delivered straight into your e-mail box. And with listservs, you get to know (and maybe even like) the various members of the list. Some lists, such as **Travel-L,** have real-world gatherings, where members meet and host one another.

As you'd expect, many of the discussions on these lists cover destination advice, such as this request from the Travel-L list: "Next week, I get to spend a day, really less than a day, in Bangkok. I will arrive mid-afternoon and leave mid-morning the next day. I am looking for suggestions about what I should see on such a short visit." Within a couple of days, several members of the list responded, suggesting a boat ride through the city, a visit to the Grand Palace, and places to dine. And some of these recommendations came from people who had recently visited Bangkok or who live there. That's one of the beauties of these lists—you have a network of correspondents who are willing, even eager, to share their knowledge. And, if you have an unlimited, all-you-can-eat Net account, which is what most people in the United States now have, it doesn't cost a dime.

In addition to the listservs just discussed (which you can think of as "two-way" lists because you can send and receive messages), there are "one-way" lists on which you sign up for dispatches sent by an organization or company. These include lists sent by individuals, dispatches sent by nonprofits, and weekly updates on travel specials, customized to your interests. Here are some examples:

- **Ecotravel** is one-way mailing list from the founder of Planeta.com, which covers eco-tourism in Latin America. Though this is a one-way newsletter, its author encourages readers to write to him with tips, scoops, or contributions. For subscription information, send e-mail to ron@greenbuilder.com.

- **Mountain Mail** is a weekly dispatch from a Web site called The Mountain Zone. It follows the progress of intrepid mountaineers in the sunny months and has ski updates through the winter. Here's a bit from an April letter on preparations for an Everest expedition: "On Tuesday, Eric Simonson reported the team was getting ready to head up with its second load of yaks. That day they were hoping to establish Camp IV on the North Col, but had been struggling with the yak drivers down here to organize our second load of 42 yaks." To learn more see **www.mountainzone.com**.

tip

■ **IRC is a multiuser chat system, where people convene on "channels" (a virtual place, usually with a topic of conversation) to talk in groups or privately. IRC was created in 1988 by Jarkko Oikarinen. Since starting in Finland, it has been used in more than fifty countries. IRC gained international fame during the Persian Gulf War. Updates from around the world came across an IRC channel, and people gathered to hear these reports. To learn more about IRC, see the IRC Networks site (www.irchelp.org/irchelp/networks).**

■ **Scoop** is an e-mail dispatch from Lonely Planet, with news updates from around the world, such as the following about Bolivia: "Lonely Planet has received a number of credible reports of the drugging and subsequent rape of women tourists who have taken jungle and pampas tours around Rurrenabaque, Bolivia, with an independent guide formerly employed by a tour company that has since closed. This individual has an excellent knowledge of the Bolivian lowlands and may be operating under a false name in other parts of the country."

Because this information is so current, it's not the type of advice you'll find in a print guidebook. Again, that's not to say that print guides are no longer valuable—I find them essential for just about every trip besides quick weekend getaways—but this updated advice can be of immeasurable help.

Another advantage of these dispatches is that they can be very specific. Many guidebooks, especially those covering an entire country, have to take a somewhat general approach, but with these lists you can get very targeted information. For example, if you're wondering where you can spend a quiet week on a deserted beach in the Greek islands, you could post this question to Travel-L and probably get some worthwhile advice. If you looked for advice in Lonely Planet, there's a good chance that "deserted isle" is now overrun by other solitude-seeking tourists.

tip

■ If you don't remember the e-mail address for the group you've joined, simply reply to a message and change the topic in the subject line of your e-mail, which will start a new discussion.

Subscribing to E-mail Lists

So maybe by now you're sold and are wondering, "How do I find interesting lists and sign up?" Well, for lists associated with Web sites, such as Scoop, simply go to the site (**www.lonelyplanet.com**, in this case), click on "Scoop," and enter your e-mail address to join. Like most mailing lists, this is free; once you enter your e-mail address, you'll start receiving dispatches.

You can join other lists, such as the Travel-L listserv, by sending an e-mail message to the list's address with the word *subscribe* in the subject field or in the body of the message. To find lists and subscription instructions, consult a listserv directory, such as **Topica (www.topica.com)** or **Liszt (liszt.com)**. These are similar to search sites like **Yahoo (yahoo.com)**, only they describe mailing lists rather than Web sites. Like a Web directory, you can drill down: Go to Liszt and click on "Recreation," then on "Travel," and you'll see about one hundred mailing lists, with instructions for signing up. Here's an entry for a list called **Student Travel:**

> Listname: Student_Travel
>
> Home Page: www.smarterliving.com
>
> Hosted at: smarterliving.com
>
> Contact person: help@smarterliving.com
>
> Description: A summary of airline, car rental, hotel and other travel discounts geared towards students.

To get more info: mail the command to moreinfo@smarterliving.com

To unsubscribe: mail the command to unsubscribe_student@smarterliving.com

If you're interested, send an e-mail message to moreinfo@ smarterliving.com, and you'll get instructions on subscribing. If you ever get tired of the list (or overwhelmed—Travel-L sometimes sends more than 20 messages a day!), you can easily unsubscribe. One way to help manage e-mail coming from popular groups is to set up a folder in your e-mail program specifically for that list. So all the Travel-L messages, for example, could be routed into a Travel-L box, and your main In box won't be overwhelmed by Travel-L messages. For advice on setting up mail folders, use your e-mail program's Help menu.

Another way to find list-servs is to search for keywords. A search for *travel* on Topica yielded 315 lists, including one called **green-travel**. The listing for green-travel at Topica makes it easy

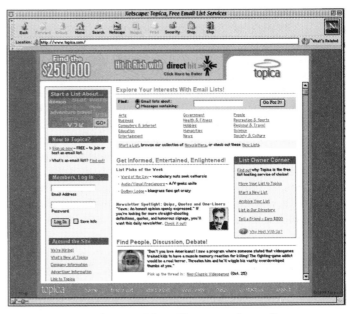

Topica (www.topica.com) is a directory of e-mail discussions, also known as listservs.

to subscribe: Just click on the subscription link, and you're set. You'll start receiving messages as soon as the next one is sent to subscribers, and if you want to unsubscribe, you can follow the instructions sent in the message confirming your subscription.

Finally, there are all sorts of mailing lists sent by travel sites, especially budget travel sites, such as Arthur Frommer's Budget Travel Online **(www.frommers.com)**, which offers a daily digest of specials culled by Arthur Frommer. And as you may know, all the major airlines have weekly dispatches of last-minute deals, and some sites (including **1travel.com** and **Smarter Living** at **www.smarterliving.com**) aggregate deals from about twenty airlines and send them in one convenient e-mail. (These are covered in chap. 7.) So whether you're interested in a dispatch from the other side of the planet or the latest airline deals, you'll probably find at least a couple of lists worth joining.

Live Chats *and* Online Events

One of the potentially most exciting, yet often most disappointing, aspects of the Net is live chat. Unlike the conversations in newsgroups and Web-site forums described earlier, chat happens in real time. This means you can have conversations almost as quickly as you can have them on the phone. Here are the main differences between chat and phone conversations:

■ You're often in a "chat room" with several other people, as opposed to a one-to-one conversation.

■ You're typing instead of speaking.

■ You can "talk" for much less than a long-distance phone call would cost.

The biggest drawback of these chats, particularly those on AOL and big search sites, is they often degenerate into soft-core porn bantering. It's really a shame because the potential here is so great. But don't despair, there are alternatives that enable you to chat with people you select or join in a moderated chat with a celebrity. Renown travel writers such as Rick Steves are occasionally available online for an hour or more to answer questions from anyone who logs on.

Sometimes, you end up in a chat in which one person really knows what he or she is talking about, while the rest of the group is mired in grade-school trash talk. An option here is to break away from the group and establish a one-to-one conversation with this person. You can send instant messages back and forth, which is like sending e-mail that gets delivered instantly. Yahoo is one of several Web sites that offers instant messaging. To learn more about this service, see **Yahoo Messenger (messenger.yahoo.com)**.

And if you're chatting on Yahoo, there are ways to have private chats that shoot off from public chats. Just double-click on someone's name in the chat box and a smaller box will pop up. Next, click on "Private Message," and you can send a message just to this person, rather than to the whole chat room. This box also gives you the option of seeing the person's profile (if it's been filled out), which lists where they live, age, interests, or any other information they've chosen to add. Of course, anyone can say anything online, so you can't know whether a profile is genuine.

For AOL Users:

CHAT

If you're in a chat room and if you want to have a one-on-one conversation with someone, you can send them an **Instant Message**. Simply hold down the control key on your keyboard and type "I" and an Instant Message box pops up. (You can also do this through the People menu at the top.) Type in the recipient's AOL name (without "@aol.com" at the end) and they'll get the message in an instant. They can reply just as quickly. The exchange can be so fast that it will almost seem like talking to the person at the other end.

Finding Online Events and Ongoing Travel Chats

Several sites list both events (such as a chat with a celebrity) and ongoing chats focused on travel. Online events are often moderated, meaning it's less likely they'll degenerate into mindless blather. The following are several Web sites that list events and chats.

Yahoo Net Events (events.yahoo.com/Recreation/Travel)

At its travel events site, Yahoo lists one-time discussions, such as a conversation with travel writer Marybeth Bond on **iVillage (ivillage.com)**. Peruse the day's online events or check Yahoo's weekly calendar of celebrity chats. Yahoo also lists ongoing travel chats on Web sites and in IRC channels.

Expedia Forums (expedia.msn.com/daily/community)

On this page Expedia combines listings for live chat events (such as an hour-long discussion on traveling solo) with its ongoing bulletin boards (such as forums on Europe, senior travel, theme parks, and many others). Some of Expedia's "special chats" include a celebrity, usually a travel writer, while others are just general discussion. Either way, you're encouraged to participate and type in any questions or thoughts that come to mind. If you miss a chat that looked intriguing, you can read through it in the archives.

OnNow (www.onnow.com)

Though OnNow doesn't have a travel category, you can type in the word *travel* into the keyword search box and get a list of dozens of travel chats and events, many of them ongoing but some are special events.

Snap (snap.com)

Go to Snap's home page and click on "Travel" in the directory area, then scroll down and click on "Chat," where you'll find a page listing Web sites that host travel chats and events. Among the sites listed are **1travel.com**, **Atevo's Traveler's Exchange**, **CNN**, and **MSNBC**'s travel bulletin boards.

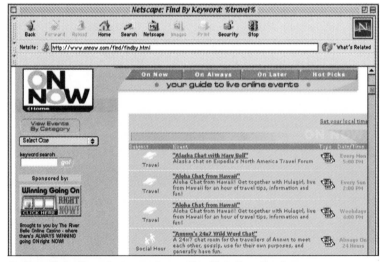

OnNow lists live chat events on the Net. See the home page (www.onnow.com) and enter "travel" in the search box to find travel-related discussions.

For AOL Users:

TRAVEL CAFE

As mentioned earlier in the chapter, AOL has lots of lively chat areas. The online service also hosts a live chat room called **Travel Cafe** (keyword: *travel cafe*). When you get to the cafe, you can enter the live chat room or look for events of interest. Many of the events are hosted on a weekly basis, For example, Caribbean Travel on Mondays 8:30–10:30 P.M. ET, European Traveler on Tuesdays from 9:00–11:00 P.M., and World Traveler on Thursdays from 9:00–11:00 P.M. To join one of these discussions, visit the cafe at the appointed time, click on the link for the forum, follow the discussion, and, when you're ready, jump in!

Summing Up

The Net can be a source of remarkably specific and useful advice from fellow travelers. You can learn a lot by simply browsing through the ongoing discussions and reading what others have posted. After lurking for a little while in online discussions to get a sense of their tone and range, feel free to post a message of your own. Though these groups might seem a little intimidating, most people are willing to be helpful. One caution, though: As in e-mail, sarcasm isn't advised as it might be misinterpreted. So stay upbeat and try to give something back to a group when another traveler has a question that you can answer.

STAYING ONLINE WHEREVER YOU GO– WITH *or* WITHOUT *a* LAPTOP

In recent years the Internet has led to vast changes in the way we travel. And perhaps the biggest shift relates to how we communicate while we're on the road. Back in 1997, when my first Internet book appeared, most wired travelers were laptop-toting mobile professionals, who often grappled with adapters and other headaches while trying to connect from the road. The consensus then was that logging on while traveling in one's own country was relatively simple, but hooking up from overseas could be a nightmare.

These days it can still be challenging to configure a laptop outside of one's native land. Electrical and telephone systems vary from country to country, and phone charges for logging on can be prohibitive, especially after hotel surcharges. Today, though, there's a cheap and easy way to log on while traveling: Web-based e-mail.

Free E-mail: Logging On without a Laptop

If you've ever traveled abroad, especially in the developing world, and waited forty minutes at a telephone office for the privilege of spending $20 for a ten-minute call, you've probably said, "There's gotta to be a better way." Well, there is, thanks to the Net. It's called free e-mail, or freemail, which enables you to check and send e-mail from any Web connection in the world. So instead of lugging a laptop around the planet, you can log on at Net cafes, copy shops, airport kiosks, friends' homes, or anywhere else you can find a computer connected to the Net. In most pay-for-access places, you'll spend between $.10 and $.25 a minute, or a set fee, such as $2.00 for each ten-minute block of time.

In the early days (1996–1997), freemail programs, especially **Hotmail (hotmail. com)**, were notoriously unreliable. Some messages never got delivered, and sometimes travelers were unable to access their accounts for days on end. According to press reports, Hotmail continued to have some problems well into 1999, but Hotmail is now owned by Microsoft, which has pledged to squash the bugs.

These problems aside, free e-mail programs are a brilliant idea. Consumers get a wonderful service, and Web sites get people who keep returning to their pages, meaning they can sell advertisements on these pages for a tidy sum. It's similar to television in that the product is free, but it is packaged with ads. Yet online ads are less intrusive—they're just like billboards and easy to ignore.

By visiting a site such as Hotmail or **Yahoo Mail (mail.yahoo.com)**, you can set up a personal e-mail account that's unrelated to your Internet service provider (ISP). Many people have a primary account through a home ISP or office connection, for example, yourname@earthlink.net or

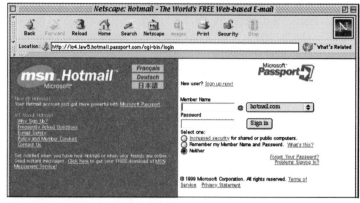

Hotmail.com (hotmail.com) is one of several leading freemail services that enable you to check your mail from any Net connection.

yourname@company.com. But with freemail accounts, you can set up a Web-based account. Mine is michaelshapiro@yahoo.com. This is a unique account—any other Michael Shapiro who wants a Yahoo Mail account would have to come up with a different name.

Though I don't use my Yahoo account much while at home, I rely on it when I'm on the road. While traveling, I set my primary account to forward all messages to michaelshapiro@yahoo.com (more on forwarding later). This way, wherever I am, I can get all my messages in one place, without having to access my home account. And then I can use Yahoo Mail to respond to any messages, just like I could through my home account. Yahoo Mail and other freemail programs also have folders for organizing messages, autoresponders for generating automatic vacation replies, address books, and attachment capability, just like more traditional e-mail programs.

Some Leading Free E-mail Sites

- **Yahoo Mail (mail.yahoo.com)**
- **NetAddress (netaddress.usa.net)**
- **Email.com (email.com)**
- **Hotmail (www.hotmail.com)**
- **iName (www.iname.com)**

Signing up is easy: Just go to any of the freemail sites mentioned in this chapter and follow the instructions. For Yahoo Mail, go to **mail.yahoo.com** and click "Sign Me Up." Then, after accepting the Terms of Service agreement, select a Yahoo ID, such as mrmagoo@yahoo.com. Next, fill out the form, which asks for your name, address, gender, and zip code. Click "Submit This Form," and you're set. (Sadly, mrmagoo@yahoo.com is already taken; you'll have to select a different name, perhaps mrmagoo2@yahoo.com.)

Another amazing feature about freemail that some people don't consider: You don't need any sort of home e-mail account, and you don't have to own a computer to use freemail. Anyone can sign up for an account to send and receive e-mail while they're on the road—or even if they don't travel much. Just log on and check mail at Net cafes, copy shops, or libraries whenever you get the chance.

Finally, and this is a killer application for freewheeling travelers, you can use freemail to stay in touch with fellow wanderers. Imagine this: You're traveling in Bali while your friends are roaming around Thailand. No one has a phone, but with freemail you can leave a message saying you'll be arriving in Bangkok on November 15, and they should meet you at a Net cafe called Cyberia. They can e-mail back to confirm or reschedule, meaning you can communicate and set up a rendezvous without ever using the phone.

Free E-mail: Frequently Asked Questions

What's freemail? Freemail is a Web-based e-mail application that lets you check your e-mail from any computer with a Net connection.

Why have these sites taken off? Because when you're traveling you don't have to dial into your home account. You can log on at an Internet cafe or kiosk and check mail by going to a Web site, such as Hotmail.com.

Who pays for it? Advertisers. Top freemail sites attract lots of eyeballs to ads that appear on these sites. Portals such as Yahoo also use freemail to encourage users to visit their other services, such as stock quotes or online appointment calendars.

Do freemail sites have the same features as the leading e-mail programs, such as Eudora? Well, not quite all the same features, and the integration isn't as seamless. But freemail programs have the most important features, such as folders, address books, and attachment capability. Yahoo and some others have recently added mail forwarding, a nice feature that means you don't have to keep checking your freemail box. However, if you sign up for this service at Yahoo, you'll be hit with "special offers, discounts, and promotions" (oh my!), so it's a mixed bag. You get the convenience of mail forwarding, but the price is getting unsolicited e-mail. It's up to you to decide if it's worthwhile.

Which freemail site should I use? Any of the leading sites should be fine. Due to the pace of innovation on the Web, when one of these sites adds a new feature, the others usually copy it, so they're all somewhat similar. But I wouldn't use just any freemail provider. For example, the San Francisco Giants' site offers freemail, but I'd stick with a company whose main business is Net-related.

Can I store all my mail there forever? In theory, you can establish a freemail account that will endure whether you change jobs or Internet service providers. But most freemail sites limit the amount of mail you can store, so delete old and unwanted messages when you no longer need them.

How can I find places to connect while on the road? Among the best places to log on are Internet cafes. Usually, the staff is helpful, and it's relatively cheap. To find cafes around the globe, visit one of the directories listed in "Finding Internet Cafes" (following).

What if I can't find a place to connect? Well, that may happen. All I can say is that I've seen too many travelers obsess over logging on, rather than exploring where they are. So wherever you may be, revel in that place, and when you get to the next city on your itinerary you'll probably be able to log on.

Using Freemail Services to Check Your Home Account

As mentioned earlier, you can use a freemail provider such as Yahoo Mail to check your home account. In other words, wherever I can find a Web connection, I can go to Yahoo Mail's home page, enter my user name (michaelshapiro—I don't need "yahoo.com" at the end because I'm already at Yahoo) and password, and then click on the link that says "External Mail." This will enable me to establish a POP3 (post office protocol) connection that lets me access the mail that's accumulated in my primary account. This access is especially handy if you haven't had your mail forwarded to your freemail account.

Now, to do this you need to know what your POP3 server is called—check with your Internet service provider to find out. Typically, it's simply the letters *pop* in front of your ISP's address, for example, pop.isp.com. When you retrieve e-mail from your home provider, you can have it sent into your In box, or, on some services, you can create a special folder for it. This may sound a bit technical, but it's relatively simple to follow the steps at Yahoo and many other freemail providers.

tip

■ Don't click "Save Password" at a public Internet terminal. If you do, your password will stay on the machine and enable others to log on to your account. And always be sure to sign off completely so that no one else can access your freemail account. If you have any questions, ask a staff person if one is available.

Some Web sites, for example, **That Web (thatweb.com)**, make it even easier to check your home e-mail. Simply enter your e-mail address and password, and click "Check Mail"—in a few seconds you'll be in your home or office e-mail box, where you can check your messages and send mail. That Web takes cares of the POP3 connection. You don't need to worry about finding the POP3 address. However, That Web may not be able to access some office e-mail systems if they're protected by firewalls. Currently, That Web is unable to access AOL accounts, but the company said it was working on this and expected to have a solution soon.

One concern I had was entrusting my password to a site I wasn't familiar with. But a spokesperson for That Web assured me the site doesn't store passwords (or e-mail addresses for that matter), and that as soon as you close the connection to your mail account, all sensitive information is purged from That Web. I felt confident enough to check it out, but if you have any hesitations, have your primary e-mail address forward to a freemail address and check your mail there.

Finding Internet Cafes

There are two primary ways to find Net cafes online: One is to use a search site such as Yahoo and combine the name of your destination with the term "internet cafe." For example, if you're going to Honolulu and want to log on, search for "Honolulu internet cafe" (without the quotes), which leads to several cafe sites. Among the listings: Honolulu's **The Internet Cafe (www.aloha-cafe.com)**, which greets visitors with an audio sample from the *Hawaii Five-O* theme.

the connected traveler

Another way to find Internet cafes is through online cafe directories, which list Internet cafes around the world (see section following). It's a good idea to check more than one directory because a cafe might appear in one but not another. Also, bear in mind the lifespan of some Net cafes is shorter than that of the common housefly, so don't count on a cafe's being there when you arrive. But if the cafe you intended to visit has disappeared, it's quite likely there's another nearby. Wherever backpackers and budget travelers congregate, it's a good bet a Net cafe or terminal is not far away. When you get to your destination ask around, and you'll probably find a place from which to log on.

tip

■ On extended journeys you can use the Net to manage your affairs; for example, many banks offer online banking so you can pay bills while traveling. Check with your bank to learn more.

Here are some online cafe directories to get you started:

- **The Cybercafe Search Engine (cybercaptive.com):** This database has listings for 2,567 verified cybercafes in 128 countries plus over 2,000 public Internet access points and kiosks. And the list will continue to grow.

- **Internet Cafe Guide (netcafeguide.com/textindex.htm):** With listings for more than 2,400 cybercafes in over one hundred countries, this is a good place to start. To search by keyword see **www.netcafeguide.com/frames.html.**

- **Internet Cafes Guide (www.cybercafe.com):** Though the name sounds the same as the previous entry, you'll notice an *s* at the end of "Cafes" and a shorter Web address. This is a nicely designed site—just enter the name of a city for a selection of Net cafes.

- **Euro Cyber Cafes (eyesite.simplenet.com/eurocybercafes):** With more than 1,000 cafes listed, this is a good source of information for Europe-bound travelers.

A Journal of Logging On without a Laptop

Through the first thirteen chapters, I've featured first-person accounts from Net-savvy travelers. At this point I'd like to share one of my own stories about logging on in New York, London, Southern California, and later Guatemala—without a laptop. What follows are some highlights from a journal I kept during these laptop-free travels.

Day 1: San Francisco International Airport

With an hour to spare before my flight, I spot a QuickAID Internet kiosk in the United Airlines departure area, insert my Visa card, and I'm online for ten minutes (cost: $2.50). I don't much care for the touch-pad pointing device, but it works well enough, and I call up Yahoo Mail, where I have a freemail account. In Yahoo Mail, I've set up an autoreply that tells anyone who sends me mail that I'm traveling, and it may take a couple of days for me to get back to them. (To create an autoreply, set up a Yahoo Mail account, click on "Options," then select "Vacation Response.")

Day 3: New York City

My grandfather and I visit the National Museum of the American Indian. After touring a display of indigenous Panamanian works entitled "The Art of Being Kuna," I notice an online component of the exhibition. I ask the attendant if she would mind if I jump from the museum's Web site over to Yahoo to check my e-mail. She gives me the green light, and I scan the twenty-three messages in my In box, then zap a quick message to an editor in San Francisco. The next day I visit a Kinko's about a block from the Empire State Building and stop to check my mail.

Day 5: London

After flying all night, I arrive in London. Later that day, I go to an old friend's flat and ask if I can log on through his home computer. We fire up his Mac, and I check my e-mail. Then, I use the Web to find the exchange rate of dollars to pounds.

Day 7: London

The afternoon is rainy and cool, and I want a respite from touring London. Just looking for a decent place for coffee, I spot Cafe Internet near Buckingham Palace and figure this will be a fine place to warm up and check my mail. Fifteen minutes of online time costs just under two pounds (about $3.00), and I notice the staff is quite helpful to those unfamiliar with using the Net.

Day 13: Los Angeles

Back in the United States after an all-night flight, I take a day to recover before finding a Kinko's and logging on. The cost is $.20 per minute, and the time is kept by the computer.

tip

■ To avoid paying excessive hotel phone charges, you might try using your phone card rather than dialing direct from your hotel room. When you dial up, insert commas between the phone company access numbers and the telephone number to which you're trying to connect. The commas cause the system to pause for a couple of seconds so the numbers don't all run together. In some cases you may have to insert two or three commas to achieve a longer pause. Though this often works, it's not foolproof and won't achieve connection in all cases.

Day 14: San Diego

After an afternoon at Ocean Beach, I check into San Diego's Point Loma Hostel, the first stop on a weeklong tour of California coastal hostels for a magazine assignment. The hostel has an iCom Network kiosk in the common area. I slide a single dollar bill into the slot and get ten minutes, enough time to check my mail and have a brief look at the local weather forecast at **The Weather Channel (www.weather.com).**

In all, I've been away more than two weeks, and I've been able to check my mail almost every day—without going out of my way to find a connection. I've spent about $11, a phenomenal bargain considering I didn't have to carry a laptop, buy adapters, or pay for phone charges to get online.

Postscript:

In 1999 I spent a week on assignment in Guatemala and left the laptop at home. I didn't know what to expect because on two previous visits (in 1990 and 1994), it was difficult to find a functioning pay phone. This time, it was a breeze to log on and check e-mail throughout Guatemala City, and I was able to find Net cafes in smaller towns, such as Antigua and Quezaltenango.

I was prepared to be offline for a couple of days while visiting the Peten jungle town of Flores near the Mayan ruins at Tikal. But lo and behold, Flores offered a choice of places to log on, though I wouldn't call these cafes. For the equivalent of about $.07 a minute, I was checking e-mail and corresponding with friends, family, and editors from a tiny, fly-ridden room, the size of a typical office cubicle. But I had no complaints whatsoever—I could get my coffee elsewhere.

Traveling *with a* Laptop

Unless you're traveling for business or plan to write extensively about your travels while on the road, it usually doesn't make sense to carry a laptop. With the ease of connection around the world today, most leisure travelers can check e-mail and surf the Web at Net cafes or other access points, which is far easier and cheaper than lugging around an expensive piece of equipment, spending lots of time trying to configure it, and paying prohibitive phone charges.

Not only are notebook computers pricey to procure, they're prized by thieves. According to Safeware Insurance Agency, which specializes in personal computer insuance, an estimated 1.5 million computers were stolen, damaged, or otherwise destroyed during 1998, the most recent year for which data were available in late 1999. These losses included about 400,000 thefts; other losses came from accidents, mostly screen breakage and power surges. Of course, this doesn't mean you should never carry a laptop. It simply dictates that if you need one, you should be very careful to protect it from being stolen or damaged.

If you're a business traveler, laptops can be essential tools, helping to maximize time on the road. Rather than have important messages and tasks pile up, you can tackle these assignments during your down time while traveling. And you can stay in touch with the office through e-mail, work on important documents or spreadsheets, and send this information back to the office without delay.

Advice for Connecting Abroad

Getting the proper equipment and configuring laptops in your home country is relatively easy, particularly if you live in the United States. One major difference between logging on at home and while traveling is that you'll likely be dialing in to a different phone number to try to make it a local call.

Consult your Internet service provider to get a list of phone numbers around the country, but be forewarned: Some ISPs only serve local areas, so you may have to make a long-distance call to log in to your home ISP. If you're traveling for work, consult your company's system administrator.

It's also possible in some places to get temporary personal dial-up accounts. My colleague Morris Dye told me recently, "The hotel where we stayed in Hong Kong had partnered with a local ISP to offer five days of unlimited local dial-up access for HK$100, or about US$13. Getting online with our own laptop was easy, simply a matter of entering a phone number, user-

tip

■ Many hotels charge for local calls, so find out whether or how much your hotel charges before logging on. If the cost is high, you may be able to log on through a pay phone with a data port, commonly found at airports.

name, and password they gave us and linking through the data port on the room phone, and it was much more convenient than the business center."

For a business traveler who visits the same place repeatedly, it might also be worth paying for a full-blown dial-up account in that place. Say you're a U.S.–based quality control engineer working for a company that has several factories in Thailand, and you visit those locations on a regular basis, it might be worth $15 a month or so for a permanent dial-up account.

For AOL Users:

ACCESS

One of the best things about AOL is that you log on with a local call in most U.S. locations. AOL also has lots of access points outside the United States. For logging on in the United States, see **Connecting to AOL** (keyword: *access*), which lists a toll-free number for access. Remember that this toll-free number should be used as a last resort. Try to find a local number first because AOL will charge you $.10 a minute for connecting through the "toll-free" number. Here's how AOL tells its members to find local access numbers:

To connect to AOL from a new location within the U.S., whether it be a hotel, airport, or private home, you need only follow these steps: In the Select Screen Name window of the AOL sign-on screen, select "New Local #." AOL will log on using a free 800 number, and you will be prompted to enter the area code of your location, and then to pick two local numbers. AOL will then sign off, and you can log back on using the New Location name you chose, accessible by clicking the Setup button.

To log on from abroad, see **International Access** (keyword: *international access*). Here, you'll find a list of access numbers, tips on logging on from foreign countries, and a price sheet (AOL imposes a surcharge when you log on from outside the U.S.). If you're still stumped, click on an ask-a-question link and submit your question—an AOL rep should get back to you by e-mail within twenty-four hours.

It would be impossible in just a few pages to cover all the different phone and electricity requirements for logging on around the globe. However, several Web sites do a pretty thorough job of outlining the equipment needed to connect in most countries around the world. Not surprisingly, some of these sites are in the business of selling this equipment. It can be a good idea to get these adapters and other gizmos ahead of time, but sometimes, you can get them cheaper on arrival, and you may be more likely to get what you need by going to an electronics store at your destination.

Here is a list of four sites that can be very useful for learning about logging on from abroad:

- **Roadnews (roadnews.com/home.htm):** Click on **"How to Travel with a Laptop"** for an extensive and well-organized archive of tips on subjects ranging from modem configuration to converting faxes to e-mail. You'll also find road reports from other mobile professionals and tricks of the trade in this section. In **Making a Connection,** for example, you'll find advice on how to go online by disassembling the telephone. This is a fantastic site for demystifying what it takes to log on. You can sign up for Roadnews's mailing list, which will send a weekly e-mail digest of questions and answers. If you're stumped and can't find the answer to your question, click on "Ask the Editor" to pose a question to Roadnews's Bob Lawson.

■ **TeleAdapt (www.teleadapt.com):** Perhaps the coolest feature about TeleAdapt is that it offers live chat support through the Web. So if you have a question about what type of equipment you need for an upcoming international trip, click on **Live Help** to start chatting. TeleAdapt sells just about everything you might need to connect from abroad, including acoustic couplers, which enable to you connect through any phone's earpiece without having to mess with the phone's wires.

■ **Walkabout Travel Gear (www.walkabouttravel gear.com):** Like some other valuable Web pages for world wanderers, Walkabout combines advice with items for sale. Click on "Come In and Browse," where you'll find sections on global electricity and international computer use. Each of these sections has an informative FAQ, as well as a summary with links to other sections of Walkabout's site. Here's a sample of the advice you'll find: "Plugging into a digital system can potentially fry your modem, because the voltage level is higher than what many modems can handle." Toward the bottom of the page, you'll find recommended products for sale. Another great source of information is **Walkabout Tips.** You'll see a link to this section on the home page.

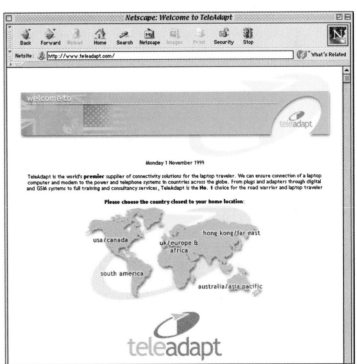

Teleadapt (www.teleadapt.com) can help you get the gear to connect to the Net while traveling abroad.

■ **Help for World Travelers (kropla.com):** Like the Walkabout site, Help for World

Travelers combines useful advice for logging on with general tips for international travel. For help with notebook computers, see the **Worldwide Phone Guide** or the **World Electric Power Guide.** Unlike the sites mentioned earlier, Help for World Travelers doesn't appear to be selling anything.

Laptop Tips *for* Mobile Professionals

Before you invest in a laptop and begin traveling with it, you may want to consider the following advice: Although laptops have been considered essential for business travelers, you may be able to get away without carrying one, even on business trips. Most hotel business centers now have computer terminals you can rent by the half hour for checking e-mail or composing documents. And airport terminals often have Net kiosks, where you can log on with a credit card or cash (carry some small bills) while waiting for your flight to depart. Of course, toting a laptop has its advantages too. If you're going to be carrying one, consider the following tips:

- **Choosing a laptop:** Ultralight notebook computers cost a bit more, but for some people they are worth the price. I use an ultralight IBM Thinkpad, which has a detachable CD drive. Because I don't usually need the CD drive, I don't have to carry it with me. (The disk drive is also detachable.) Remember though that ultralights (in the four-pound range) can be a bit more fragile than their slightly sturdier counterparts. Another point to consider: You'll pay more for the latest technology—ask yourself if you really need to have the fastest machine. If you don't, you can save a bundle and still get the features you need. Also, consider purchasing a spare battery—standard battery life is two to three hours, barely enough to fly halfway across the United States. Finally, if you just need to handle some basic functions and don't mind a small keyboard, you might consider a compact Windows CE machine.

- **Watch out for carry-on baggage ripoffs:** Laptop theft at airport security checkpoints is a common scam. Try not to get in a situation where you're delayed at the metal detector, either by people ahead of you or by your own metal items.

- **Back up before flying:** You should back up your data before each flight and keep your backup disks separate from your computer.

- **Beware of digital phone systems:** Though more and more hotels throughout the world are providing safe data ports for connecting your modem, some still use digital phone systems. If you try to jack into these systems, you can fry your modem. Check with the front desk to find out the best way to log on and avoid unnecessary risks.

- **Prove you own it:** Carry some proof of purchase. Two copies is probably best: one with the computer and one somewhere else to show its value if it's stolen. In many destinations, it's important to show that you're not planning to sell it; on reentering the United States, the point is to demonstrate you didn't buy it abroad.

- **Printing:** A small portable ink-jet printer can be very useful—bring extra ink cartridges. For travel overseas, you may want to bring U.S. size paper and envelopes.

Other Tools for Business Travelers

Chapter 11, "Taking Care of Business," discusses several tools for business travelers, such as the Palm Pilot. There are also a couple of tools that help you stay in touch through the Net: roaming networks and fax-to-e-mail conversion.

Roaming Networks

Although national or international Internet service providers, such as **Netcom (www.netcom.com)**, can be the best choice for frequent travelers, you may still be able to log on locally if you're a member of a small ISP. Some smaller ISPs have hooked up to a roaming network such as **iPass (ipass.com).** If your ISP is a member of iPass, you can log on throughout the world, usually through a local call to a local ISP that's part of iPass's network. There is a surcharge for this service, typically $.05 to $.25 a minute. If you haven't selected an ISP yet and you travel often, choose one that covers where you travel or check with iPass for a list of ISPs that are part of its network.

Fax-to-e-mail Conversion

Though e-mail could some-day render the fax machine obsolete, faxes are still widely used. While away on business, you may not want to wait until you get home to read your faxes, and there are services that will convert incoming faxes to e-mail and drop them in your e-mail box. Some services convert e-mail messages into faxes and send them to a phone number you choose.

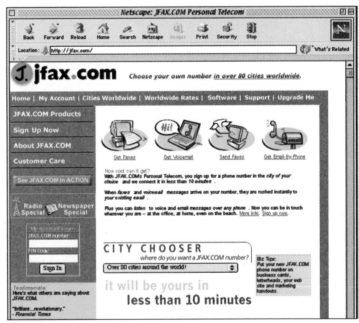

Jfax.com (jfax.com) lets you receive faxes in your e-mail box.

For sending faxes, try **Fax4Free (www.fax4free. com)**, which lets you send faxes to any phone in the United States. Faxes include banner ads on the printed pages and can take a while to arrive, so this is not a full-time substitute for a fax machine, but it is a good alternative while traveling. Registration is required but free, as you'd guess from the name. Another alternative for sending faxes is **Swiss Click (www.hotcorp.com/swiss click)**, where you don't have to register. Not only are these services useful for business, they're a great way to keep Net-deprived friends and relatives updated on your travels. If your Aunt Millie has a fax machine but not a computer, you can send her a fax when you log on at a Net cafe or through your laptop.

Receiving faxes is a bit more involved because you need a phone number. Remarkably, **jfax.com (www.jfax.com)** will give a you free phone number for receiving faxes and will convert incoming faxes (including images) into a graphical e-mail attachment and send it to your e-mail address. The phone number will probably not be in your home area code, but if it's important for you to have your fax number be local, you can sign up for jfax's business package. The business package costs $12.50 a month and provides a fax number in the city you choose, the ability to receive multiple faxes simultaneously, and some other services.

The Promise *and* Perils *of* Documenting Trips Online

The Net offers almost limitless possibilities for documenting trips, from sending basic e-mail dispatches to constructing elaborate Web pages, complete with images—and even sound or video. More and more travelers are choosing to create travelogues *as they travel,* but many veteran wired travelers are saying that just because you can doesn't mean you should.

Several people interviewed for this book said that some of their greatest travel moments involved documenting their journeys. But these same travelers said a lot of frustration resulted from failing to connect or having a laptop damaged or stolen. Ultimately, the key is balance: Document trips if it turns you on, but don't spend your entire journey trying to splice phone wires or hunkered down in a Net cafe. And remember, you can keep a pen-and-paper journal while you travel and put that beautiful Web page together when you get home.

> **tip**
>
> For advice on putting together a Web page and other general Internet wisdom, get ahold of *The Internet* by Angus Kennedy, published by Rough Guides.

Travelers' Tales

As travel writer Jeff Greenwald approached his fortieth birthday, he decided to circumnavigate the globe. To get away from the rut of commuting, he chose to completely avoid air travel and circle the globe with on-the-ground transport: trains, boats, cars, and on foot. Every couple of weeks he filed a dispatch for the GNN Travelers' Center (now defunct). "While my brain was telecommuting at the speed of light, my body was still compelled to travel at a snail's pace, face down in the sand," he said.

There were days when Greenwald cursed the wires, couplers, and laptop he dragged with him on his quest. One such day was during a festival in Oaxaca, Mexico. Mariachi bands played in the town square, children paraded in costumes down the street, and Greenwald was stuck in the dank offices of Teléfonos de Mexico trying futilely to get his dispatch to the travel editor back at GNN in California. Each successive attempt thinned his wallet, but not one dispatch got through. Months later, when he was halfway around the world, Greenwald realized that the entire travesty may have been due to his failure to flick a switch from tone to pulse dialing.

At other times, however, Greenwald was ecstatic that as he traveled through Guatemala, Istanbul, Nepal, and more than a dozen other countries, he could share his adventures—almost instantaneously—with friends, family, and fascinated followers half a world away. "I had this sense of being almost on fire, that the excitement and heat my journey was providing me was something I could broadcast in no time at all," he says. "It was a very giddy feeling."

The Loss of a Laptop

When Jeff was in Nepal, his state-of-the-art laptop was stolen on an overnight bus ride. "I was devastated, more depressed than I'd ever been in my life. The laptop, more than the most useful tool I was carrying, had become a companion to me. I was pouring my emotions into it—all the best things I was doing on my trip, the best writing, the best feelings, the best observations were all being confided to that machine, which became a companion, almost in the way an android, like Data from *Star Trek,* would be a companion. I just really respected the machine's ability and its incredible versatility and portability; it (was) almost my little therapist."

Jim Klima, who discusses planning his overland trip in chapter 8, also had a devastating experience while carrying a laptop. The following is an excerpt from his site (see **www.jetcity.com/~suebee** for the entire travelog; **www.jetcity.com/~sue bee/52.shtml** for the page that includes this excerpt):

tip

■ Jeff Greenwald's dispatches are no longer online but are part of a book entitled *The Size of the World* (Ballantine Books).

First Person: Jim Klima

In Abeoketa (Nigeria) we set up the tents behind a fancy hotel. After dinner I entered the lobby and persuaded the desk clerk to let me plug my laptop into a power point. Time disappeared and all of a sudden it was 3:00 A.M. I packed up and stepped out into a dark parking lot. Suddenly I felt vulnerable and several shadowy figures in the corner of my eye didn't allay my fear. Walking quickly I followed the driveway, paying more attention to the figures behind me than the terrain in front of me. Stepping over the curb into a shadow I abruptly found myself falling. One square in the string of large tiles covering the sewer running alongside the road was missing and I scored a bull's-eye.

The sewer was deep. I flung out my arms to catch myself after dropping three feet. Unfortunately one hand held the laptop, which slammed against the pavement. I prayed that the laptop's soft case had cushioned it sufficiently. Safely back inside my tent I carefully unpacked the computer and powered it up. Disaster—it would not boot because it could not find the hard drive. The disk must have crashed! How could such a freak accident occur after all the special care I had taken to protect the laptop? How am I going to deliver travel stories to the five sites that agreed to post them? My disappointment is profound. For me the trip is over. It is little consolation that the last thing I did before leaving the hotel was backup everything on a floppy disk.

Both Greenwald and Klima traveled extensively with a laptop in the mid- to late 1990s. Today, however, both say they'd rather be free of their laptops for future trips. "Nowadays when I see people sitting around filing Internet dispatches from foreign countries, I roll my eyes," Greenwald said. "I get lots of e-mail asking how to send back dispatches over the Net, and my advice is, 'Leave your computer at home and enjoy your trip. You'll have a much better time keeping your eyes open and writing postcards.'"

Miles *from* Nowhere, Minutes *from* Contact

Despite the hazards of traveling with a laptop, some people are so thrilled by the prospect of documenting a trip that it becomes the focus of their journey. Though the computer is sometimes viewed as an antisocial tool, says Marlene Graham, one that tends to isolate us from in-person encounters, the exact reverse has been true for the Graham family of Wichita, Kansas. The family's site **(www.usatrip.org)** documents their van-and-tent trips to all fifty of the United States.

First Person: Marlene Graham

For three years now our lives—travels, joys, fears, fights, and frustrations—have been unfolding in front of an audience of millions, and the result has been the most exciting, incredible experiences as a family. It all started when we walked away from our hectic life to spend time together as a family traveling the fifty states. And they (people following our journey online) write to us. They give us tips on places to go, things to see, even invite us into their homes. They ask travel questions. They reminisce about their own adventures. They express concern about our welfare when our notes fall behind. Are we okay? And they provide helping hands in times of distress.

Once, for example, Radio Shack was flooded by e-mails when I talked about our video camera breaking down, and how desperately we needed it for video reports being filed weekly with a local television station back home. Just days later an e-mail came to us from a Radio Shack vice president in L.A. He said he had been apprised of our situation and wanted to let us know that the next Tandy Service Center on our route would be glad to fix the camera for us as we waited. Imagine our surprise when the bill was presented as NO CHARGE. All through the assistance of anonymous Internet friends. The funny thing is, when we set out on our first Internet adventure, we just thought the net would be a way for our families to follow our adventure.

(*Headfirst into America!* by Marlene Graham chronicles the family's adventures. It's published by Alexander Books.)

Riding Into the Sunset

With the goal of broadcasting updates as he rode across the country, motorcycle enthusiast Greg Elin embarked on a transcontinental motorcycle ride across the United States, which he called "Silicon Alley to Silicon Valley" and later staged the **Alley to Valley Rally (www.avr.org)**. Using a Connectix camera, Greg routinely broadcast images to his Web site to complement the text descriptions.

tip

■ For a list of travelogue directories, see "Adventure Travelogues" in chapter 8.

During his trip, Greg found time to visit his parents in Chicago and get them on the Net. A week and a half later, he pulled his motorcycle to the side of the road, took a digital photo of a stunning sunset, and quickly uploaded the image to his Web site. Within minutes, his mother and his girlfriend (and anyone else with a Net connection) could see an image of the sunset Greg had just witnessed. "It has the potential to be so personal," he said. "All I needed was a computer, the Net, a phone, and a camera, and they were seeing live pictures from my motorcycle in New Mexico."

Over and over, travelers who make the Net a part of their trips—whether by carrying a laptop or logging on at Net cafes—emphasize how outstanding a tool it is for making personal connections. "The Net is not this faraway vision of cyberspace, but real people you can visit," Greg says. And keeping that conduit open leads to more connections as one travels, creating those sublime encounters that make a journey rewarding and memorable.

Other Chapters to Check

Chapter 8: "The Ultimate Adventure"—Travelogue directories
Chapter 11: "Taking Care of Business"—Tools and techniques for wired business travelers

---

GLOSSARY

Bookmarks: A feature in Netscape's browser that lets you store Web page addresses and return to those pages with one click.

Browser: An application such as Netscape Navigator that enables you to download and view Web pages.

Case sensitive: Term meaning that upper or lower case is relevant. For example, an e-mail address is not case sensitive and could be written name@domain.com or Name@domain.com. But some parts of a Web address can be case sensitive.

Clickable map: An image, such as a world map, that you can click to reach other Web pages.

Domain: The main part of a Web site's address. Those that end in *.com* are usually commercial entities; those ending in *.gov* are governmental. Other domain name endings include *.net*, *.org*, and *.edu*.

Drill down: To find information at a search engine or other Web site by clicking on a series of increasingly specific categories. For example, to find ecotour outfitters, go to yahoo.com and click on "Travel" then "Ecotourism" then "Ecotour Operators."

E-mail: Electronic mail sent over the Internet, as opposed to "snailmail" sent via the postal service.

FAQ (frequently asked questions): Many Web sites and other online resources have a FAQ section where common questions are answered.

Favorites: A feature in Microsoft's Internet Explorer browser that stores Web page addresses and lets you return to those pages with one click.

Home page: A Web site's main or front page. Also refers to the first page that appears on your browser when you launch it. You can choose any Web site to be your home page.

Icon: A small image on a Web page that carries meaning. For example, browsers have icons of padlocks. If the padlock is shown locked, that means the site is in secure mode and will encode sensitive information, such as a credit card number.

Imagemap: See clickable map.

Internet: The ungoverned global network of millions of computers. The Internet, or Net, is decentralized. Anyone who's connected to it can view and post Web pages or other documents.

ISP: Internet service provider, a company that offers access to the Net, usually for a monthly fee.

Keyword: In America Online this means a word that links to a page or resource on AOL. For example, the keyword "travel" leads to a page of travel resources. In other contexts keywords can be words you're searching for more information about.

Link: A word, phrase or image that when clicked leads to another Web page or other online resource.

Mailto: A link connected to a recipient's e-mail address. A Web page may have a mailto link you can click to send e-mail to the page's author.

Net: See Internet.

Online: Refers to any resource on the Internet, including the Web, e-mail, and services such as AOL.

Online service: A company such as AOL or CompuServe that offers Internet access and a gated community of highly organized online resources. Users can stay in the gated community or venture out onto the Web.

Password: A word or phrase unique to each user that grants access to online resources.

Portal: A site like Yahoo that offers a set of Web-based resources including a search engine, yellow pages, appointment calendars, weather forecasts, and news headlines.

Pull-down menu: A list of options, found by clicking on an arrow, that displays the choices.

Query: A search for a keyword.

Radio button: A clickable button designed to input information into a Web site.

Scroll bar: The bar along the right side of a browser or other computer application that enables you to move up and down the page.

Search engine (also known as search directory): A site such as Lycos that lets you search for Web pages related to key terms.

Site: See Web site.

Spam: An unwelcome e-mail message often sent to thousands of people simultaneously.

URL (Uniform resource locator): A Web address, such as www.frommers.com. Also: the system of assigning Web addresses.

Usenet: Online discussion groups accessible through browsers or via the Web site Deja.com. Short for users' network.

Username or user ID: A usually self-selected and unique name to gain access to a Web site, online service, or other computer resource.

Web: Also World Wide Web or WWW. A network of linked documents, comprised of text and images, and in some cases audio and video feeds.

Web site: A virtual place on the Web consisting of any or all of the following: text, images, sound and video. Can be one page or lots of linked pages.

Want to learn about terms not listed here?

See the following sites:
Webopedia (www.webopedia.com)
What is? (www.whatis.com)

APPENDIX B

AOL'S TRAVEL CHANNEL
One-Stop Shopping for Booking, Destinations & Chat

An Introduction to AOL's Travel Services

America Online offers two terrific advantages for its members: First, it's relatively easy and inexpensive to connect to AOL from just about anywhere in the United States and from many foreign destinations as well. Second, it has organized lots of useful services in one place. By starting at the *AOL Travel Center* (insert the keyword *travel* or select "Travel" from the Channels screen), you can book a flight, access online guidebooks, get maps and directions, and chat with other AOL users. You can also find highly specific information, such as advice on traveling with pets.

AOL Travel provides tools for trip planning and booking.

This is not to suggest that you can find everything you need within AOL's vast gated community—the World Wide Web is a rich source of information, and it's wise to use the resources there as well.

Access the Web through AOL by clicking the Internet tab at the top of AOL's screen and selecting "Go to the Web."

AOL has teamed with many leading providers of travel services, such as Travelocity and Fodor's, to give its members familiar brands. Of course these brands have paid dearly for the privilege of delivering their services through AOL. Travelocity alone spends millions of dollars each year to reach AOL members. In the end, it appears to be a pretty good package for AOL users, who get access to some leading travel services in a simple, user-friendly format.

Just before wrapping up this book, I spoke with Mark Rogers, AOL's senior programming manager for travel, who said AOL is planning to add a complete vacation center, including about eight subcategories, such as adventure, resorts, and bargains. AOL hopes to expand its destination guides by adding new partners, such as Rough Guides, he said. The goal for 2000 and beyond is to offer a broader range of services so members can select one that best suits them, or visit more than one guide (for example Fodor's and Lonely Planet) for a more complete picture of a destination.

What follows is a guide to ten of AOL's most essential travel services, accompanied by an alphabetical directory of other important AOL travel sites. The AOL keyword for each page appears in parentheses. To go directly to a page, log on to AOL and hit "Ctrl K" (hold down the control key and type *k*) which triggers a keyword box. Enter the keyword, click "Go," and you'll be on your way.

AOL's Top Ten Travel Resources

(the keyword is in parentheses)

1. **AOL Travel** *(travel)* is AOL's launch pad for travel services and includes links to booking for flights, hotels, and rental cars; destination information from leading guidebooks; vacation bargains; message boards; a business travel center; and seasonal features, such as a beach guide. Most of these sections are described in this appendix.

AOL's Cruise Critic includes advice, news, bargains, and editor's picks.

2. **Destination Guides** *(destinations)* features indepth advice from Fodor's and other guides. Click on "Worldwide Tourism Info" for information from tourism offices and other official sources for thousands of destinations worldwide.

3. **Reservations Center** *(travel reservations)*. By partnering with Preview Travel, AOL offers most of the same services Preview offers on the Web (see chap. 2), including best-fare price quotes and booking for flights, hotels, and rental cars. To book travel through AOL, click on the Preview Travel icon, then click on "Air, Car and Hotel Reservations," which takes you to Preview's Web site. (*Note:* Preview has agreed to merge with Travelocity, so this will likely change to Travelocity in spring 2000.)

4. **Resource Center** *(resource center)* includes trip planning advice and sections on passports, money, health and safety, and packing, among other topics. The center also includes timely features, such as a recent piece on drinking water abroad. If you don't see the subject you're interested in, try the center's search box.

5. **Maps and Directions** *(mapping)* offers driving directions between any two U.S. addresses. You can also generate maps for cities, regions, states, and countries.

6. **Travel Bargains** *(travel bargains)* lists a wide range of deals on flights, lodging, car

rentals, and cruises. There are also deals for seniors, students, and families. Other specials are targeted by region—for example, a $49 deal on flights from San Jose to Lake Tahoe.

7. **Cruise Critic** *(cruise critic)* includes news and bargains, advice to help you choose, tips for first-time cruisers, and picks from cruise critic Anne Campbell. Also see AOL's **Cruise Center** *(cruise)*, which offers a cruise selector and includes links to late-breaking bargains, as well as a forum of members' opinions.

8. **Business Travel Center** *(business travel)* includes the same booking features found in AOL's general travel section. Added to this are some mapping features (including airport maps and point-to-point directions), city guides, and MaxMiles's tool for managing frequent flier accounts.

9. **Travel Interests** *(travel interests)* has sections on travel for families, women, gays and lesbians, honeymooners, RVers, theme park enthusiasts, and many more. The subject matter in Travel Interests is similar to the Web content covered in chapter 10, "A Perfect Vacation."

10. **Member Opinions** *(member opinions)* is AOL's hub for travel chat. See what others are saying or jump into the fray! There are message boards for destinations (United States, Europe, Caribbean, etc.), for travel issues (family travel tips, rail tips, etc.) and for interests/activities (cruising, adventures, etc.). You can create a Travel Home Page here and show off your travel photos.

Other Valuable Travel Pages on AOL

Adventure & Active *(adventure travel)* is a good jumping-off point for adventure planning with sections on biking, climbing, fishing, and scuba diving. A section called **Planning Guides** links to adventure Web sites, and another link goes to AOL's version of Outside Online (from *Outside* magazine). Adventure & Active links to related AOL pages, such as **Parks & Camping** and **Safaris & Ecotours.**

Airline Center *(airline)* is the place to book flights, find bargains, learn about frequent flier programs, and check for special offers.

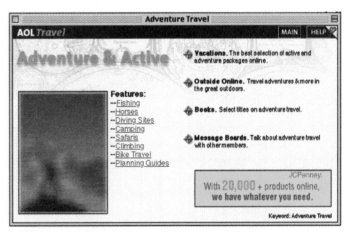

AOL's Adventure & Active pages include features, advice, and message boards.

Bargain Box *(bargain box)* offers daily and weekly specials on flights, lodging, car rentals, vacation packages, and more. Some discounts are solely for AOL members, and other deals are for certain types of travelers, such as seniors. But no matter how good a deal looks, shop around. You may find a better price elsewhere.

Bed & Breakfast Guide *(B&B)* links to the **BedandBreakfast.com** Web site, which lists more than 20,000 inns. For more details, see the B&B section in chapter 3.

Car Renter Center *(car rental)* links directly to AOL sites for Hertz, and Avis, with special deals for AOL members, such as free upgrades or $25 off a weekly rental. Whether these deals are better than those published elsewhere is debatable. AOL teams with Preview Travel to offer **Carfinder,** where users select an airport and see the best rates from car rental companies at that airport.

Digital City *(digitalcity)* includes dozens of city guides for U.S. cities. Use the clickable map to select a city where you'll find listings for entertainment, dining, hotels, sports, and more. For international cities, type in the keyword *international.*

Family Travel Network *(family travel network)* is chock-full of ideas including trips listed by interest (kids' museums, dinosaur treks, etc.) and bargains for family travel. The **Destinations** section includes planning advice and features for top vacation spots, as well as sections on the best places for families to stay.

Hotel Center *(hotel)* includes everything from big chain hotels to tiny B&Bs, as well as a listing of lodging bargains. Use **Hotel Finder** to find top hotels reviewed by Fodor's, or reserve online through an AOL service provided by Preview Travel.

Independent Traveler *(traveler)* has a section called **Travelers' Journeys** with reports from other travelers who have recently visited exciting destinations such as Costa Rica. Other sections include resources for savvy traveling, an online bookstore, and late-breaking bargains to exotic destinations. And of course, The Independent Traveler has plenty of online forums where you can learn from others or share your thoughts.

Inside Flyer Online *(inside flyer)* links to the WebFlyer site, the definitive online source of frequent flier information. For more, see chapter 11.

The Knot *(knot)* is a general wedding site that has a link to Honeymoon Escapes, which lists top honeymoon destinations and sorts trips into categories (adventure, beach, exotic, Hawaiian, European, etc.).

Lonely Planet Guides *(lonely planet)* includes some of the same features available at LP's Web site (see chap. 1).

News and Features *(news & features)* ranges from travel literature to money-saving advice and covers provocative travel issues.

Outdoor Adventure Online *(outdoor adventure)* has sections such as Guides and Tours, and Destinations and Resorts. Or click on the link for "250 Ultimate Adventures" organized into sixteen categories by OAO. This terrific resource also includes instructional features such as "Getting Certified on Your Vacation" in the scuba section. You can

tip

■ Most of AOL's restaurant coverage has been incorporated into its Digital City site. You can access Digital City's restaurant reviews by typing in the keyword *"restaurants"* or by going to a city page (enter the keyword *"miami,"* for example) and search the restaurant listings for that city. You can also discuss restaurants in AOL's many forums.

participate in OAO's forum or scroll down the box in the lower right corner for listings by state.

PlanetOut Travel (pno travel) for gay and lesbian travelers, includes destination guides, travel features, events calendars, and message boards for hooking up with others.

Ski Vacations *(ski vacations)* has lots of resort reviews and you can check snow conditions here.

Traveler's Advantage *(TA)*. This program promises 5 to 25 percent off the regular advertised price on over 100 quality vacation packages, but take a close look before signing up. Many vacation packages are generally sold below "the regular advertised price" so this might not be such a great deal. And after a three-month free trial, this program costs $59.95 per year.

Travel Classifieds *(travel classifieds)*. Stuck with a condo rental you can't use? Looking for a deal? Check AOL's travel classifieds.

Travel Search and Explore *(travelsearch)* is a directory of AOL's travel pages listed alphabetically. This is a good place to check because AOL continually adds new travel sites and sometimes changes their names and keywords.

Travel File *(travelfile)*. Find events calendars, discounted vacation packages, tourism offices, and more. The lists of restaurants and hotels are short as only paid advertisers seem to be mentioned.

Vacation Center *(vacation center)* includes sections on cruising, adventure, theme parks, casinos, and many more. **Bargains** lists trips by departure city and by type (resort packages, specialty vacations, etc.). You'll also find a section listing deals from travel suppliers such as Renaissance Cruises.

APPENDIX C

TRAVEL AGENTS IN THE INTERNET AGE

Travel Agents Can Survive—and Thrive

With the ability of travelers to book trips online, an obvious question arises: "Are travel agents doomed?" In short the answer is: "Not the good ones." Travel agents and agencies that embrace the Net can cut their costs and increase their customer base. In fact, the only travel agents who have to worry about the Internet are those who fail to integrate it into their business.

As my colleague Morris Dye has said for years, travel agents have traditionally sold two services: their expertise and access to booking systems. Now that everyone with a Net connection can book their own trips, agents have only their expertise to sell. Those agents who develop this expertise, and market it through the Net, certainly have a bright future ahead.

This appendix shows how agents can use the Web to parlay their expertise in a region (Hawaii) or type of travel (spa vacations, theme parks, etc.) and use this knowledge to develop an international clientele. Even if you're a generalist, you can use the Net to get exposure, on services that list travel agencies such as **ASTAnet (www. astanet.com).**

Also in this appendix: Travel agents who are thriving in this wired era share their strategies and demonstrate how they have made the Net work for them.

Transforming Crisis into Opportunity

With the emergence of the Internet, many travel agents are beginning to fear that their clients will abandon them and do all their trip planning online. But many travelers simply don't want to bother with the details of trip planning. Most big online booking agencies, such as **Expedia.com** have a look-to-book ratio of up to 50-to-1. That means that for every person who books online, there are up to 50 people window shopping. When it comes to purchasing, many of these people want to buy their travel through an experienced professional. And since they're already online, that's where they may begin their search for an agent.

Listing Your Agency Online

The Net offers several places where you can publicize your agency at little or no cost. Following are some of the best:

ASTAnet (www.astanet.com): The home page of the American Society of Travel Agents has a listing of agencies that's open to consumers. Your agency can be listed in the Travel Directory and Trip Request sections. There's also an area specifically for ASTA's more than 26,000 members.

Internet Travel Network (www.itn.com): ITN is unlike most online agencies in that it turns bookings over to travel agents and keeps a small fee for the referral.

1travel.com (onetravel.com): 1travel.com works with agents and refers customers to those agents it believes are offering the best bargains.

TravelHub (www.travelhub.com): TravelHub helps travelers find agencies near their home. You can be listed by destinations or types of trips in which you specialize — for example, Caribbean, golf, cruises, or seniors.

Yahoo (yahoo.com): Getting listed on search engines is essential to building your business through online referrals. Yahoo is the largest, but don't ignore the others: Excite, Go, Infoseek, LookSmart, Snap, and Lycos. A service called **Submit It** (www.submit-it.com) will, for a fee, submit your Web site's address to more than a dozen search engines.

TravelBids (www.travelbids.com): TravelBids is a reverse auction site (see chap. 7) where travelers submit the trips they want and the agent who offers the lowest prices gets the business. Commissions can be smaller than usual but you won't have to spend a lot of time on trip planning—usually you simply get the information, book the trip, and collect the commission.

No Substitute for Service

Today, most of the information to which travel agents had almost exclusive access is available free on the Net. Integrating this new reality means agents must recognize that, whether they like it or not, this information is going to be available to their customers. Rather than ignoring the Net, agents should encourage their customers to use it. Clients can get a sense of their options online and then turn to an agent to close the deal.

"Nothing will replace personal service," says Annette Sorscher of Annette's Travel in Boca Raton, Florida. "I don't think the Net will put anyone out of business unless they don't offer personal service. Loyalty depends on how you treat your clients."

To provide such service in this new environment means travel agents need to get online. Says Sally Lewis, who serves as marketing manager for **1travel.com,** "Today, coupons and special deals change by the instant. Agents with their fingers on the pulse can save you lots of money." Lewis is mystified that agents will spend thousands of dollars to advertise locally but hesitate to spend some money to get online. "You can get a huge return on your investment," she says.

Setting Up Shop on the Web

Simply putting up a Web site and leaving it unattended like a billboard ad is not a winning strategy. "Just because a travel agent puts up a Web site doesn't mean people will be knocking on their door. You have to be set up to respond quickly," Lewis says. In other words, if you have an online presence, check your e-mail every day—several times a day, in fact—because clients expect rapid replies to their e-mail queries.

"If you're a smart businessperson and an aggressive salesperson, you can make this work. A lot of travel agents are order-takers: they're not used to going out there and actively selling. You need to do that on the Net." While some agents are intimidated by the new technology, they actually are ahead of professionals in many other fields, because they know how to use a computerized reservation system (CRS). If you can master a CRS, the Net should be a snap, though, like a new destination, it does take some time to know the territory.

Nancy Zebrick, of All Destinations Travel in Cherry Hill, New Jersey **(www. alltravel.com)**, says more than 90 percent of her business today comes to her through the Net, up from 20 percent just two years ago! Zebrick advises agents to use their expertise to specialize and aggressively promote that specialty. The Internet has changed the orientation and nature of her business, Nancy says, giving it access to clients around the world.

First Person: Nancy Zebrick

I don't consider us local anymore. I consider us global. Right now I'm working with a client from Oslo [Norway] arranging a trip to Club Med and Disney World here in Florida. He found us through the Net.

I used to be a dietitian and I got into this business to do my own ticketing. People who make it on the Net are really specialized. Because of my background in diet and fitness, I'd been to thirty-nine fitness spas. Some were real spas—others just a resort with a massage therapist on duty. I knew which were the real spas and used this expertise to build my business.

It wasn't like I just opened a site and business came through the door. I had to develop the trust and confidence of clients. To do that, I got back to each one within twenty-four hours with a price and recommendation. The key to making it is to follow up quickly and work the leads. We don't just send e-mail—we call to develop a more personal bond.

Also, we don't accept any advertising on our site. I give honest opinions, tell people what's good, what's bad, and what's ugly. So when they see that I've recommended a spa, they know it's truly one of my favorites.

Nancy says there's no magic formula to success on the Net. Like just about any business, it's a lot of hard work. Some leads are good; others are junk, she says, but her agency follows up on each one, just as they would follow up on phone inquiries.

For the next couple of years, knowing how to employ the Net will give savvy agents a significant competitive advantage. Farther down the road, the knowledge they gain about the Internet, its demographics, and its culture could mean the difference between survival and failure.

The Advantages *of* E-mail *and* Online Research

As computers become more prevalent, people expect to be able to make their travel arrangements online. Rather than pick up the phone and get put on hold for an agent, many would much prefer to shoot their questions to their agent via e-mail. And e-mail saves time and money for agents as well.

"Using e-mail I can transmit a message with little or no chance of misunderstanding to a client I might never meet, at a cost lower than using the telephone," says Bob Ensten of American Made Travel Adventures in Novato, California. Through e-mail, agents can give thoughtful consideration to each part of the client's message, respond comprehensively, and even include referrals to online documents, such as a useful Web page.

You don't need to create your own Web site to begin reaping the benefits of the Net. For $15 to $22 a month, you can get an account with an Internet service provider such as Netcom or Earthlink. This account will allow you to browse the Net, monitor and post to newsgroups, and, most importantly, send and receive e-mail.

Ensten also uses the Web to research trips for clients. "Recently, a client wanted to plan a trip to Croatia. Not knowing anything about Croatia, I searched the Web for any articles/information about that country—and found several," he says.

By using e-mail, agents don't have to wait for their clients to visit their site—they can take the initiative and contact them directly, perhaps with a mass mailing of specials each week or month. Sending e-mail to past or prospective clients should be done judiciously, however. Early in the relationship, you should ask clients whether they want to receive travel alerts and other information via e-mail, or have a place on your Web site where people can sign up for these dispatches. Otherwise your well-meaning e-mail may be viewed as spam (junk e-mail).

> **tip**
>
> Your e-mail address (and Web site address, if you have one) should be on all your literature, including business cards and brochures.

Luring Clients in Online Discussion Groups

A good way to generate business is through online discussion groups (see chap. 13). By monitoring these discussions and offering knowledgeable commentary, you can reel in clients. The subtle approach works best, responding to individuals' questions rather than posting a blanket message.

Kimberly Barker, a former travel agent who publishes **The Fam Connection** online newsletter **(www.redshift.com/~talisman/FamConnection.html)**, says: "When people post in newsgroups, answer their questions with timely and useful information. Be a consultant. Show your stuff by offering genuine help. The same person who asked the weather question may come to you when it's time to plan that trip. Being there to offer guidance and experience as an agent may not guarantee you business . . . but finding your niche in these places and offering your services can often pay off in spades."

Finding Your Niche on the Net

Sally Lewis, quoted earlier, says finding your niche is the best way to go. "Agents have been squeezed by airline caps—airlines themselves are heading towards direct distribution. Many travel agents see the light and know that they need to niche themselves as some sort of travel expert online to survive. No matter how electronic we become, there will always be a need for expert advice in certain categories of the travel business."

By using the Internet, agents reach travelers in their chosen medium. Rather than curse the fact that travelers can find and arrange travel on the Net, smart agencies are staking their claims in cyberspace. In chapter 10, honeymooner Leslie Camino-Markowitz tells how she used the Net to find a travel agent on the Mediterranean island of Ibiza. Because the agent, James Benjamin of Festive Travel & Tours **(www.festive travel.com)**, lives at this destination, he's familiar with the best accommodations and made her honeymoon a delight.

"When we decided to start a site on the Net we really had no idea what to do," Benjamin says. "We started late in the season and just put a few pages together to try to promote the area. In no time at all we were receiving e-mail with requests from all over the world. We were very excited by the response. In the short amount of time we rented hotel rooms, rental cars, apartments, villas, flights, and the requests continue to roll in. Living in a place does help in the planning of a holiday."

When Leslie and her new husband arrived in Ibiza, James met them at the airport, showed them to their hotel, and then shared a bottle of sangria to congratulate the newlyweds. So, in this case the Net facilitated a strong business relationship that led to a new friendship.

Your Web Site: More Than *a* Flyer That Glows

In the retail business, they call advertising signs "silent salesmen" because they work around the clock. A Web site can be seen as an interactive version of an advertising sign. It's not only an inexpensive way to get a travel agency's message out, it's also a way to leave the office open twenty-four hours a day, seven days a week.

"Traditionally, planning and booking a cruise with a client would only be done during my office hours, making it convenient for me and my staff but not necessarily for the client," says Gordon Merritt, who runs **Internet Cruise Travel Network (www.cruisetravel.com)**. "By going online, we are able to receive and send messages from and to clients anytime of the day or night. We respond rapidly to our clients and potential clients, many times within the half hour."

Merritt's site serves as an interactive travel brochure, yet it does far more than any printed brochure could do—and it can be easily updated with new specials or features. Internet Cruise Travel Network is a smartly organized site that tells potential clients about cruise types, itineraries, special deals, and monthly features. While many potential clients may come solely for the information, Merritt's mentality is like that of any smart merchant: Get 'em into the store, and they may just buy something.

ICTN does something else that's very smart: It offers a free membership program. At press time the site claimed more than 420,000 members. What do members get for taking a few minutes to fill out a form? Special discounts, a cruise newsletter delivered periodically via e-mail, and a cruise profile that enables them to specify interests so they can get updates about bargain cruises that meet their specs. Offering these memberships doesn't really cost the agency anything, and it helps create a clientele that's more connected to the site, whether or not a client is local. The one thing I don't like about ICTN's site is that the only way to get in the door (past the home page) is to become a member. It's better to let people browse whether they want to become a member or not.

Seven Tips for a Successful Web Site

Most of the following tips come from Tom and Mary Kay Aufrance, who run the **Lake Tahoe Home Page (highsierra.com)**.

1. **Choose a reliable Internet service provider. If your site is down, you're out.**

2. **Prominently identify your company, services, and how to make contact with you (such as your toll-free number).**

3. **Right on top, you need an attractive photo that allows the reader to imagine, "That's me there in that exotic place! Where do I sign up?"**

4. **Make sure your call to action is interspersed throughout the text. ("Click here to reserve now!") This "Click Here" button should lead to a reservation request form that includes all the information you need to replace that first phone call, such as name, address, phone number, e-mail address, desired service, and arrival/departure dates.**

5. **Your request form should send you an e-mail message (which means you need your own e-mail account) so that you or your staff can respond within twenty-four hours, before the lead goes stale.**

6. **A search on your site is like a magnet for readers. The High Sierra site logs show the most readership on pages that are titled "Search for Your Dream Vacation" or something like that, says Tom. "People love the interactivity, and also the ability to customize their search criteria to fit their personal desires."**

7. **Don't put a site up for the world to see until it meets some minimum requirements for completeness. There is nothing more irritating to users than a site that promises tons of information but is "under construction" for an extended period of time.**

tip

■ Surf the Web constantly to see what other agencies are doing with their sites and learn from their innovations.

Summing Up

Whether you simply want to get Net access and e-mail to communicate with clients or establish your own Web site, one thing is clear: You can't afford not to get online. Clients expect you to be able to communicate by e-mail, but more important, the Web offers an almost limitless array of services for agents. As the competition among agents increases, you'll have to employ every tool at your disposal to remain competitive. Both your prospective customers and your competitors will be using the Net. If you're not, you may be out of the game.

Most of the agents profiled above jumped online for commonsense business reasons. But after they got on the Net, they found a whole new world had opened to them, a world that included new ways to attract clients, novel methods for researching destinations, and broader connections with their colleagues. So while many agents rightly feel they must get online to survive, there are lots of side benefits to being on the Net. Don't wait too long to share in this adventure.

APPENDIX D

TRAVEL WEB SITES
by TOPIC

Below you'll find hundreds of Web site listings in twenty-five categories. The most useful are denoted Five-Star Sites; you may want to check these first. But each site here has something to offer. To learn more about how to best use these sites, check the chapter that related to the topic heading—this is listed next to each category for easy reference. No printed listing can be comprehensive, but if a site changes, we'll try to update its address at the companion site to this book (www.internettravelplanner.com). Another way to find new sites is to check your favorite search engine. Happy surfing!

Adventure Travel (Chapter 8)

Active Travel (activetravel.about.com): A vast roundup of links to active travel sites, with categories ranging from bicycling to wildlife safaris.

⭐ **Adventure Seek (www.adventureseek.com):** Promising to revolutionize the way travelers choose adventure trips, this site offers detailed listings of adventures by activity and destinations. Trip reviews from traveler reports and its own experts, as well as personalized content, make this site special.

Adventure Travel Society (www.adventure travel.com): Find tour operators, exotic lodgings, and boat charters around the world. The focus here is on sustainable tourism.

Adventure Quest (www.adventurequest.com): An extensive directory of things to do and places to go.

⭐ **Art of Travel (artoftravel.com):** An online treatise on the art of budget travel.

Cyber Adventures (www.cyber-adv.com): Read online travelogues from intrepid travelers.

Eurotrip.com (eurotrip.com): Just about everything you need to know for backpacking around Europe.

Fielding's Danger Finder (www.fieldingtravel.com/df/index.htm): A guide to the world's most dangerous places and how to survive in them.

⭐ **GoSki (goski.com):** Resort reports, snow conditions, live views of the slopes and gear advice. Also see **iSki (iski.com)**.

⭐ **Great Outdoor Recreation Pages (www.gorp.com):** The Web's definitive outdoor recreation site, with listings and features on outdoor attractions and activities around the world.

Green Tortoise Adventure Travel (www.green tortoise.com): Refurbished buses let you enjoy "alterna-tours" throughout the United States and Central America.

⭐ **Mountain Travel Sobek (www.mtsobek.com):** Guided adventures to far-flung destinations around the world.

⭐ **Outside Online (www.outsidemag.com):** The online version of *Outside* magazine combines lively features, interactive forums, and general advice.

5★ Planeta.com: Eco Travels in Latin America (www2.planeta.com/mader): Resources for planning an ecotour and essays for learning about the region.

Specialty Travel Index (www.spectrav.com): Find tour operators by activity or by location.

Airports & Airlines (Chapter 2)

Most airline sites offer flight schedules and booking, last-minute deals, and sometimes incentives for booking online. Airline directories and other air sites are listed at the top of this category; airlines sites follow below. For online agencies such as **Expedia.com,** see the Booking Sites section of this appendix.

Airline Information FAQ (www.iecc.com/airline): A frequently updated guide to airline information on the Net.

5★ Airlines of the Web (www.flyaow.com): A guide to hundreds of airline sites, last-minute air deals, and toll-free phone numbers.

Airport Strategies (trip.com/strategies/airport): Tips for moving efficiently through airports.

QuickAID (www.quickaid.com): An extensive directory of links to airport sites around the world.

Office of Airline Information (www.faa.gov/asafety.htm): Information on airline safety.

Rules of the Air (www.onetravel.com/rules/rules.cfm): See excerpts from airlines' rulebooks.

American Airlines (aa.com)

British Airways (www.british-airways.com)

Continental Airlines (www.flycontinental.com)

Delta Air Lines (www.delta-air.com)

Northwest Airlines (nwa.com)

Southwest Airlines (southwest.com)

TWA (www.twa.com)

United Airlines (www.ual.com)

US Airways (usairways.com)

Virgin Atlantic (www.fly.virgin.com)

B&B Directories (Chapter 3)

5★ BedandBreakfast.com (www.bedandbreakfast.com): Travelers find B&Bs and innkeepers learn to promote their inns.

InnCrawler (www.inncrawler.com): Search dozens of B&B directories simultaneously.

5★ InnSite (www.innsite.com): A massive directory listing tens of thousands of inns. Search by keyword or browse geographically.

5★ Pamela Lanier's Travelguides (www.travelguides.com): More than 27,000 B&B listings along with other lodging options.

Booking Sites (Chapter 2)

At online travel agencies you can research flights, lodgings, car rentals, and package vacations. These sites also offer booking through the Net and tools such as low-fare alerts. Below are some of the leading online agencies.

Atevo (atevo.com)

5★ Expedia.com (expedia.com)

intelliTrip (intellitrip.thetrip.com)

Internet Travel Network (www.itn.com)

5★ Preview Travel (www.previewtravel.com)

Travelocity (www.travelocity.com)

Budget Travel (Chapter 7)

5★ 1travel.com (www.onetravel.com): Deals on domestic and international flights, cruises, hotels, and all-inclusive resorts such as Club Med. Saving Alert compiles last-minute deals based on your preferences and e-mails them to you.

Airtech.com (www.airtech.com): Rock-bottom prices on flights for those who can be flexible about when they fly.

5★ Arthur Frommer's Budget Travel Online (frommers.com): Savvy strategies for saving, a daily newsletter, hot tips, and lively features from the guru of budget travel.

Bestfares.com (bestfares.com): Lists lots of great air deals, but for some you must sign up for a paid membership.

Cheap Tickets (www.cheaptickets.com): Discounted fares on domestic and international air tickets and hotel rooms.

Click-it Weekends (www.travelweb.com/TravelWeb/clickit.html): Last-minute weekend deals on hotel rooms, from TravelWeb.

Council Travel (www.counciltravel.com):

Another agency that negotiates volume discounts and than may have better deals that you find through mainstream channels.

Go4Less.com (go4less.com): Deals on vacation packages, cruises, airline tickets, hotels, and car rentals.

Hostelling International (www.iyhf.org): The official directory of the International Youth Hostels Federation.

⭐ **Hostels.com (hostels.com):** A broad-based directory that includes lots of hostels that don't belong to the IYHF. You'll also find budget travel advice and travelers' tales here.

International Association of Air Travel Couriers (www.courier.org): Learn how to fly as an air courier for next to nothing.

⭐ **International Home Exchange Network (www.homexchange.com):** Swap your home for a house at your destination and save a bundle.

LastMinuteTravel.com (www.lastminute travel.com): A clearinghouse for trips from all sorts of travel suppliers, including airlines, cruise lines, tour packagers, and more. Smaller companies, such as B&Bs, can participate.

Lowestfare.com (www.lowestfare.com): Discount air deals, mostly on TWA.

Priceline.com (priceline.com): An auction site where you can name your price. Priceline has strict restrictions, so know what you're getting into before you bid.

Shoestring Travel (www.stratpub.com): An e-zine of advice for traveling on the cheap.

⭐ **Smarter Living (www.smarter living.com):** Best known for its e-mail dispatch of weekend deals on twenty airlines, Smarter Living also compiles lists of deals on its site.

Ticket Planet (www.ticketplanet.com): Steep discounts on international air tickets for multi-city and around-the-world trips.

tiss (www.tiss.com): A database of discounted consolidator flights.

Travelbids.com (www.travelbids.com): Pick a trip and let travel agents bid to see who'll give you the best deal.

TravelFacts (www.bid4travel.com): An auction site where you can bid on trips.

Worldwide Courier Association (www.walls tech.com): Give up your baggage allowance to a courier company and fly on the cheap.

Business Travel (Chapter 11)

⭐ **Biztravel.com (biztravel.com):** Book flights, hotels, and cars and get the most from your frequent travel programs.

Business Travel News (www.btnonline.com): Focusing on the needs of corporate travel planners, this twice-monthly magazine can help corporations make informed decisions about travel expenditures.

Business Traveler Online (www.btonline.com): Combining lively features with destination information, this is a worthwhile site for business travelers, especially those heading to Europe.

⭐ **CNNfn Travel Center (www.cnnfn.com/ travelcenter):** CNN business travel stories, tools such as booking services, and city guides.

⭐ **Doing Business Abroad (www.get customs.com/omnibus/dba.html):** Although buried deep in the Get Customs site, this is a fantastic resource for knowing how to act in various countries.

Executive Woman's Travel Network (www.delta-air.com/womenexecs): Tips on laptops, luggage, and frequent flying, as well as useful sections called Family Matters and Health and Fitness on the Road.

Expedia.com: Business Travel (expedia.msn.com/daily/business): A nice roundup of resources for business travelers, from one of the big booking sites.

⭐ **Gestures of the World (www.webof culture.com/edu/gestures.html):** Learn how to avoid inappropriate gestures and get a handle on respectful conduct for business meetings around the globe.

New York Times: Business Traveler (www.nytimes.com/library/travel/business): An archive of updates, usually with four or five short items per column.

⭐ **Roadnews.com (www.roadnews.com):** Chock-full of informative articles, this is a must-visit site for road warriors.

⭐ **Trip.com (trip.com):** Flight, hotel, and car booking, as well as lots of tools and features for mobile professionals.

U.S. State Department: Business Travel (www.state.gov/www/about_state/busi ness/business_travel.html): Guidelines for personal security, advice for protecting business information, and links to travel warnings and consular information sheets.

Car Rental Sites (Chapter 5)

Online car rentals can be made directly with suppliers (such as Hertz.) or through online agencies such as Travelocity. Car company sites are listed below; for online agencies see the Booking Sites section above.

Alamo (www.goalamo.com)

Avis (www.avis.com)

Budget (www.budget.com)

Dollar (www.dollar.com)

Enterprise (www.enterprise.com)

National (www.nationalcar.com)

Thrifty (www.thrifty.com)

Cruise Sites (Chapter 9)

In the first part of this listing you'll find general cruise sites, such as those that list reviews; after these are cruise lines' own sites.

CDC Vessel Sanitation Program (www.cdc.gov/nceh/programs/sanit/vsp/scores/scores.htm): Centers for Disease Control ranks ships on cleanliness and sanitation.

Cruise Fun (www.cruisefun.com): An online agency that can put you in touch with a cruise specialist in your hometown.

Cruise Lines International Association (www.cruising.org/index2.htm): This extensive database from CLIA, a major cruise line trade association, can help you select a cruise—but you won't find critical analysis here.

Cruise News Daily (www.reply.net/clients/cruise/news.html): A matter-of-fact daily update on cruise news.

Cruise News (www.cruise-news.com): News on seasonal and themed cruises and information about upcoming launches of new ships.

CruiseOpinion.com (www.cruiseopinion.com): Thousands of personal reviews, sorted by cruise line and ship, with numerical rankings for about forty categories, from midnight buffets to shore excursions.

Fielding's Cruise Finder (www.fieldingtravel.com/cf/index.htm): Each line is reviewed and more than a dozen categories are covered, including tips on the ships, cuisine, and who should (and should not) go.

Freighter World Cruises (www.freighterworld.com): Ride along on a cargo ship in more comfort than you might expect.

Get Cruising (www.getcruising.com/cruising): Input your preferences—such as price—and scan a list of suggested cruises.

Internet Cruise Travel Network (www.cruisetravel.com): An online cruise agency where you can check prices and look for special deals.

TravelPage.com (www.travelpage.com/cruise): Expert assessments of hundreds of cruises and a forum where you can see postings from others or ask a question of your own.

Carnival (www.carnival.com)

Celebrity Cruises (www.celebrity-cruises.com)

Crystal Cruises (www.crystalcruises.com)

Cunard (www.cunardline.com)

Disney Cruise Line (disney.go.com/DisneyCruise)

Holland America Line (www.hollandamerica.com)

Norwegian Cruise Line (www.ncl.com)

Princess Cruises (www.princess.com)

Royal Caribbean International (www.rccl.com)

Seabourn Cruise Line (www.seabourn.com)

Windjammer Barefoot Cruises (www.windjammer.com)

Windstar Cruises (www.windstarcruises.com)

Destination Guides (Chapter 1)

Arthur Frommer's Budget Travel Online (www.frommers.com): Destination guides, budget travel advice, a daily newsletter, and features from Arthur Frommer's Budget Travel magazine.

CitySearch (www.citysearch.com): Produced in cooperation with local media outlets, CitySearch covers dining, lodging, attractions, nightlife, and lots of other topics for travelers.

Digital City (www.digitalcity.com): This AOL city guide, offering advice on dining and entertainment, is available on the Web at the above address.

Fodor's Travel Online (www.fodors.com): Create a custom miniguide based on your interests, and see Fodor's hotel and restaurant reviews for about one hundred destinations.

Lonely Planet (www.lonelyplanet.com): Destination overviews, guidebook updates, and travel news advisories from the guidebook that conquered the globe.

Planet Rider (www.planetrider.com): A directory of a few recommended sites for hundreds of destinations worldwide.

⭐ **Rick Steves' Europe Through the Back Door (www.ricksteves.com):** Destination advice for fourteen European countries and travel tips from the master of "back-door" travel.

⭐ **Rough Guides (travel.roughguides.com):** The complete texts for dozens of RG's guides are published online.

⭐ **Time Out (www.timeout.com):** Combining irreverent attitude with provocative features and entertainment listings, Time Out has guides for most major European cities and several U.S. metropolises.

Dining Guides (Chapter 4)

In addition to the sites below, you can find restaurant reviews at city guides such as **CitySearch** or **NYToday,** and online guidebooks such as **Fodor's.** And there are many local restaurant guides—see chapter 4 for advice on how to find them.

CuisineNet (www.cuisinenet.com): Reviews and diners' comments for restaurants in sixteen U.S. cities.

The Gumbo Pages (www.gumbopages.com): Restaurant advice and more for New Orleans.

Kosher Restaurant Database (www.shamash.org/kosher/krestquery.html): Perhaps the most extensive database of kosher restaurants.

The Sushi World Guide (sushi.to): A worldwide guide to sushi restaurants, compiled from sushi lovers' recommendations.

World Guide to Vegetarianism (www.veg.org): The Net community recommends veggie places around the globe.

⭐ **Zagat.com (zagat.com):** This highly regarded guide surveys diners and lists leading restaurants with information on price, cuisine type, and decor.

Disabled Travelers (Chapter 10)

⭐ **Access-Able Travel Source (www.access-able.com):** Travel recommendations and advice, along with a list of travel agents who specialize in trips for the disabled.

Dialysis at Sea Cruises (www.dialysis-at-sea.com): Learn about cruises in the Caribbean and other destinations, all on ships outfitted to care for dialysis patients.

Dialysis Finder (www.dialysisfinder.com): Find a dialysis unit anywhere in the United States.

Emerging Horizons (www.candy-charles.com/Horizons): An accessible travel magazine and newsletter.

Family Travel (Chapter 10)

⭐ **Disney Theme Parks (disney.go.com):** Disney's main site is the launch pad for virtual forays into Disneyland and Disney World.

Family.com (family.go.com/Categories/Travel): An extensive set of resources to help you find and plan your family's next trip.

Family Travel (expedia.msn.com/daily/family): Vacation packages for families, tips from author Eileen Ogintz on taking the kids, an airport survival guide, and forums where you can discuss family trips with other travelers.

Family Travel Forum (familytravelforum.com): Deals, news, trip reports, and family travel guides to lots of destinations.

Pamela Lanier's Familytravelguides.com (family travelguides.com): Travel tips, destination advice, suggestions for enjoying the great outdoors, and special deals for family travel.

Free E-mail (Chapter 14)

Free e-mail (or freemail) services include just about all the features found in more traditional e-mail programs—and they let you log on from any computer with a Net connection. For Internet cafe directories, see the Internet cafe section below or in chapter 14.

Email.com (email.com)

Hotmail (www.hotmail.com)

IName (www.iname.com)

Mail.com (mail.com)

NetAddress (netaddress.usa.net)

Yahoo Mail (mail.yahoo.com)

Also: To check your POP3 (home) e-mail box from any Web connection, see:

MailStart (mailstart.com)

That Web (thatweb.com)

Frequent Flier Programs (Chapter 11)

ClickRewards (clickrewards.com): Offers miles whenever you buy from participating merchants, such as Barnes & Noble. These miles are good for most major U.S. airline programs —you choose which program you want your miles placed in.

Frequentflier.com (frequentflier.com): A terrific site for advice on choosing a program, maximizing miles, and late-breaking frequent flier news.

⭐ **WebFlyer (webflyer.com):** The definitive site for frequent fliers can help you understand and get the most from your frequent travel programs.

Gay and Lesbian Travelers (Chapter 10)

Note: You can find lots of gay/lesbian city guides through search sites such as Yahoo.

Alyson Adventures (www.alysonadventures.com): Active vacations for gays and lesbians.

Gaytraveling.com (www.gaytraveling.com): A gay guide to select locales, including Key West.

Olivia Cruises & Resorts (www.olivia travel.com): Olivia specializes in cruises and other tours for women.

⭐ **Out & About (www.outandabout.com):** Destination info, a newsletter, gay travel health, tour operator listings, and links to other gay travel sites.

⭐ **PlanetOut Travel (www.planetout.com/ pno/travel):** A destination guide to insider advice for gay and lesbian travelers.

Travelook (www.travelook.com): Meet other LBG travelers through home exchanges, vacations, businesses, clubs, online events, and chat.

Health Advice (Chapter 12)

CDC Travel Information (www.cdc.gov/travel/ travel.html): Updates and advisories from the U.S. Centers for Disease Control.

Healthy Flying (www.flyana.com): Advice for staying healthy in the air.

International Society of Travel Medicine (www.istm.org/clinidir.html): Lists clinics around the world which are members of this organization.

MedicAlert (www.medicalert.org): ID bracelets for those with chronic medical conditions.

Pills, Ills and Bellyaches (www.lonelyplanet.com/health/health.htm): Road-tested remedies for those nasty bugs.

⭐ **Staying Healthy in Asia, Africa, and Latin America (www.moon.com/staying_ healthy):** Info on immunizations, malaria, blood transfusions, and signs of dangerous illness.

Travel Health Online (www.tripprep.com): International health conditions with other foreign travel advice.

Your Health Abroad (www.armchair.com/ info/health.html): Topics from health insurance to insect bites.

Hotel and Resort Directories (Chapter 3)

All Hotels (www.all-hotels.com): Tens of thousands of listings for hotels throughout the world.

Hotel Reservations Network (www.hotel discounts.com): Rooms at up to 65 percent off retail rates. Sometimes rooms are available at hotels that are "sold out" through regular channels.

HotelsTravel.com (www.hotelstravel.com): Links to more than 100,000 hotels in more than 120 countries.

HotelView (www.hotelview.com): See images of hotel rooms or take an audiotour with a slide show.

Leisure Planet (www.leisureplanet.com): Listings for more than 45,000 hotels, including 13,000 with color photos. Book a flight, rent a car, and find guidebook information here.

⭐ **Local Hotels (www.localhotels.com):** An uber-directory of local hotel directories around the globe.

⭐ **Places to Stay (www.placestostay.com):** Thousands of resorts and inns around the world, many of which don't appear on sites that focus on the big chains.

TravelBook (travelbook.com): Rooms for under $100 a night in New York and some other U.S. cities.

TravelWeb (www.travelweb.com): An extensive directory to major chain hotels.

VacationSpot (vacationspot.com): Lists one-of-a-kind lodgings around the world.

WorldHotel Finder (worldhotel.com): Discounted rooms outside the United States; claims a directory of almost 200,000 listings.

Internet Cafe Directories (Chapter 14)

Use the directories below to get online—without a laptop computer—wherever you travel.

Cybercafe Search Engine (cybercaptive.com)

Euro Cyber Cafes (eyesite.simplenet.com/eurocybercafes)

Internet Cafe Guide (netcafeguide.com/text index.htm)

Internet Cafes Guide (www.cybercafe.com)

Magazines and Travel News (Chapter 1)

Big World (www.bigworld.com): A fresh, unpretentious travel magazine that celebrates the joy of exploration.

⭐ **CNN Travelguide (www.cnn.com/TRAVEL):** Travel news and destination info.

Concierge.com (concierge.com): Features from *Condé Nast Traveler* and one-stop shopping for the upscale traveler.

⭐ **The Connected Traveler (www.connectedtraveler.com):** Travel stories with sound and video.

Monk.com (www.monk.com): Two self-described mad monks live on the road and write about their adventures.

No Shitting in the Toilet (www.noshit.com.au): A celebration of everything that is perverse about travel.

⭐ **Planeta.com (www.planeta.com):** A journal of ecotravel in Latin America.

⭐ **Salon Travel (salon.com/travel/index.html):** Travel literature from leading writers.

Split (www.splitnews.com): An alternative travel journal.

Travel Channel (travelchannel.com): Online version of the cable channel of the same name.

Web Travel Review (webtravel.org/webtravel): One of the first online travel magazines

continues to shine with stories from the U.S. and around the world.

Outdoors and Camping (Chapter 8)

⭐ **Art of Travel (artoftravel.com):** A full-length manuscript with lots of great advice for traveling gracefully.

⭐ **Great Outdoor Recreation Pages (www.gorp.com):** Vast database for planning your outdoor adventure or finding an outfitter.

⭐ **Green Travel Network (www.greentravel.com):** Research destinations and read trip reports at this "active travel center created by travelers for travelers."

⭐ **Mountain Travel Sobek (www.mtsobek.com):** Guided tours to remote destinations.

⭐ **MountainZone.com (mountainzone.com):** Live reports from climbing expeditions, ski and snowboard reports, and mountain biking coverage and tips.

⭐ **Outside Online (www.outsidemag.com):** The online version of *Outside* magazine.

⭐ **Round-The-World Travel Guide (www.Travel-Library.com/rtw/html):** Just about everything you need to know to plan a trip around the globe.

Specialty Travel Index (www.spectrav.com): An index of travel outfitters by location and activity.

Rail Sites (Chapter 6)

Amtrak (www.amtrak.com): Timetables, fares, and special offers.

Cyperspace World Railroad Lounge Car (www.mcs.com/~dsdawdy/Parlor/parlor.html): Take a virtual ride through others' stories or plan a rail journey of your own.

European Railway Server (mercurio.iet.unipi.it): The best links for rail travel, organized by country, city, or region.

NMRA Directory of World Wide Rail Sites (www.ribbonrail.com/nmra): This directory of more than 3,600 different train trip sites can help you plan a rail vacation.

⭐ **RailEurope (www.raileurope.com):** Timetables, fares, and online booking for trains throughout Europe.

RailPass Express (www.railpass.com): Research and buy Eurail passes online.

RailServe (www.railserve.com): A directory with links to major rail sites around the world.

⭐ **Rick Steves' Eurail Guide (www.rick steves.com/rail):** Sage advice on whether, when, and how to buy Eurail passes.

Rail Travel Center (www.railtvl.com): Itinerary dates, prices, and some stunning images of high-end train tours.

⭐ **Subway Navigator (metro.ratp. fr:10001/bin/cities/english):** Maps, routes, and estimated trip times for more than sixty metropolitan subway systems around the world.

VIA Rail Canada (www.viarail.ca): Timetables and fares for traveling in Canada.

Search Sites

Some of the sites below have travel pages that typically include trip booking, destination information, and travel tools such as weather forecasts or flight status. For search sites with travel centers, you'll find two Web addresses, the first for the home page and the second for travel center.

About.com (about.com)

Excite (www.excite.com or www.excite.com/travel)

Go Network (go.com or travel.go.com)

Looksmart (www.looksmart.com)

Lycos (www.lycos.com or www.lycos.com/ travel)

Snap.com (snap.com): From the home page, click "Travel and Reservations" to get to Snap's travel center.

⭐ **Yahoo (yahoo.com or travel.yahoo.com)**

Senior Travel (Chapter 10)

American Association of Retired Persons (www.aarp.org/travel): Travel stories, an interactive forum, and information on AARP's travel discount program.

⭐ **Elderhostel, Inc. (www.elderhostel.org):** Learn about courses for seniors at inviting locations around the world.

ElderTreks (www.eldertreks.com): An online catalog for this adventure travel company dedicated exclusively to people fifty and over.

SeniorNet (www.seniornet.org): A general site for seniors that has a lively forum where you can discuss travel issues.

⭐ **Yahoo Seniors' Guide (seniors.yahoo.com/seniors/travel/index. html):** Online resources, special trips, and links to deals for seniors.

Tools for Travelers (Chapter 12)

AccuWeather.com (accuweather.com): Check forecasts around the world. Also see **Weather.com** or **intellicast.com**.

⭐ **Foreign Languages for Travelers (www.travlang.com/languages):** Basic terms for more than seventy languages. Click on underlined words to hear the audio files.

Mastercard's ATM Finder (www.mastercard. com/atm): International listings for ATMs that accept MasterCard or Cirrus.

Passport Services (travel.state.gov/ passport_services.html): Get advice from the U.S. State Department, but don't expect to order passports online.

Universal Currency Converter (www.xe.net/ currency): Find out how much your money is worth in another country's currency. Also see **Oanda Currency Converter (www.oanda.com)**.

Visa ATM Locator (www.visa.com/pd/atm): Locate automatic teller machines that accept Visa around the world.

Travel Advisories (Chapter 12)

CIA World Factbook (www.odci.gov/cia/ publications/factbook): Basic information on just about every country on the planet.

Kroll Travel Watch (www.krollassociates. com/KTS): Country overviews and advisories from a private firm.

U.S. State Dept. Travel Warnings (travel.state.gov/travel_warnings.html): International advisories—check the date on each one to see how current it is.

APPENDIX E

WEB SITES
by DESTINATION

One of the Web's finest features is that it enables you to get timely and extensive destination information online, advice that even the best guidebooks can't include. You can find events calendars, interactive maps, trip reports, underground guides, dining advice, the inside scoop on attractions, and much more. Print guides are essential—I never leave on an extended trip without one. However, the sites listed below can be the ideal complement to a good print guide. Following are key sites for more than twenty-five top destinations around the world.

Note: For most cities below, you can find excellent advice at multicity guides, such as **CitySearch (citysearch.com)** or **TimeOut (www.timeout.com)**. Similarly, you can finding dining guides for many cities at **Zagat (zagat.com)** or **CuisineNet (www.cuisinenet.com)**. Online guidebooks, such as **Arthur Frommer's Budget Travel (frommers.com)** and **Rough Guides (travel.roughguides.com)** are also excellent sources for destination information, as described in chapter 1. The directory below doesn't include these general guides but instead focuses on sites specific to each city, such as **Boston Insider**.

Arizona and the Grand Canyon

Arizona Central (www.azcentral.com): The online home of the Arizona Republic, this site offers information on local attractions and nightlife and restaurant reviews.

Arizona Guide (www.arizonaguide.com): Weather reports from around the state, a trip planner, an events guide, and city listings, plus an extensive section on the Grand Canyon.

Best of Tucson (www.desert.net/tw/bot/index.htm): Details about food, shopping, outdoors, bars, cafes, and city life.

Grand Canyon Explorer (www.kaibab.org): A passionate Canyon guide with maps, hikes, weather, and lodging.

Grand Canyon National Park (www.nps.gov/grca): All the basics from the National Park Service. Also see **www.thecanyon.com**.

Ultimate Arizona Vacation Guide (www.webcreationsetc.com/Azguide): Official site of the Arizona tourism bureau lists everything from hotel deals to campgrounds.

Australia

Australian Tourist Commission (www.aussie.net.au): City guides and advice for exploring Australia's natural wonders.

Destination Australia (www.austtravel.com.au): A country guide with transit tips and advice on customs, banking, tipping, and more.

Great Barrier Reef Visitor Bureau (www.great-barrier-reef.com): Links to lodging, tours, transportation, maps, and event calendars.

Melbourne Visitors Guide (melbourne.8m.com): Images of local attractions, transit tips, and more.

Sydney Travel Guide (www.travelsydney.com): Detailed descriptions covering attractions, budget travel, transportation, weather, parks, and beaches.

Boston

Boston By Foot (www.bostonbyfoot.com): Descriptions of the walking tours, most for under $10, by this nonprofit group.

Boston CityPass (www.citypass.net/boston.html): Order these passes online for discounts at participating museums.

🏅 **Boston.com** (from the Boston Globe) **(www.boston.com):** An excellent all-around site featuring entertainment listings, weather, and city events.

🏅 **Boston Insider (www.theinsider.com/boston):** Tips for discount on theater, museums, and books, along with restaurant advice.

Boston Magazine (www.bostonmagazine.com): Reviews of theater, music, dance, museums, restaurants, and family activities.

Boston Phoenix (www.bostonphoenix.com): Critical reviews of theater productions, restaurants, movies, dance, and art exhibits.

BostonUSA (Convention and Visitors Bureau) **(www.bostonusa.com):** Search by location for lodging, dining, museums, theater, and nightlife.

Caribbean

Calabash Skyviews (www.skyviews.com): Advice on dining, lodging, and sightseeing for about twenty islands.

Caribbean Online (www.caribbean-on-line.com): A general interest guide to the Caribbean that can help you find tour operators, golf courses, sailing trips, and more.

Interknowledge: The Caribbean (www.interknowledge.com/indx02.htm): Advice from local tourism bureaus on golfing, fishing, beaches, and points of interest.

Island Connoisseur: Caribbean SuperSite (caribbeansupersite.com): A nice collection of

links to Web sites featuring everything from dining to travelogues.

TravelFacts (www.travelfacts.com): Pick a destination for extensive listings on sightseeing, tours, dining, lodging, and shopping.

Chicago

Art Institute of Chicago (www.artic.edu): A virtual tour of permanent and upcoming exhibitions.

Blues in Chicago (nitescape.com/chicago/blues): Reviews of Chicago's blues clubs and links to their Web sites.

Chicago Guide (www.chicago-guide.com): Music calendar for blues, jazz, country and western, folk, bluegrass, and rock.

Chicago Tribune (chicagotribune.com): Listings and reviews for music, movies, dining, performance art, and museums.

Exploring Chicago (www.ci.chi.il.us/Tourism): Official city site helps you learn about the city's attractions.

Sears Tower (www.sears-tower.com): Check out the (virtual) view from the top of the world's tallest building.

Costa Rica

Costa Rica Accommodations (www.accommodations.co.cr): A well-rounded list of more than 300 lodging options.

Costa Rica Naturally (www.tourism.co.cr): A guide from the national tourism office includes sections on adventures, rental cars, hotels, and national parks.

Costa Rica Tourism Board (www.tourism-costarica.com): A nice all-around guide to Costa Rica, including slide shows of its natural wonders.

🏅 **Costa Rica Supersite: Visitor Center (incostarica.net/centers/visitor):** An extensive tourism site from *La Nacion,* Costa Rica's leading newspaper.

🏅 **Costa Rica Travel Web (www.crica.com):** A well designed, easy-to-use site listing hotels, car rentals, tours, and adventures.

Rain Forest Aerial Tram (www.rainforest tram.com): Learn about this ninety-minute tram ride through the jungle canopy, which helps promote conservation in Costa Rica.

Rios Tropicales (www.riostro.com): White-water rafting and sea kayak tours: descriptions, images, prices, and river reports.

Tico Times (www.ticotimes.co.cr): English language edition makes it easy to find out what's happening in Costa Rica.

Web Travel Review: Costa Rica (webtravel.org/cr): Lively text and beautiful photos of sloths, volcanoes, and great egrets.

England and the United Kingdom

A2B Travel (www.a2btravel.com): Plan and book trips and use this site's tips for getting around.

⭐ **Automobile Association–UK (www.theaa.co.uk):** This outstanding guide includes extensive lodging listings and restaurant reviews.

⭐ **Britannia (www.britannia.com):** This expansive site is much more than a travel guide: It's chock-full of lively features, history, and regional profiles.

Cathedrals of Britain (www.cathedrals.org.uk): This well-designed site features dozens of cathedrals organized by region.

Dine Online (www.limitless.co.uk/dine): This site publishes independent reviews sent in by diners from all around England.

English Tourist Board (www.travelengland. org.uk): This official site covers a lot of ground but doesn't go very deep.

Knowhere: A User's Guide to Britain (www.knowhere.co.uk): Travelers from around the world comment on restaurants, attractions, shops, and more.

Royal Shakespeare Company (www.rsc.org.uk): Schedules for upcoming performances in London, Stratford, Newcastle, and Plymouth.

Tower of London Tour (www.toweroflondontour.com): An extensive and illuminating photographic tour.

Westminister Abbey (www.westminster-abbey.org): A superb historical tour with lots of photos of one of the world's most magnificent Gothic churches.

What's On Stage (www.whatsonstage.com): Theater listings and ticket information for London and the rest of the U.K.

Europe (General Sites)

Europe (www.visiteurope.com): Advice by country on passports, visas, international phone codes, and more.

Europe Online (www.europeonline.com): Links by country related to travel categories.

⭐ **Rick Steves' Europe Through the Back Door (www.ricksteves.com):** Country and rail information along with insider advice.

⭐ **TimeOut.com (www.timeout.com):** An outstanding guide to more than a dozen European cities, with a focus on entertainment listings.

Florida and Disneyworld

Come to the Sun (www.goflorida.com): A guide to South Florida, including Miami, Fort Lauderdale, Palm Beach, Boca Raton, and the Florida Keys.

Everglades National Park (www.nps.gov/ever): Attractions, activities, lodging, camping, fishing, and climate for this remarkable park.

⭐ **FLA USA (www.flausa.com):** Attractions, beaches, golfing, and water sports; from Florida's tourism bureau.

⭐ **Go2Orlando (www.go2orlando.com):** Detailed practical information on attractions, dining, lodging, shopping, beaches, and recreation.

Kennedy Space Center (www.kennedyspacecenter.com): Images and descriptions about the myriad attractions here, including the Rocket Garden, Space Shuttle Plaza, and Astronaut Memorial.

SeaWorld (www.seaworld.com): Information on attractions, ticket prices, vacation packages, and special programs.

⭐ **Universal Studios Florida (www.usf.com):** Information on tickets, vacation packages, attractions, and what's shooting.

⭐ **Walt Disney World**—Official Site **(disney.go.com/disneyworld):** A virtual wonderland designed to help you take care of real-world tasks necessary to make your Disney fantasy come true.

France

Eiffel Tower (www.tour-eiffel.fr): Read a history of the tower and enjoy virtual views from the top.

Enjoy France (www.enjoyfrance.com): Search for a restaurant, hotel, guest house, or ski resort around the country. Most listings include basic contact information and photos.

FranceWay (www.franceway.com): Especially heavy on information about Paris, this guide covers dining, lodging, and transportation.

Louvre Museum Official Website (mistral.culture.fr/louvre/louvrea.htm): Descriptions of guided tours, permanent collections, and temporary exhibitions.

Maison de la France (www.franceguide.com): This practical guide to France gives advice on using transportation and finding lodging.

5★ **Paris Pages (www.paris.org):** An events calendar, shop listings, map of attractions, and photo tour.

Also see:

Burgundy: Land of Great Art and Good Living (www.burgundy-tourism.com)

Chateau Versailles (www.chateauversailles.com)

Giverny and Vernon (giverny.org)

Provence Touristic Guide (www.provence.guideweb.com)

Riviera Cote d'Azur (www.crt-riviera.fr)

Hawaii

Aloha Insider (www.theinsider.com/Aloha/index.html): An extensive island-by-island activities guide with lots of photos.

5★ **Go Hawaii (www.gohawaii.com):** An excellent, all-around guide to activities, tours, lodging, and events from the Hawaii Visitors & Convention Bureau.

5★ **Honolulu Star-Bulletin (starbulletin.com/doit):** A well-rounded guide to nightlife, outdoor events, movies, and more.

Honolulu Weekly (www.honoluluweekly.com): An extensive dining guide and entertainment calendar.

Island Highlights: Big Island of Hawaii (www.gohawaii.com/hokeo/islands/bigisland.html): A superb all-around guide to Big Island dining, lodging, shopping, and activities from the Hawaii Visitors & Convention Bureau.

Also see:

Haleakala National Park (www.nps.gov/hale)

Hawaii Volcanoes National Park (www.nps.gov/havo)

Kauai: Island of Discovery (kauai-hawaii.com)

Maui: The Magic Isles (visitmaui.com)

Maui.net (www.maui.net)

Visit Oahu (www.visit-oahu.com)

Hong Kong

5★ **Hong Kong: City of Life (www.hkta.org/home.html):** Attractions, dining advice, bargains, events, and history are all nicely presented here.

hongkong.com (www.hongkong.com): A city guide that focuses on local events and news.

Hong Kong Travel Information (asiatravel.com/hkinfo.html): A basic city guide including transportation, airports, hotels, tours, and "Hong Kong in a Nutshell."

India

All India Guide (www.allindiaguide.com): A wide-ranging guide with a focus on adventure travel.

Destination India (www.destinationindia.com): Attractions, cuisine, hotels, shopping, train information, and more.

India Guide (www.india-guide.com): Although this site is slow to load, it has nice profiles of more than 250 India destinations.

India Travel Network (www.inetindia.com/travel/index.php3): A directory of tours, hotels, attractions, transit, and more.

Italy

Dolce Vita (www.dolcevita.com): The self-proclaimed "insider's guide to Italy" is all about style as it pertains to fashion, cuisine, design, and travel.

5★ **In Italy Online (www.initaly.com):** This extensive lodging site also includes tips on shopping, dining, driving, and art.

Italian Tourist Web Guide (www.itwg.com): Recommends itineraries for art lovers, nature buffs, and wine enthusiasts.

Italy Hotel Reservation (www.italyhotel.com):
With almost 10,000 listings solely for Italy, IHR is a good place to research and reserve lodgings.

Milan City Center Map and Guide (www.CityLightsNews.com/ztmimp1.htm): A big map shows the location of Milan's highlights.

Rome Guide (www.romeguide.it):
Hotel/restaurant listings, walking tours, nightlife, airfares, and more.

Rome: Traveling with Ed and Julie (www.twenj.com/romevisit.htm): Seasoned travelers advise novices on what to do when in Rome.

Tuscany: Know it All (www.knowital.com): As the name suggests, this travel guide does seem to know it all about lodging, dining, and, expectedly, wine in the Italian region of Tuscany.

5★ Wandering Italy (www.wandering.com): Virtual reality tours of spots such as the village of Marciana Marina and the Piazza San Marco.

The Baby Boomer's Venice (www.writing.org/venice.htm): For the post-backpacker and pre-senior-tour set, this guide hits the spot.

Japan

Japan Information Network (www.jinjapan.org/index.html): Click on "Regions & Cities" for local information.

5★ Japan Travel Updates (www.jnto.go.jp): Regional information, events, maps, lodging, agencies, and more from Japan National Tourist Organization.

Japan Web Guide (www.gol.com/jguide/index.html): Attractions, hotels, regional info, and practical advice. See **Rob's Japan FAQ (www.gol.com/jguide/rob.html)** for some personal tips.

5★ Schauwecker's Guide to Japan (www.japan-guide.com): Entertainment, dining, and tourism combined with etiquette, history, and tradition.

Las Vegas

Best of Las Vegas: Las Vegas Review Journal (www.lvrj.com/lvrj_home/bestoflv): Editors and readers vote for their favorite dining, shopping, lodging, and entertainment spots.

Caesar's Magical Empire (caesars.com/palace/right.htm): Las Vegas meets ancient Rome.

Casino Legends Hall of Fame (www.lvbegins.com): A hall of fame that's all about the gamblers, musicians, and showgirls who built Sin City.

Las Vegas Casino Gaming Lessons (www.vegaswebworld.com/casino/game lessons.html): Learn how to play the house before you bet the farm.

5★ Las Vegas.Com (www.lasvegas.com/visit.html): A city guide, events calendar, and reviews of restaurants and buffets.

Las Vegas Weekly (www.lasvegasweekly.com): Reviews of bars, cafes, nightclubs, restaurants, and amusement parks.

Los Angeles

Audiences Unlimited (www.tvtickets.com): Get free tickets to dozens of sitcoms.

5★ Disneyland: The Official Site (disney.go.com/Disneyland/index.html): A virtual wonderland of attractions, park information, and vacation planning tips.

Getty Museum (www.getty.edu/museum): See what's on display at the Getty and find out how to get there by public transit.

Knott's Berry Farm (www.knotts.com): Visitor information and virtual rides.

Los Angeles Times (www.latimes.com): California's leading newspaper offers an extensive calendar of events and entertainment reviews.

Six Flags Magic Mountain (www.sixflags.com/magicmountain/nonflash. cfm): From the Riddler's Revenge to corkscrew coasters, this site is a virtual ride through Magic Mountain.

Universal Studios (www.universalstudios. com/unicity2/ush.html): Virtual rides, visitor information, and games you can play online.

Mexico

EcoTravels in Mexico (www2.planeta.com/mader): If you're looking for a vacation a bit off the beaten track, this is a good place to start.

Mexico Connect (www.mexconnect.com): Offering a collection of magazine-style features, this site is a nice complement to a good guidebook.

Mexico: An Endless Journey (www.mexico-travel.com): This is an almost endless site from Mexico's Ministry of Tourism.

⁵⭐ Mexico Desconocido (www.mexdesco.com/indice.htm): Extensive descriptions and stunning images for Colonial Mexico, Copper Canyon, Maya World, Sea of Cortez, and other categories.

Mexico Travel Guide (www.go2mexico.com): This far-reaching site has listings by category as well as by location.

Also see:

All About Cancun (www.CancunMx.com)

⁵⭐ Baja Travel Guide (bajatravel.com)

Cozumel.net (www.cozumel.net)

Mexico City Virtual Guide (www.mexicocity.com.mx/mexcity.html)

Maya: Portraits of a People (www.nationalgeographic.com/explorer/maya/more.html)

⁵⭐ Puerto Vallarta Complete Guide (www.puerto-vallarta.com)

New Orleans

Best of New Orleans (www.bestofneworleans.com): Editors' choices for the best in dining, music, theater, events, and more.

Gumbo Pages (www.gumbopages.com): This insider's guide includes advice on restaurants, festivals, music, and "how to tawk rite."

Inside New Orleans (www.insideneworleans.com): A well-rounded guide from Cox Communications covering dining, lodging, shopping, and much more.

OffBeat (www.offbeat.com): New Orleans's most thorough music magazine includes club listing, events, and Jazz Fest.

New Orleans French Quarter (www.frenchquarter.com): An extensive events calendar and hotel guide plus sound files of musicians recorded in Jackson Square.

New Orleans Jazz and Heritage Festival (www.nojazzfest.com): The official home of Jazz Fest.

⁵⭐ nola Live (www.nolalive.com): From the *Times-Picayune* comes this lively city guide, with dining reviews and local festival information.

Virtually New Orleans (www.yatcom.com/neworl/vno.html): A personal and insightful guide, this site is like having a good friend show you around.

New York

Carnegie Hall (www.carnegiehall.org): Concert calendar, box office, and virtual tour.

Central Park (www.centralpark.org): Maps, upcoming events, and a tour of the park.

Ellis Island (www.ellisisland.org): An online tour of the former immigration center that was the gateway to the United States for millions of immigrants.

Empire State Building (www.esbnyc.com): Tour information, facts, history, and kid stuff at the official site of New York's most famous skyscraper.

Lincoln Center (www.lincolncenter.org): Schedule of events, such as classical music recitals, and online ticket purchasing for many performances.

New York City! (www.nycvisit.com): Essentials: The Web site for the New York Convention & Visitors Bureau.

New York Today (www.nytoday.com): Arts, restaurant, and entertainment reviews and listings from the *New York Times*.

NYC Museums (www.go-newyorkcity.com/museums/index.html): A guide to the city's leading museums and current exhibitions.

Radio City Music Hall (www.radiocity.com): Schedule of events and online tour of the place where you can see the glitz, glamour, and gusto of the Rockettes.

Rockefeller Center (www.nyctourist.com/rock_center1.htm): Art deco marvel, graced by a statue of Prometheus, comes alive during the holidays with its famous Christmas tree and ice rink.

Portland

Oregon Live (www.oregonlive.com): An events calendar and much more from Oregon's leading newspaper.

Oregon Museum of Science and Industry (www.omsi.edu): Online exhibits and visitor information.

Portland Saturday Market (www.saturdaymarket.org): The lowdown on perhaps the largest open-air arts-and-crafts market in the United States.

Visit Portland (www.pova.com): An events calendar, visitor information, and museum listings.

San Diego

Gaslamp Quarter Online (www.gaslamp.com): Listings and basic contact information for restaurants, cafes, nightclubs, galleries, theaters, and shopping in the neighborhood.

Home Port of San Diego (www.homeport-sd. com/fun): A vast Web directory to link out to museums, theaters, dining guides, and sports and outdoor recreation.

San Diego Convention and Visitors Bureau (www.sandiego.org): Official advice on lodging, transportation, shopping, dining, arts, sports.

⑤★ San Diego Insider (www.sandiego insider.com): This well-rounded guide contains bar, club, and movie reviews.

San Diego Magazine Online (www.sandiego-online.com): Local features, ideas for outdoor excursions, and venues for performing arts.

San Diego Zoo (www.sandiegozoo.org): Details on tours, directions to the zoo, operation hours, and admission prices.

SeaWorld (www.seaworld.com): Attractions, park information, tickets, and killer whales.

San Francisco

Alcatraz (www.nps.gov/alcatraz): The National Park Service posts tour schedules and history of The Rock.

BayInsider (www.bayinsider.com): Reviews and listings of attractions, restaurants, and local entertainment.

Best of the Bay: San Francisco Bay Guardian (www.bestofthebay.com): Edgy, opinionated suggestions on excursions, restaurants, shopping, and budget activities.

Eguide: SF Gate (www.sfgate.com/eguide): Advice on dining, nightlife, museums, and galleries, from the *San Francisco Chronicle* and

Examiner. Also see **sfgate.com** for news, sports, and local events.

Exploratorium (www.exploratorium.edu): Especially fun for kids, this hands-on science museum site includes exhibit information, directions, admission, hours, and a schedule of events.

Fisherman's Wharf (www.fishermanswharf.org): Preview the shops, nearby restaurants, hotels, and wax museums of what's arguably the city's most touristy area.

Ghirardelli Square (www.ghirardellisq.com): This old chocolate factory has been transformed into a collection of upscale of shops and restaurants.

Golden Gate Bridge (www.goldengate.org): Photos and descriptions about this San Francisco landmark.

San Francisco Museum of Modern Art (www.sfmoma.org): Brief descriptions with pictures of current and upcoming exhibits show what's happening in the galleries. Get contact information, hours, and admission.

Also see:

Angel Island State Park (www.angelisland.org)

California Wine Country: Vinescape (vinescape.com)

Muir Woods National Monument (www.nps.gov/muwo)

Oakland.com (www.oakland.com)

Seattle

Pike Place Market (www.pikeplacemarket. com): An online tour of Seattle's famous market. Find out what's fresh today!

Seattle Center (www.seattlecenter.com): Entertainment, cultural events, and attractions, including the famed Space Needle. Also see **www.spaceneedle.com**.

Seattle Dining (www.seattledining.com): A full-fledged online newspaper concerned primarily with the culinary treats of Seattle.

Seattle-King County Convention and Visitors Bureau (www.seeseattle.org): A calendar of events and attractions, including museums, theaters, shopping, and sports.

Seattle Post-Intelligencer (www.seattle-pi. com): Seattle daily newspaper includes attractions for kids and adults.

Spain

⭐⭐ **All About Spain (www.red2000.com):** Take an online region-by-region, city-by-city photo tour of Spain.

Cyberspain (www.cyberspain.com): Whether you want to see some Picassos or get a feel for Spanish *futbol* fanaticism, this site offers a taste of a colorful Spain.

Tourist Office of Spain (www.okspain.org): Hotels and villa reservations, culinary tips, and advice for a cultural or active vacation.

⭐⭐ **TuSpain (Your Spain) (tuspain.com):** Arts and culture, news, embassies, transportation, food and wine, and museums.

Also see:

Barcelona: A Different Point of View (members.xoom.com/barcy)

Catalonia Tourism Guide (www.travelcat.com)

Madrid: Madridman (www.madridman.com)

Madrid: Museo del Prado (museoprado.mcu.es)

Madrid: Soft Guide (www.softguides.com/index_madrid.html)

Thailand

Bangkok.com: Travel Stories (www.bangkok.com/stories): Travelers share their stories on Bangkok.com, a directory of Thai Web sites.

Bangkok Post (www.bangkokpost.net): Find out what's happening locally from Bangkok's English-language newspaper.

Thai Focus (www.thaifocus.com): An extensive guide to Thailand's regions, lodging, cuisine, and major attractions.

Thailand Hotel and Tour Information (www.tiscoverasia.com/thai): A guide (with images) to hotels and resorts that offers online booking.

Tourism Authority of Thailand (www.tat.or.th): Attractions, dining, festivals, shopping, and planning tips from Thailand's official tourism agency.

Also see:

Chiang Mai Online (www.tiscoverasia.com/thai)

Phuket, Thailand (www.phuket.com)

Welcome to Chiang Mai and Chiang Rai (www.infothai.com/wtcmcr)

Washington, D.C.

The Kennedy Center (www.kennedy-center.org): Find out what's playing at the center and listen to live broadcasts through the Net.

National Capital Parks Central (www.nps.gov/nacc): This site from the National Park Service includes links to about a dozen memorials and monuments, such as the Washington Monument.

⭐⭐ **Smithsonian Institution (www.nasm.si.edu):** Detailed information on the many museums that comprise the SI.

⭐⭐ **Style Live (www.washingtonpost.com/wp-srv/style/front.htm):** An events calendar, nightlife advice, theater and dance listings, and much more.

Washington DC: The American Experience (www.washington.org): A product of Washington's visitors bureau, this site gives a broad overview of what to see and do in D.C.

⭐⭐ **Washingtonian Online (www.washingtonian.com):** Click on "Visitors Guide" or "Arts & Entertainment" for advice on where to stay and dine and what to see.

⭐⭐ **WashingtonPost.com: Destination D.C. (www.washingtonpost.com/wp-srv/local/longterm/tours/guide2.htm):** A very long Web address, but it's worth entering for terrific advice here.

The White House (www.whitehouse.gov): Click on "Tour Information" to learn about seeing the White House and upcoming public events.

Also see:

Library of Congress (www.loc.gov)

National Gallery of Art (www.nga.gov)

The National Garden (www.nationalgarden.org)

INDEX

Michael Shapiro is a travel journalist whose features appear regularly in national magazines, including *Arthur Frommer's Budget Travel, Yahoo Internet Life,* and *Trips,* as well as in Sunday newspaper travel sections of the *San Francisco Examiner* and *Dallas Morning News.* His earlier book, *NetTravel: How Travelers Use the Internet,* was the first book to discuss how travelers can use the Net to enhance their travels. He is also the creator and writer of a series of online directories in Frommer's travel guidebooks.

Michael received a 1999 Society of American Travel Writers Lowell Thomas award in the category Travel News/Investigative Reporting. He has appeared on national television shows, including ZDTV's *Call for Help,* PBS's *Computer Chronicles,* and CNET's *CNET Central.*

Michael lives north of San Francisco and volunteers as a white-water rafting and sea kayak guide with a group that takes disabled people on wilderness trips.